£10.99 TK D

# Pressure Groups

## Books in the Politics Study Guides series

*British Government and Politics: A Comparative Guide*
Duncan Watts

*International Politics: An Introductory Guide*
Alasdair Blair, Steven Curtis and Sean McGough

*US Government and Politics*
William Storey

*Britain and the European Union*
Alistair Jones

*The Changing Constitution*
Kevin Harrison and Tony Boyd

*Democracy in Britain*
Matt Cole

*Devolution in the United Kingdom*
Russell Deacon and Alan Sandry

*Elections and Voting in Britain*
Chris Robinson

*The Judiciary, Civil Liberties and Human Rights*
Steven Foster

*Political Communication*
Steven Foster

*Political Parties in Britain*
Matt Cole

*The Politics of Northern Ireland*
Joanne McEvoy

*Pressure Groups*
Duncan Watts

*The Prime Minister and Cabinet*
Stephen Buckley

*The UK Parliament*
Moyra Grant

# Pressure Groups

**Duncan Watts**

Edinburgh University Press

© Duncan Watts, 2007

Edinburgh University Press Ltd
22 George Square, Edinburgh

Typeset in 11/13pt Monotype Baskerville by
Servis Filmsetting Ltd, Manchester, and
printed and bound in Spain by
GraphyCems

A CIP record for this book is available from the British Library

ISBN 978 0 7486 2439 3 (paperback)

The right of Duncan Watts to be identified as author of this work has been
asserted in accordance with the Copyright, Designs and Patents Act 1988.

# Contents

Y0065030

# Boxes

# Tables

# Introduction

## Contents

### Overview

In modern societies, there is a vast array of groups that are formed for an infinite variety of purposes. Many exist primarily to benefit the interests of members or to advance some specific cause. When such groups are concerned in some way to influence public policy, they are known as pressure groups.

In this chapter, we explore the extent of group activity and why it has developed in every democracy. We then set out to define relevant terminology before assessing the significance of group activity.

### Key issues to be covered in this chapter

- The tendency of individuals to form associations or groups
- The extent of group activity
- The development and proliferation of groups
- The terminology associated with groups
- The distinction between movements and groups
- The distinction between political parties and groups
- The importance of groups
- An introduction to the main perspectives by which group activity can be assessed

## The growth and extent of group activity

Pressure groups are not a new phenomenon. They have been a feature of the political scene for centuries, although it is only in the post-1945 era that they have become a subject of academic study. They are as old as politics itself, having existed whenever a group of individuals has banded together to achieve an end that demands some kind of pressure on those who make the decisions about how their country should be run.

Forming groups is a natural thing for people to do, for humans are essentially social creatures. But there is also another sound motivation for joining together with other people. Individuals are rarely sufficiently influential on their own that they can hope to influence policy and decisions that affect their lives. Therefore, taking advantage of their democratic rights to free expression and free assembly, they act together to secure the introduction, prevention, continuation or abolition of whatever measures they feel are important to them. After visiting the United States in the 1830s, Alexis **de Tocqueville**[1] was impressed by the way in which 'Americans of all ages, all conditions, and all dispositions constantly form associations' which had in his view become a 'powerful instrument of action'. In his view their existence was to be celebrated as an indication – indeed a bastion – of a healthy democracy.

In the early to mid-nineteenth century, the Anti-Slavery Society and the Anti-Corn Law League were familiar features of political life. By the end of the century, there were in several democracies powerful interests that were successful in promoting their special political agendas – agricultural, business, railway or labour groups among them. These were what we now call interest groups (see page 30), which Wilson[2] defined as 'organisations, separate from government though often in close partnership with government, which attempt to influence public policy'. In the late nineteenth and early twentieth centuries, however, a variety of other public groups developed as government expanded into areas such as education, health care, leisure and welfare. Some were interest groups but many others were campaigning bodies that were concerned to promote policies of general benefit, rather than of personal advantage, to their members. We can see the range of activities covered by such groups by looking at developments in one particular sphere of activity, that concerning the environment.

Associations and campaigning groups have been active in the environmental field for well over a century. According to Lowe and Goyder,[3] there have been four main bursts of activity in Britain over the last 100 years:

1. At the end of the nineteenth century, there was an upsurge in the growth of organisations such as the Royal Society for the Prevention of Cruelty to Animals (RSPCA), the National Trust and the Garden Cities (later the Town and Country Planning) Association, which were all concerned with the quality of life and desire to preserve its best features. These were conservation bodies interested in preserving the countryside, its inhabitants and fine buildings.

2. The interwar era saw the emergence of organisations more concerned to encourage people to benefit from what the countryside could offer them in a pre-television age – for example, The Ramblers Association and the Pedestrian Association.

3. The late 1950s was a period in which groups were developed that sought to preserve the best of the past and avoid the horrors of modern life by organising such movements as the Civic Trust, Victorian Society and Noise Abatement Society.

4. The early 1970s and after saw the formation of many new groups, such as Friends of the Earth, Greenpeace, Transport 2000, and a host of amenity groups, many of which affiliated to the Civic Trust.

## The proliferation of groups

Since the 1960s, there has been an astonishing rate of growth in the formation of issue and cause groups, some national, others operating at grass-roots level. So dense is the modern group system that most people belong to at least one voluntary association, be it a church, a social or sports club or an organisation concerned to promote civil liberties or rights. Minorities and women have been active in organising to demand access to the social and political benefits long denied to them. Women have sought to ensure that their rights are recognised in law, as well as speaking out on central issues of procreation and reproduction.

The associative tendency discerned by de Tocqueville and inherent in the developments we have just described, constitutes a country's **civil society**, a term more often deployed than defined. Held[4] has provided a useful definition, using the term to refer to 'areas of social life – the domestic world, the economic sphere, cultural activities and political interaction – which are organised by private or voluntary arrangements between individuals and groups outside the direct control of the state'. It comprises those public groups that are above the personal realm of the family but beneath the state and covers a variety of bodies of differing degrees of formality, autonomy and power. It includes 'registered charities, development non-governmental organisations, community groups, women's organisations, faith-based organisations, professional associations, trades unions, self-help groups, social movements, business associations, and advocacy groups'. Businesses are usually excluded, for they are not voluntary bodies emerging from society.

There are many pressure groups which inhabit the political landscape from time to time. Some are long-lasting, others are transient; some are national, others local; some are giants firmly rooted in the public mind, others are little known. There is a multiplicity and a diversity of groups ranging, as Baggott[5] points out, from those so important that they are primarily known by their initials (the British Medical Association and the Trades Union Congress, the BMA and the TUC respectively), to the much less high-profile British Toilet Association and English Collective of Prostitutes. The former campaigns for better public toilets for all. The latter offers help and support to women working in the sex industry, seeking human and civil rights for prostitutes and urging the abolition of the existing laws on the world's oldest profession.

Peele[6] points out that, in addition to the wide range of explicitly campaigning and defensive groups already alluded to, there is in Britain a vast array of more than half a million voluntary organisations: 'Not all have charitable status, although some 190,000 do (such as the Sunshine Home for Blind Babes, the Royal National Institute for the Deaf and Barnardo's)'.

**Why have pressure groups proliferated in the modern age?**
As we have seen, pressure-group activity is not a recent phenomenon, although the increase in the number and range of organisations has been dramatic in recent decades. There are several reasons for this:

1.  The growth in the extent and scope of governmental activity in the second half of the twentieth century in the areas of national economic management and social services. Ministerial decisions constantly and significantly influence the daily lives of the majority of citizens, so not surprisingly those people who share a common interest tend to band together to preserve and advance their interests. They recognise that one voice is likely to be markedly less effective than a collection of voices in highlighting their demands. The influence of any body tends to increase as its membership grows, thus providing an impetus to recruit new members or to amalgamate with other groups of similar viewpoint. Governments do not wish to embark lightly upon policies that are offensive to many voters.

    Despite the extent of welfare provision in areas such as education, health and housing, there is always more that can be done. Expectations having been created, and many people want to see more and better facilities and benefits. In addition, new problems emerge and gain recognition. A plethora of groups has emerged to articulate the views of the poor, the homeless, the old and the mentally and physically handicapped, among many others.

2.  The growing complexity and specialism of modern life. People belong to many subgroups, not least those based on their occupation. For instance, those working in the medical field may not belong to one main union of health-sector workers, but to more specialised associations such as those for ambulance drivers and paramedics .

3.  Improvements in communication have facilitated the trend towards association and organisation, and further stimulated group development – as with the use of e-mails and other such innovations by those protesting against globalisation.

4.  The development since the middle of the last century of a **multi-ethnic** and **multi-cultural society**. This has encouraged the formation of a variety of groups to represent particular minorities, including bodies such as the British Sikh Federation, the Forum of

British Hindus and the Muslim Council of Britain. As well as these groups working to promote and defend the interests of sections of the community, there are other groups that have emerged to counter discrimination and combat racism, such as the Anti Nazi League.

5. The emergence of new issues and the development of post-materialist attitudes. Whereas many voters were once primarily concerned with bread-and-butter matters affecting their lifestyles – their home, their work, their income – in recent decades, ideas such as **ecologism**, feminism and gay rights have come on to the polit-ical agenda. Many younger, better-educated voters share post-materialist attitudes and want to express their views on causes such as the creation of an aesthetically pleasing environment, their dis-approval of nuclear power, their rights to freedom of expression and the need for social and political empowerment.

## Some matters of definition

Some studies have deliberately shunned the use of the term 'pressure group', preferring labels such as 'the lobby', 'organised', 'sectional' or 'interest' groups. Americans tend to speak of 'interest groups' to refer to the whole range of organised groups whereas, in Britain, the term describes groups that cater for a specific interest in society, such as farming or big business. The term is not really suitable as a label for the various bodies that propagandise on some issue of social concern or public benefit.

'Pressure groups' is the more all-embracing British term but this, too, has its detractors. The word 'pressure' is a problem for those who think of it as implying the threatened use of force. There are some groups that do threaten the use of sanctions if their demands are not acknowledged but most do not do so for much of the time. More importantly, the explicit or implied use of force is not a characteristic of many forms of association at all. They rely on reason and argu-ment as they make requests and advocate their chosen causes. It would be grossly unfair to many socially innocuous and entirely peaceful organisations to suggest that their activities are bolstered by any kind of intimidation. This is why many of those that exist to promote a cause which members think is to the betterment of society or of the world at large have in recent years often preferred the name

**non-governmental organisations** (NGOs). Environmental, aid and other campaigning groups find that the term has a greater public appeal. It is much used in the media which, as Grant[7] notes, thrives on the good visual stories that they often uncover. According to the Union of International Associations website, there were nearly 50,000 of them at the turn of the new millennium.

Perhaps in seeking alternative terms to pressure groups, some writers exhibit an undue delicacy of approach. The problem of precise definition is one that affects the study of groups in all countries, but there is little doubt as to the array of organisations that are being analysed. Truman[8] offered a broad definition of the territory under discussion by writing of 'any group that, on the basis of one or more shared attitudes, makes certain claims upon other groups in society for the establishment, maintenance or enhancement of forms of behaviour that are implied by the shared attitudes'. Here, we shall refer to such organised groups as pressure groups and use the term interest groups as the label for an important subcategory of them.

Many legislative chambers have adjoining lobbies in which elected representatives and their constituents (or their chosen spokespersons) can informally meet and talk. It was out of this practice that the word 'lobbying' emerged to describe the efforts by representatives of pressure groups to persuade public officials or members of legislatures to support their aims. To lobby, therefore, is to make a direct representation to a policy-maker, using persuasion or argument. Here, we use the term lobbyist to describe spokespersons for, and campaigners of, pressure groups in general.

There are two other areas of definition that need to be clarified before we examine pressure groups in greater detail: the relationship of pressure groups to movements and to political parties.

## Movements

Movements comprise large bodies of people who organise themselves in support of some broad area of policy such as environmentalism, feminism or single-sex relationships. Accordingly, we speak of the Green Movement, the Women's Movement or the Gay Movement. The goal of their members is often to articulate a common identity (such as Gay Pride) and take action in support of the issue, idea or concern. They strive to change attitudes and perceptions, and make institutions more responsive to their needs. Movements often arise at grass-roots level and evolve into national groups. Their members often see themselves as adopting a position that is morally unassailable whereas the approaches of their opponents are at best misconceived, at worst morally flawed.

Movements and pressure groups have some features in common. They focus on a single issue or range of issues. They do not seek to attain political power but, rather, try to influence it. They speak up for people who feel 'left out' of government, whose interests might otherwise be ignored. Despite the overlap in their preoccupations and activities, however, there are differences. They are often more loosely organised than pressure groups, lacking their precise memberships, subscriptions and leadership.

We can illustrate the difference by looking at the Women's Movement. At the public level, women began to acquire a sense of group consciousness in the nineteenth century. Their wish to do so sprang from a sense of powerlessness, as well as in response to social problems that concerned women, such as care of children, divorce, illiteracy and alcohol. Pioneering women demanded equal rights in marriage, property contracts, trades and professions. They saw the acquisition of the right to vote as an important first step, forming groups such as the moderate suffragists and the more militant suffragettes. Thereafter, many women pursued specific causes, such as abortion, child care, equal pay and an end to discrimination in employment. Many pressure groups were formed to represent these particular concerns. But members still retained an abiding commitment to the overall issue of womens' rights.

The Women's Movement comprises all those women's organisations that campaign for the better treatment of women and a recognition of their distinctive needs. Inevitably, it has within its broad umbrella, individuals and groups who may disagree about particular issues (abortion, for example) or broad tactics (gradualist or more militant approach). But those who belong see themselves as united by a common desire to protect and promote the interests of women.

Movements, then, are less organised and often less specifically focused than pressure groups. They comprise many different pressure groups operating in the broad field. The Animal Rights Movement has been one which has aroused popular interest and support in recent years. Within its broad remit of concern to care for and protect animals and promote their welfare, there are some individuals and groups that adopt reformist strategies and others whose methods are quite different. Militants within the movement may resort to 'extreme' tactics that sometimes terrorise those who oppose them.

## New social movements

In fact, there is nothing new in single-issue protest movements. Today's popular movements are often referred to as new social movements, the term seeking to differentiate current movements with those of yesteryear. The 'old' social movements of the nineteenth century included a myriad of small groups and combinations who were protesting against harsh industrial conditions, with workers struggling to achieve a new social order in which they could enjoy better living and working conditions. They were challenging the dominant ideas and power structure of their day.

Single-issue campaigning was a feature of the 1950s and 1960s when many contemporary politicians engaged in anti-apartheid or anti-Vietnam protests. These were the forerunners of what is often called the 'new politics' practised by the new social movements of the present day. They are new in that they challenge a new set of dominant ideas and are concerned with new issues and concerns. They employ techniques previously unavailable to those involved in popular campaigns. Ease of communication (particularly in recent years by such techniques as e-mailing and texting) has made it easier to organise protests at a national and even global level. Whereas parties and pressure groups operate at the home level, today's global communication makes it possible to co-ordinate activity on a world-wide scale, whether the cause be anti-capitalism or the 2003 war in Iraq. As Hague and Harrop[9] observe: 'The ability of social movements to mushroom in this way – even without any central organisation or leader – confirms their capacity to articulate authentic public concern at a transnational level. Social movements are a form of participation that is well-suited to a more global world.'

As we see from the above, new social movements have a radical edge and visions of a world transformed by their demands. Shunning the traditional forms of pressure-group activity, they are committed to open, and often ultrademocratic, modes of operation and are more willing to engage in direct action. They seek to disrupt the taken-for-granted routines of normal, everyday political life.

Many new social movement protesters operate on the political Left. Some have post-materialist values that directly contradict the dominant materialist views of modern society. Others, especially in poorer parts of the world, are motivated by the basic considerations of survival and security. In 2004, in the advanced Western World, supporters of the Make Poverty History campaign represented many organisations whose sympathies were aroused by scenes of desperate suffering on the African continent. Their motivation was very much concerned with bread-and-butter issues today, rather than the post-materialist values preached by utopian and other commentators.

Some movements represent the forces of the political Right, their members seeking to restore the social order or standards of a bygone age. The Campaign for Moral Re-armament of the 1960s was concerned to arrest what its members perceived as a decline in moral standards in society. The movement in 2000 against high taxation of petrol and the activities of the Countryside Alliance have been good examples of protest politics in which many of the individuals and groups involved took an anti-Labour government stance. As with other social movements, they are less formally led and funded than many ordinary pressure groups and their supporters are more likely to employ unconventional tactics including **direct action** to achieve their ends.

## Political parties and pressure groups

There are basically three differences between political parties and pressure groups which, between them, provide a clear distinction. Firstly, parties put up candidates for election in the hope of winning power and forming a government. Pressure groups do not usually stand for elective office. Pressure groups are voluntary associations designed to influence the policy and conduct of government, rather than themselves wishing to accept the responsibilities of office. Secondly, parties need to be all-embracing as they seek the support of a wide section of the electorate. They need to maintain a broad appeal and to do so cannot afford to be the prisoner of any particular group. They advance aims and programmes which they hope will be of general appeal. Pressure groups do not usually seek to command widespread support from a range of groups in society. They have a narrower programme, their concern being one area of policy. Thirdly, the work of parties is almost entirely political. The role of groups varies according to the nature of the organisation. For some, the search for political influence is continuous and extremely important. For others, it is just an occasional activity and is regarded as a minor aspect of the group's *raison d'être*. In the case of the Rose Growers' Association, they only become interested in politics only as the need arises, an infrequent occurrence. Many campaigning groups are likely to be dissolved when their cause is achieved.

The two types of organisation are more closely linked than these distinctions imply, however: Both inhabit similar areas of territory; they are concerned with the formation and implementation of government policy; they act as intermediary means by which the public can be involved in the political process; they are together the major means of participation, representation and political education. Nor are the differences outlined above as clear-cut as they may at first seem, for:

1. Pressure groups may field candidates, particularly at by-elections, mainly for publicity purposes. On occasion, they put up candidates in a general election, the Pro-Life Coalition having put up more than fifty candidates in 1997. The Christian Peoples Alliance is a minor political party that emerged directly from the non-party-based Movement for Christian Democracy. Having secured over 240,000 votes in the London Assembly and European elections of 2004, it put up nine candidates in 2005. These groups have no chance of forming a government and are concerned to make their cause better known. They are, in reality, pressure groups trying to influence political decisions, rather than parties wishing to exercise power.
2. Labour has close connections with the trade union movement, ties which are financial and organisational, as well as emotional and historical. The Conservatives have traditional links with big business, some large companies having been generous donors to the party in the distant and more recent past.
3. Parties can themselves be an arena for pressure-group conflict, each having factions representing a spectrum of views. The

Conservatives have the Tory Reform Group which takes a one-nation stance on political and social issues, whereas Conservative Way Forward and the No Turning Back Group advocate a more right-wing programme. Both are concerned to induce the party to adopt certain policy stances.

4. There are also **think-tank**, policy-research organisations that work alongside political parties and have an overlap of membership and some shared goals but which, nonetheless, have an independent status and life of their own. British examples include the broadly Conservative-supporting Centre For Policy Studies and the Labour-inclined Institute for Public Policy Research.

5. There is often an overlap of personnel between parties and campaigning groups. Group activists frequently seek to enter Parliament and Former MPs sometimes assume prominent roles in voluntary bodies. There is a natural affinity between parties of the Centre–Left and groups working in the social field, all of whom are in the business of seeking to change society. Groups often find that

**Table Int.1  The characteristics of parties and pressure groups: a summary**

|  | Pressure groups | Political parties |
| --- | --- | --- |
| Purpose | Promote a specific cause or protect a specific interest. Achieve influence over government. | Win a general election, with a view to gaining public office. Implement their programme. |
| Membership | Promotional groups are open to all. Protective groups have a closed membership. | Open to anyone who accepts party principles. |
| Methods | Persuasion, via discussions in Whitehall and Westminster, and possibly Brussels: attempt to win public approval. Protest, direct action. | Putting up candidates for election. Getting MPs into government. |

their staffs, supporters and objectives sit more easily with a Labour administration which at least shares some of their values and priorities (however much it may disappoint them), than with a Conservative one.

Having discussed their nomenclature and distinguished groups from movements and parties, a definition is needed which caters for the distinctions advanced so far. We have noted certain characteristics: groups do not wish to become the government; they seek to influence public policy over a relatively small area, often a single issue or range of issues; they are not the same as political parties, nor are they usually a faction of them; they are more organised than popular movements; and they tend to use conventional tactics, even if direct action has become more common in recent years. In the light of such features, we may conclude that *a pressure group is an organisation which is not a political party but which seeks to influence government through the political process, in order that it can affect the development of public policy.*

## Why groups matter

**Pluralist societies** provide an arena for competition between multifarious pressure groups which compete for influence. Government is usually willing at least to listen to all the significant voices it can hear in the political debate before making up its mind on how to act. Group representatives are involved at all stages of the decision and policy processes, from raising issues and agenda-setting to policy implementation and monitoring. There are, however, differing viewpoints about the way pluralism functions and of how closely or otherwise groups should be involved with government, as we see in the next section.

Movements, well-known pressure groups and all manner of smaller voluntary associations and clubs play an important role in modern social and political life. They comprise an essential part of a democratic society, channels through which the government is informed of views of sections of the public. Larger bodies have the resources to match those of the government agencies they are seeking to influence. They are often highly professional and skilled in the art of lobbying. Their involvement in politics is extensive and continuous.

For the smaller fry, their involvement in the political process is more sporadic, as when a recreational centre for the elderly campaigns for a pedestrian crossing or a residents' association protests against the late-night noise coming from a local social club.

In either case, pressure groups represent an important channel through which people can participate in decisions about their welfare and well-being. They act as a link between ordinary people and decision-makers, the freedom to organise and collectively represent views being an important democratic principle. They help to organise the opinions of the electorate, their information helping to educate voters in the issues of the day and enabling them to formulate and develop their opinions. At a time when membership of political parties is in decline, people are more likely to join pressure groups and movements. In this way, they make a continuing contribution to democracy.

## Studying pressure groups: theoretical perspectives on group power

Governments are elected by the people and are answerable to them for their deeds. They alone are ultimately responsible for determining the shape, broad thrust and detail of policy. But in almost every democracy the role of groups in the processes of policy formation and implementation is greater than such a view implies.

Various theories help us to achieve a better understanding of the operations of pressure groups and their importance in political life. In particular, they help to explain how peak organisations, such as those representing employers and employees, perform a role in government alongside that of the state. With the exception of the final one, all of the theories outlined see groups as having a significant role. They differ considerably, however: in how they view group involvement in the political system; in their perceptions of the balance of power between groups; and on whether or not such associations enhance or undermine democratic life.

Two other introductory observations are worth making. Firstly, the perspectives all have application not only to Britain but to other democracies as well. In two cases, they have originated in, or been influenced by, research conducted in the United States although they are often discussed in the context of European countries. Secondly, within each category, different writers often disagree in significant respects with others who subscribe to the same model.

Two theories have dominated investigations into the relationship of government and groups and group behaviour: those advanced by pluralists and those advanced by corporatists. The former first emerged and continue to hold sway in the United States, where it flourishes in a broadly open and very fragmented political system. Power in America is dispersed in several locations: in central government and in the states; in government departments and in **executive agencies** such as the Department of Veterans Affairs. The latter is more significant in continental Europe. Both views are described below.

### The pluralist approach

Group theory was for a long while dominated by the pluralist model which was originally advanced by Arthur Bentley[10] in the early twentieth century. Bentley saw group activity as essential to the political process, his approach being summarised in the observation that 'when the groups are adequately stated, everything is stated'.

Similar views were developed and expounded at length by David Truman[11] in 1951. According to Truman and subsequent pluralists, American groups – of which he was writing – were an entirely natural, and healthy, feature of political life. They benefited the political system in various ways:

- Their preoccupations reflect those of ordinary people who are entitled to air their views.
- They provide informed views and specialist expertise about issues of concern.
- They allow minority voices to be well articulated, helping to achieve a necessary balance in a democracy between minority and majority rights.
- They cater for the representation of a heterogeneous population, allowing the diverse views of ethnic and other groups to organise and be heard.
- They prevent any single group from exercising disproportionate influence because there are opportunities for other groups to form and compete with them.

In the same decade, an eminent American political scientist, Robert Dahl,[12] similarly argued that major decisions in US politics emerged as a result of negotiation between competing groups. These groups served to defend the individual from government and to promote democratic responsiveness. Deploying findings derived from his studies of the power structure in local communities, he claimed support for the assertion that no single group was able to dominate the process of policy-making. This was because political power was so fragmented. He concluded that: 'All the active and legitimate groups in the population can make themselves heard at some crucial stage in the process of decision.'

Galbraith[13] contributed an explanation for this lack of dominance. He claimed that there was an equilibrium in group activity based upon the idea of 'countervailing powers'. In his view, the success of one strong group – big business, for instance – inspired rival interests, labour or the consumers, to match its efforts so that rough balance was naturally achieved.

The essence of the pluralist case is that power should be dispersed in society and that diversity should be encouraged. It stresses that there are no barriers to the formation of groups and no single group monopolises political resources. Access to the political system is open to all and they can put forward their case without significant difficulty. The government may take advice from, indeed, sometimes rely upon the advice of, groups in making and implementing their policies. Groups are recognised as having sectional interests, however, and accorded no special favours. Numerous groups compete for influence over a responsible government which holds the ring, 'more umpire than player'.

For all of the reasons outlined, pluralist writers portray pressure groups as having a benign impact on the political system. Far from posing any form of threat, their existence serves to enhance democracy. Indeed, they are 'the very stuff of the democratic process'.[14]

By the 1970s, a more critical and qualified form of pluralism was beginning to emerge. Charles Lindblom[15] highlighted the strong, dominant position that big business holds in Western democracies, seeing it as undermining their claims to be as wholesomely democratic as they would wish others to believe. Some subsequent commentators have similarly doubted the view that competition prevents any group from achieving undue influence. They feel that power is not equally dispersed and that access to government is not open to all.

These neo-pluralists of the last three decades lament the fact that pluralism in its purest sense is not being upheld. They acknowledge a stronger role for government in relation to group activity, accepting that today it is not so much an umpire between opposing groups as an active participant in group politics, conferring status on some of them so that in any country there are some who are winners and others losers. Dahl[16] himself adjusted his earlier theories to become an exponent of neo-pluralism, accepting the disproportionate power of some groups and recognising a stronger role for government in relation to groups than he had previously accepted.

In no country does pluralism operate in an ideal way in which no single group achieves a dominant role. Some groups are inevitably more powerful than others, particularly if they are well resourced and can provide government with essential information or services. If they contribute such expertise and assistance, and occupy a significant position in the national economy, then they are likely to have a close – perhaps a rather cosy – relationship with government, with real opportunities for political influence.

### The corporatist approach

As a theory, corporatism is a means of incorporating organised interests into the process of government. Corporatists place greater emphasis on the close links that exist between certain types of groups and the state in industrialised countries, enabling manufacturing groups to have access to the government and play a key role in shaping and implementing policy.

Corporatism is difficult to describe for the term is used differently by many of those who claim to adhere to it. Its meaning can range from the institutional involvement of interest groups with the state to a much weaker version involving bargaining between the state, employers and employees about the conduct of economic and social policy, often known as **tripartism**.

In the 1960s and 1970s, there was a broad drift towards corporatist thinking and practice in several European countries. In the 1970s, governments in Britain sought to achieve agreement between employers and employees on a prices and incomes policy. In a sense, corporatism provided for a fusion of the idea of the capitalist economy, based as it is on a mainly privately owned business sector, with the socialist tradition of planning and democratic consultation. As such, the British version was able to endure through the period of the Heath Conservative administration (1970–4) to the era of Wilson/Callaghan Labour rule (1974–9). (See pages 48–9 for further discussion of British experience).

Critics portray corporatism as overly reminiscent of Mussolini's Fascist-dominated Italian state in which consultation was enforced by government decree and the role of the legislature reduced to near impotence. They regard corporatism as inherently unhealthy, a threat to representative democracy. They see Parliament as the place where conflicts should be resolved. Whereas pluralism involves groups supplementing the democratic process, corporatism sees decisions being taken in closed locations, beyond the means of public scrutiny and democratic accountability. Yet Germany and Sweden both have effective tripartite arrangements and, in the case of the Swedish Riksdag in particular, an effective, strong legislature. Because of the association of corporatism with past authoritarian regimes, some commentators employ the term liberal corporatism to describe the way in which organised interests in mature democracies are enabled to play such a role.

Many states in which there is very close tripartite co-operation nonetheless fall short of outright corporatism, hence the name neo-corporatism to describe the way it currently works in democratic states.

The pluralist versus corporatist debate is central to democratic politics for it sets out the framework for discussion of society and the state. Hague and Harrop[17] put it well: 'Pluralists see society dominating the state: corporatists view the state as leading society . . . the debate reflects contrasting views of the proper role of government. Pluralists see the state's task as responding to interests expressed to it. Corporatists, by contrast, favour an organised, integrated society in which the state offers leadership in pursuit of a vision shared with society.'

### The New Right approach
In the late 1970s and 1980s, the **New Right** developed a different view of group activity. Its exponents questioned the value of groups

in democratic life, portraying them as sectional bodies primarily concerned with advancing their own interests rather than those of society at large. In particular, they expressed alarm about the role and power of some groups. They noted the preponderance of producer interests (employers and employees) and their easy access to government. In comparison, the viewpoint of consumers, taxpayers and promotional groups was neglected.

Adherents of the New Right were more generally doubtful of the benign influence of groups for they saw them as distorting the proper role of the executive and legislature. Their influence over both

## Box Int.1  Mancur Olson

New Right thinking was influenced by Mancur Olson,[18] an American who, in the late 1960s, had written an influential book in which the author sought to demonstrate that it was highly irrational for people sharing a set of beliefs to join a group in pursuit of collective goals that, if achieved, would be granted to both members and non-members of that group. In other words, a free-rider problem exists: individuals can gain whatever benefits a group wins without paying the costs in terms of money and time. From this, Olson concluded that there were only two valid reasons for joining a group. Either, the individual had no choice because there was some kind of coercion (e.g. the trade union **closed shop**) or the group offered special elective benefits as part of its membership package, such as cheap health insurance or access to holidays. There is a logic in Olson's argument but, although it is strong in theory, some would argue that, in practice, it fails to explain why millions of people in Western democracies 'irrationally' join groups without any coercion and – in the case of cause – group, without any special benefits to offset their membership costs. An extensive green lobby has developed in recent decades without members of environmental groups being able to receive a direct benefit.

In a later work, Olson was scathing about pressure-group activity seeing it as a major determinant of the prosperity or failure of particular states. Pointing to Britain in particular, he concluded that there was a strong link between the existence of well-organised and powerful business, union and professional associations and a decline in economic growth and national prosperity.

branches of government made it more difficult for ministers and officials to resist the demands of consulted groups and act in the general good and for MPs to represent all viewpoints among their constituents.

In the minds of many New Right critics, the British tripartism of the past decade was associated with national economic decline. They detected a clear connection between corporatism and excessive government control, seeing it as responsible for policies involving burdensome levels of public expenditure.

Anti-corporatists of the New Right school were much influenced by the thinking of Mancur Olson (see Box Int. 1 on page 19). Their preferred model is based on individualist and market-based ideas, its adherents admiring entrepreneurs and self-reliant, buccaneering adventurers and being disdainful of social groups and collective bodies. In this spirit, during the Reagan and Thatcher years the United States and Britain both embarked on deregulation of the economy and – in Britain – the dismantling of corporatist institutions.

**The Marxist approach**
A very different analysis has been provided by members of the radical Left. They see real control in society as being exercised by the ruling economic group that takes decisions to serve its own interests. As the owners of productive wealth, they control the levers of political power. For Marx, the state was 'nothing but an executive committee for the bourgeoisie' and under capitalism the dominant groups – primarily business interests – rule to their own advantage, exploiting the bulk of society in the process and perpetuating the existence of gross inequality. Whether the system of group activity was described as pluralist or corporatist, in either case the dominant ruling group in the power structure would prevail.

Marxists draw attention to the unequal distribution of power between employers and employees, pointing out that business interests exercise disproportionate influence. They control economic resources, possess status and access to government. Trade unions lack such power, status and access. Moreover, in any case they tend to accept and work within the capitalist system, as long as it enables them to achieve some modest benefits.

## Table Int.2 Models of group influence: a summary

| Theory | Characteristics | General observations |
|---|---|---|
| Pluralism | Sees groups as essential to democracy, providing additional opportunities for participation and representation.<br><br>Decision-making the result of interaction between government and a wide range of groups. Access to government is generally open, allowing all lobbyists and campaigners the opportunity to get their views across.<br><br>Groups can act as a useful check on the power of government.<br><br>There is nothing to stop any section of society from forming a group.<br><br>No group is predominant in society, for the influence of one is offset by that of another (the Galbraithian idea of counterbalance) – e.g. anti-abortionists vie with pro-abortionists in seeking to influence decision-makers. | Most writers on pressure groups have adopted the pluralist perspective, much of the literature being based on US experience.<br><br>Critics doubt the ease of access which all groups in society have to the political system.<br><br>Neo-pluralists have reinterpreted the traditional case. They accept that producer groups are at an advantage, business interests especially being better resourced than others. They also note the ways in which governments try to persuade groups to support their proposals.<br><br>The proliferation of cause groups suggests that it is relatively easy to form new groups, as pluralist suggests.<br><br>Because many people belong to more than one group, this helps prevent the dominance of particular groups. |
| Corporatism | Form of close and stable consultation between major interest groups and government over broad range of economic and social policies. | Theory applicable mainly to producer groups who are involved with government in formulation and implementation of policy. |

## Table Int.2 (Continued)

| Theory | Characteristics | General observations |
|---|---|---|
| | Government has the initiative in shaping the way in which dialogue proceeds. In return for their involvement, groups offer co-operation and seek to ensure compliance of their members.<br><br>A modified variant is the tripartism or neo-corporatism of Britain in the 1970s, an era in which the CBI, TUC and government representatives agreed on the broad thrust of a counter-inflationary prices and incomes policy, behind closed doors. | Corporatist practice in broad decline since the 1980s, although they continue in 'consensus democracies' such as Austria and Scandinavia, especially where centre-left parties are in power. Britain was never a fully fledged corporate state. Its short experiment with tripartism was ended in the Thatcher years. No likelihood of any return to corporatist notions.<br><br>Often criticised for its lack of accountability and public involvement and supervision. |
| New Right thinking | Influenced by Olson's analysis of collective action and critique of groups.<br><br>Critical of group activity which throttles democratic politics and imperils economic growth.<br><br>Dislike of corporatist approach, associated with national decline in Britain of the 1960s and 1970s. Accused advocates of corporatism of wrecking the economy.<br><br>In particular, hostile to excessive power of major sectional, economic interests which did deals | Ideas highly influential in inspiring a backlash against tripartism and hastening its decline in the 1980s. Influence not confined to Britain, relevant on parts of Continent and in the United States.<br><br>Under the Conservatives and subsequently New Labour, governments have kept CBI and TUC at a distance, according 'no special favours'.<br><br>Not sympathetic to role and importance of groups in general, seeing producer professional groups (doctors, teachers) as wielding too much |

with government away from the public gaze and in the process undermined Parliament and democratic accountability.

No involvement of consumers and taxpayers.

influence over welfare policy. But thinkers of the New Right were to be found in various think tanks and right-wing business organisations – e.g. Freedom Association.

Marxism

Sees the fundamental problem in society as being the unequal distribution of wealth and power associated with capitalism.

Pressure groups seen as relatively ineffective, in that they cannot bring about major change.

Recognises that inevitably the interests of big business and manufacturing will predominate; they will act to their own advantage, in an exploitative way which entrenches and perpetuates economic and social inequality.

Labour organisations will be in a weaker position, unable to challenge the problems caused by the capitalist system. They can exert only modest influence, although Miliband sees unions as 'groups which governments have to reckon with'.

Marxists would argue that capitalism has survived because rulers have bought off the working classes by making concessions to them. Critics of their viewpoint would question the past marginal role of unions and suggest that workers have achieved benefits because of trade-union promotion of welfare state policies, full employment, better wage deals and workers rights etc.

Miliband[19] and others suggest that – contrary to usual Marxist thinking – other organisations can be influential. They note that women's, peace and environmental movements have at times had an impact, as have pro-immigrant bodies. All can modify the impact of capitalism and ultimately have the capacity to become agencies for the transformation of capitalist society.

•••••••••••••••••••••••••••••••••••••••••••••••••••••••••••••••••••••••••••

## ✔ What you should have learnt from reading this chapter

- Pressure groups are an important part of the political landscape in every democracy.

- They derive from man's natural wish for association with other individuals, in order to fulfil common goals.

- Their number has proliferated in recent decades and they represent many diverse causes.

- There is disagreement about the best term to describe them.

- They differ from social (popular) movements in that they are more formally organised and tend to use more conventional tactics.

- They differ from political parties in that they do not wish to assume the responsibilities of office but, instead, wish to influence those responsible for making public policy.

- They are a significant feature of pluralist societies, providing a channel of communication between the government and the governed, and assisting those in authority with the making of their decisions.

- There are different views of the role and value of pressure groups in modern societies, primarily those of pluralists, corporatists, New Right thinkers and Marxists.

## 🔍 Glossary of key terms

**Civil society**  A term embracing the various voluntary public bodies and private associations and their spokespersons which occupy the space between the family and the state and which contribute their ideas to the development of society. A strong civil society is often seen as a sound basis for a healthy democracy.

**Closed shop**  An industrial establishment in which there exists a contract between a trade union and an employer permitting the employment of the union's members only.

**De Tocqueville (1805–59)**  A liberal French aristocrat, writer and politician, Alexis de Tocqueville visited the United States as a young man, was impressed and wrote his study of *Democracy in America*.

**Direct action**  Any action beyond the usual constitutional and legal framework, such as obstructing access to a building or the building of a motorway. Terrorism is an extreme form. Essentially, it is an attempt to coerce those in authority into doing something they would not otherwise do.

**Ecologism**  The ideas concerned with ecology, the study of the relationship between living organisms and the environment. Ecologism starts not from a conception of humanity or human needs but from a vision of nature as a network of precious but fragile relationships between living species, including the human species, and the natural environment. Ecologists stress the network of relationships that sustain all forms of life. In contrast, an environmentalist is a person concerned with the issues that affect the environment, a light green. An ecologist, a deep green, has a more radical view, the good life being very different from the one we presently lead. He or she challenges the direction of our materialistic way of living.

**Executive agencies**  The forty or so agencies in the United States that provide special services either to the government or to the people – e.g. the Department of Veterans' Affairs.

**Multi-cultural/multi-ethnic society**  In a multi-cultural society, there is a diverse range of ethnic groups and cultures. Multi-ethnicity refers to the diverse range of ethnic groups that make up society.

**New Right**  A blend of right-wing ideas with some traditional conservative elements (strong government, plus an emphasis on leadership, defence, law and order, family values and patriotism) and some neo-liberal attitudes such as support for free markets, individualism and minimal state intervention. A prevalent strand of thinking in the 1980s among British Thatcherite Conservatives and US Reaganite Republicans.

**New social movements**  Organisations that have emerged since the 1960s in order to influence public policy on broad issues such as the environment, nuclear energy, peace and women's rights. They have wider interests and are more loosely organised than most pressure groups, tend to have supporters rather than members, and do not operate via detailed involvement with government. They are concerned to bring about fundamental change in society.

**Non-governmental organisations**  A term often applied to non-profit-making voluntary sector bodies to indicate that they are formally separate from government, even if their campaigning activities are directed at influencing ministerial policy. Often used by group representatives in the environmental and aid sectors, to describe their status.

**Pluralist societies**  Pluralism refers to the belief that power in modern societies is widely distributed between a multiplicity of competing interests. From time to time, new groups emerge, ensuring that there is further competition in the political market place. Pluralist societies are ones in which group activity can flourish, the various organised groups each having the opportunity to articulate their diverse demands.

**Think tanks**  Organisations formed specifically to conduct independent research, develop policy proposals and campaign for their adoption among opinion-formers and policy-makers. They have been more significant in British politics since the 1970s when a variety of bodies pushed for radical changes in economic and social policy and exercised an influence on the development of Conservative thinking. Right-wing think tanks include the Adam Smith Institute, the Centre For Policy Studies and the Institute of Economic Affairs. Centre-left organisations include Demos and the Institute for Public Policy Research.

**Tripartism**  A loose, less centralised form of corporatism (sometimes known as neo-corporatism) that involves close government consultation with business organisations and the trade unions over the conduct of economic policy and in particular over wage and price restraint. It was operated under governments of both British parties in the 1960s and 1970s. It is a rather weaker variety of corporatism than that often practised on the Continent where corporatist decision-making has often been institutionalised.

## Likely examination questions

Define a pressure group. Why is there some controversy over the definition of pressure groups?

Why is the distinction between pressure groups and political parties often unclear?

How do pluralists and corporatists view the role and value of pressure groups in modern democratic societies?

## Helpful websites

For basic information on pressure groups, their characteristics and influence, and on pluralism, consult:

www.historylearningsite.co.uk/pressure-groups.htm

www.psr.keele.ac.uk/parties  A university website providing links to international and national groups and social movements

www.uk-p.org/Organisations/Pressure_Groups  The UK Politics Directory that can be used to find the web addresses of a range of British pressure groups

For information on the ubiquitous nature of group activity, consult:

www.uia.org/index  Union of International Associations

www.politicalresources.net/ A list of national and international organisations

Otherwise, see the individual sites of various groups such as:

www.nationaltrust.org.uk  The National Trust

## Suggestions for further reading

*Useful books:*

R. Baggott, *Pressure Groups Today*, Manchester University Press, 1995.

P. Byrne, *Social Movements in Britain*, Routledge, 1997.

B. Coxall, *Pressure Groups in British Politics*, Pearson, 2001.

W. Grant, *Pressure Groups and British Politics*, Palgrave, 2000.

D. Simpson, *Pressure Groups*, 'Access to Politics' series, Hodder & Stoughton, 1999.

## CHAPTER 1

# Classifying Pressure Groups

## Contents

## Overview

Pressure groups are very numerous and very diverse, some being vast and permanent national organisations, others being short-lived local action groups. This makes it difficult to categorise them neatly. Nonetheless, academics have devised various classifications of groups.

In this chapter, we are concerned with three typologies: we divide groups according to the sector to which they belong, by the purpose for which they exist, and by their strategy to and relationship with government.

## Key issues to be covered in this chapter

- The Finer classification
- The traditional protective v. promotional classification, its merits and difficulties
- The Grant classification, its merits and difficulties
- Alternative typologies

## Opening observations

Attempting any classification of pressure groups is a difficult task, but one which all writers on the subject feel the need to tackle. There is such a multiplicity and diversity of associations and – as we have seen in the introductory chapter – they vary enormously in their degree of organisation, durability, influence and status. The confusing American usage of the term interest groups to embrace all of them serves only to make the issue more difficult. Three typologies have been distinguished with which we will deal in the order in which they were advanced.

## The sectoral approach

In his early study of the world of pressure-group activity, *Anonymous Empire*, Finer[1] produced a 'rough classification' of the more prominent and typical associations. This was done by categorising groups according to the sector in which they were active. He divided them into eight types:

• The business lobby
• The labour lobby
• The Co-operative Movement
• The professions
• Civic groups
• Special sections of the population
• The churches and evangelical groups
• Educational, recreational and cultural groups

Finer admitted that there was 'no sanctity' about his typology and that other classifications would do as well, 'perhaps even better'. His view was that even a half century ago groups were so 'innumerable and ubiquitous' that such broad groupings were a useful means of dividing them. His approach has been followed by many textbook writers in the United States ever since. As Walker[2] has shown that around three-quarters of American groups are based on business and occupational interests, the use of the term interest groups seems appropriate in American usage and it is convenient to speak of those concerned with manufacturing, labour, agriculture, the professions and so on. Indeed, writers such as Jillson[3] describe the remaining groups (those involved in campaigning for a particular cause) as interests as well, delineating two categories:

- Public interest groups, comprising a diffuse set of membership groups, law firms, think tanks, lobbying groups, and community organisations
- Social equity interest groups, civil rights organisations such as those representing women and ethnic minorities, which work to ensure that there exist equal opportunities for all Americans.

The problem with the sectoral approach is that the categories tell us little about the sort of work that an organisation does and its relationship with government, whether or not it has influence in the corridors of power. Indeed, the fact that Finer himself gave an interest and a promotional example for each grouping suggests that he recognised the desirability about being more specific about the groups involved.

## Protective and promotional groups

For several years, many writers preferred the approach outlined by Stewart,[4] the division of groups into those which defended an interest (variously known as interest, defensive, sectional groups) and those which advanced a cause (also known as attitude, cause, propaganda or ideas groups). Here, we use the more usual terms of **protective** and **promotional groups**.

Protective groups, referred to in the previous section as interest groups, represent the sectional interest of certain groups in society, their function being primarily to defend the material interests of, and provide a service to, their members. They are concerned with the self-interest of a particular section of the population, such as big employers and employees (see Box 1.1 opposite), farmers, doctors, lawyers and teachers. Such groups tend to be highly organised, well staffed and resourced, highly durable and – with some exceptions – have access to government. They comprise only those who operate in the sector.

Promotional groups are concerned to promote or propagandise on behalf of particular causes or ideas, arising out of the attitudes and beliefs (rather than the self-interests) of their members. They are concerned to advance what they see as the general good of society,

## Box 1.1  Employers' and employees' organisations: articulating the viewpoint of 'big business' and the unions

**Employer's organisations**

Business interests are among the most powerful players in pluralist democracies such as Britain. They are of strategic importance in the economy, and governmental interests and their own often tend to coincide. Many of them are represented in **peak organisations** which bring together within one organisation a whole range of other bodies and co-ordinate their activity and speak on their behalf. Such umbrella groups may represent the broad interests of capital (the Confederation of British Industry and the Institute of Directors, often referred to as the CBI or IoD) or the firms belonging to specific industries (Motor Manufacturers and Equipment Association, Food and Drink Federation).

The Confederation of British Industry is the premier lobbying organisation for British business on national and international issues. It works with the British government, international legislators and policy-makers to help British businesses compete effectively.

In addition to their membership of peak business and trade organisations, many large companies have their own public relations departments and engage in their own lobbying of government departments.

**Employee's organisations**

Employees are organised in trade unions. There is one British peak organisation representing the cause of labour, the Trades Union Congress (TUC). It has seventy affiliated trade unions (not all trade unions affiliate to the TUC). In many democracies, union power has been in decline in recent years and the TUC has lost membership since its heyday of the 1970s. It now represents just fewer than 7 million trade unionists.

Trade unionists are represented more directly by their individual unions. The largest are UNISON (1,300,500 members), AMICUS (1,061,199) and the Transport and General Workers Union (835,351). Membership of individual unions has dropped significantly in recent decades, from a high of 13.2million in 1979 to around 7million today.

In recent decades, trade unions have lost much of their bargaining power in Britain, Europe and America. The decline of manufacturing industry and high levels of unemployment in the 1980s, the trends to globalisation of national economies and the increase in new and less unionised employment have seriously affected their membership and have generally taken a toll of union influence.

helping groups other than their own members: their members do not stand to benefit materially from the end they seek to achieve. Heywood[5] provides the useful reminder that Save the Whale is an organisation *for* whales, not one *of* whales, and is therefore an example of a promotional rather than a protective group. Such groups often – but not always – operate on more limited resources; are inadequately staffed; are prone to division and secession; have open memberships and are often relatively short lived, disappearing once their task is completed. As a generalisation, they are less powerful than protective groups. They flourish in areas such as animal and human rights, the environment and welfare. Examples include Amnesty International, Friends of the Earth, the Child Poverty Action Group (CPAG) and the Royal Society for the Protection of Birds (RSPB).

There are problems with this classification. Many of the protective groups as usually defined would also argue that they devote themselves to the public welfare as well as to protecting their own self-interest. Bodies such as the British Medical Association (BMA) and the National Union of Teachers do campaigning work on behalf of promoting health care and provision, and education, respectively. Most protective groups do have a wider concern than solely advancing their members' good. The Automobile Association is primarily an organisation providing breakdown, insurance and other motoring services to those who annually subscribe to it. But it also takes a strong interest in motoring questions generally. Its views are sought by government ministers and journalists on issues ranging from speed limits to road safety more generally. In the same way, although a promotional group, such as the Campaign for the Advancement of State Education, has an open membership, in reality its supporters are heavily drawn from teachers in state schools who, as Coxall[6] points out, 'stand to gain professionally from the success of their cause'.

It is because of this overlap in function that some writers from Finer onwards have distinguished a third group within this classification, hybrid groups. He quoted the example of the Roads Campaign Council, founded by a group of trade and road-users' associations to campaign for better highways. Financed by 'interests', much of its work is propagandist. Similarly, the Royal College of Physicians was a prime mover in the creation of Action on Smoking and Health (ASH), as part of its bid to reduce smoking. We have already referred to the British Toilet Association which laments the decline in the quality of the country's public toilets 'once the envy of the world'[7] and campaigns for improved provision. But the list of backers – many of whom attended the 2005 World Toilet Summit – gives the game away. Its corporate champions range from Armitage Shanks to Enviro-Fresh Sani-Sleeve, from Danfo Public Conveniences to Healthmatic, companies all with an interest in providing 'away from home' toilet facilities.

From the above review, it may appear that protective groups, based on clear occupational interests, are more powerful than promotional ones. But there are some groups in the category that may lack power or even influence because they do not fulfil a key role in the national economy and have few sanctions to apply. As we have seen, trade unions as a whole have lost much of the power they exerted three or four decades ago. Finally, there are the **NIMBY groups** (Not In My Back Yard) who wish to see airport runways, asylum centres, prisons or roads built 'anywhere but here'. Local action groups designed to fend off some change of land use deemed detrimental to the interests of local residents have mushroomed in recent years. Technically protective groups, they are not the powerful, well-staffed bodies that immediately spring to mind when thinking of that genre. Their members often claim to be working for the good of the whole community. Under the right circumstances, they can achieve their objects and prevent unwanted development affecting their localities.

Writing from the late 1970s onwards, Grant[8] finds the protective versus promotional distinction unsatisfactory for another reason. Underlying it, in his view, there tends to be the assumption that protective groups are more influential than cause groups because they represent powerful interests. Also, it is easy to assume that promotional groups are of greater benefit to society than protective ones because they are more concerned with the general good rather than personal advantage. This led him to develop an alternative typology, as set out below.

## Insider and outsider groups

In the 1970s, Benewick[9] had tried to distinguish pressure groups in a different way by discerning three groups, each of which was characterised by the kind of relationship it had with government. There were:

- Those well-resourced groups seen as legitimate by government with which they had a stable and continuous relationship (the first world).
- Groups not short of resources or devoid of legitimacy which had less frequent contact with government (the second world).
- Groups not perceived as legitimate by government and which did not benefit from the kind of access accorded to the first two groups. Inevitably, these were seen as exerting less influence on government policy (the third world).

Benewick's division into the 'three worlds' of pressure groups did not have a profound effect on subsequent surveys. He himself came to recognise that some groups in his third category could have more impact in shaping public policy than he had originally believed, if only in helping to set the agenda for discussion. But his emphasis on group access to those with the power of decision was resurrected in Grant's research and publications.

Grant's[10] preferred approach is based on the relationship of groups with the central decision-makers in government. For him, the key issues are whether any particular group wants to gain acceptance by government and, if it does, whether or not it achieves that status. In his words: The principle on which such a typology is based is that in order to understand pressure groups, one needs to look not just at the behaviour of the groups but also at the behaviour of government.

Grant divides groups according to whether they are **insider** or **outsider** ones. Insider groups are regarded as legitimate players and are regularly consulted by government, having good – almost 'cosy' – access to the corridors of power. Outsider groups either do not want access or legitimacy, or are unable to attain such recognition. They are obliged to take a more public route in their search for influence. Many, but not all, protective groups are insider bodies and have con-sultative status. In most cases, promotional groups are outsider organ-isations, campaigning against the political mainstream. But there are several exceptions, such as the Campaign to Protect Rural England (CPRE), the Howard League for Penal Reform and the Royal Society for the Protection of Birds, all of which are in frequent touch with representatives of government. The status of others fluctuates over a period.

The Grant typology has itself come under some criticism:

- Baggott[11] has pointed out that it tends to assume that insider groups are more influential than outsider ones: 'This is not necessarily the case. Insider status may constrain groups who oppose government policy but do not wish to lose their privileged status. Secondly, outsider groups can exert influence over public attitudes and the political agenda and may ultimately have an impact on government policy.'

- There are different types of insider group, Jordan, Maloney and McLaughlin[12] distinguishing between core insiders who provide important information (e.g. the National Farmers Union and the BMA, on agriculture and health respectively), specialist insiders identified with a narrow area of policy (e.g. food safety) and peripheral insiders who have limited access and a fairly marginal impact on policy.

- More groups have insider status than Grant originally suggested. It is not hard to be consulted – some 200 are on the list for consultation on issues relating to motor cycles but their influence may be marginal. In other words, consultation is not a special privilege.

- Some groups pursue insider and outsider strategies at the same time so that the distinction is not clear-cut. Tactics, such as peaceful public demonstrations and letter-writing campaigns, are compatible with insider status but more violent direct action is not. In Greenpeace, from time to time, some tensions have existed over tactics. Over the years, it has shifted towards more dialogue with government and business while maintaining direct-action activities that attract money and popular support.

- In recent years, governments have been keen to show that they are not too beholden to pressure groups. Departments of state have tried to protect themselves from the accusation that they are held captive by powerful special interests and are less keen to provide economic pay-offs, whatever pressure they may under. The Blair government has been unwilling to bow to a range of union demands, such as large pay increases for many workers in the public sector. By contrast, ministers may today be more willing to

## Table 1.1 Selected groups from the three main classifications and their characteristics

| Sector | Group | Protective or promotional | Insider or outsider | Influence wielded |
|---|---|---|---|---|
| Big business | CBI | Protective | Insider | Significant, if not as great as in corporatist era (see pages 48–9). Well financed, staffed and resourced. In regular dialogue with government. |
| Labour | TUC | Protective | Insider: an outsider in the Thatcher–Major era in spite of its past importance. Now consulted more and in regular contact with Labour government. | Well financed, staffed and resourced but lost much of its influence and bargaining power in 1980s when there was an attack on union power and there was anti-union legislation. Consulted today, but granted 'no special favours' (see page 94). |
| Farming | NFU | Protective | Insider | Proud of its consultative status. In regular dialogue with Whitehall which values its specialist information and help in policy implementation. |

| | | | | |
|---|---|---|---|---|
| Professions | BMA | Protective | Insider | In regular dialogue. Seen as important in Whitehall for it offers specialist advice and co-operation in several policy areas. Also, representative of majority of doctors. |
| Public interest: conservation | RSPB | Promotional | Insider | Highly influential, consulted regularly on policy matters. Has vast membership and resources. |
| Public interest: the environment | Greenpeace | Promotional | Outsider | On occasion, able to express views in Whitehall but no regular dialogue. Members reluctant to get too close to ministers for fear of compromising their position. Sometimes likes to use direct action to grab public and ministerial attention. |

take note of the views of well-organised pressure from outsider groups, particularly if they have the ear of the media.

- If the insider versus outsider distinction was valid several years ago, it is less valid now because new forms of politics have arisen in the 1990s and subsequently. Pressure-group politics has changed, with more middle-class involvement in animal welfare and anti-roads protests. Also, there are more arenas than before, most obviously the devolved bodies and the European Union. Several British groups now concentrate much of the time on Brussels and this gives a new dimension to talk of access to the corridors of power in Whitehall.

- Finally, whereas the protective/promotional division can be usefully applied to pressure groups in Britain and worldwide, the Grant approach is inappropriate for use in a country such as the United States because of its structure of government. The American Constitution, based on the notion of a **separation of powers**, gives a greater role to the legislature than in Britain. Any United States administration lacks the capacity of a British government to push its programme through the legislative chambers so that there is much more concentration by large pressure groups on Congress. Grant's approach is better geared to democracies in which priority is placed on influencing the executive.

## Box 1.2  Alternative means of classifying groups

Other typologies of pressure groups have on occasion been employed. Some distinguish between primary and secondary groups. The former exist solely to lobby for political purposes, the latter primarily for other than political purposes – although they find themselves from time to time making representations on behalf of their members. Professional lobbying companies (see pages 88–9) and national cause groups, such as Charter 88 and local amenity groups, fall into the first category. Charities, churches, motoring organisations, trade unions and universities fall into the second one, their primary purpose being to cater for charitable, religious, motoring, workers' and higher-educational needs. The distinction is useful in reminding us that most groups are concerned with more than one task and do not spend all of their time on political activity. But it has been catered for in the section on the distinction between protective and promotional groups where we have referred to the fact that protective bodies often do promotional work and that some organisations are of the hybrid variety.

There are other taxonomies of groups. One advanced by Almond and Powell[13] in 2000 distinguishes them according to whether or not their objectives are primarily political. Under this classification, there are:

1. Associational groups are specifically organised to advance the political objectives of their members. The BMA is a British example, Common Cause an American one. The BMA well understands that, in protecting the professional and financial interests of its members, its professional staff and members take many actions to influence the policies of the British government concerning health provision. In both cases, members pay a membership fee. In the case of the former, they do so for the protection and services it provides, as well as to maintain the organisation. In the case of the latter, they pay up in order that the lobbying activities of a central staff can be sustained.

2. Institutional groups are primarily preoccupied with non-political goals although they may also pursue political objectives. Leaders of occupational groups well understand that, although they have other preoccupations, the actions of decision-makers in the political system will have less impact upon their own interests. Hence, they need to engage in lobbying.

3. Non-associational groups are more fluid groupings of individuals who share some common views and may on occasion become politically active on an issue. But they are not joined together in any permanent organisation. Local action groups come into this category.

4. Anomic groups are short-lived, spontaneous collections of individuals who share a common set of interests or grievances and express them in a generally disorganised and often emotional manner, perhaps in some sudden form of direct action that quickly comes to an end.

In their recent study, Newton and Van Deth[14] distinguish between the vast range of voluntary groups by dividing them into three categories:

1. Episodic groups which are not usually in any way concerned with public issues and seek to avoid them because involvement may be contentious and divisive. A local football team falls into this category. Only if its main amenity, its pitch, is threatened by some development is it likely to be involved in lobbying,

2. Fire brigade groups (see pages 57 and 64) are established to contest a particular issue. They fade away when the cause is won or lost.

3. Political groups (such as trade unions and business associations and many other associations, including campaigning environmental groups, health and welfare groups) are set up to operate in the political arena but engage in other non-political work as well.

In this case, the writers again seek to differentiate the world of the 'politically active' groups and those voluntary organisations whose work is 'non-political for most of the time'. They refer to any voluntary organisations that perform a political role at any time as pressure groups and then proceed to distinguish between Interest groups representing sectional interests and the rest which are labelled as cause groups. In other words, we come back to the second taxonomy described earlier in the chapter, the main point of this categorisation being to highlight the level of political activity in which a group engages.

Finally, in his 2005 study of the British political system, Moran[15] recognises that no classification can be definitive. Having alluded to the traditional distinction between interest groups whose members share a common interest and groups that promote a cause, he tries to capture the differences between them by using his own preferred terms. He opts for:

1. Functional groups: all those groups which 'reflect the occupational and industrial specialisation by which our economy operates'. They include groups whose members are individuals (e.g. the BMA) and those whose membership comprises organisations (e.g. the CBI). He stresses the importance of the division of labour in any modern economy and argues that such groups are important to the governing process because 'they create and deliver goods and services . . . the language pf "function" expresses this importance: these groups represent people and institutions that perform functions vital to social and economic life'.

2. Preference groups refer to those associations that are 'united by some set of common preferences'. Their range is potentially infinite for people may share a common interest in anything form religious affiliation to gay rights. Indeed, as he observes, they may be linked by a combination of these preferences, as in the formation of gay Christian groups. Preference groups cut across the functional category in that they include people who have different functional interests. He quotes the example of churches whose membership contains both employers and employees.

## Summary

We have already referred to the difficulties in classifying groups which come in so many different forms and varieties. Categories tend to overlap and be less than clear cut. They have their uses for convenience of academic study and provide some insight into how groups work politically and how successful they are likely to be in achieving influence or power.

The traditional protective versus promotional division is a useful one, focusing as it does on the purpose for which groups exist and the sort of people who belong to them. It features strongly in the rest of this study. But the broad thrust of debate on the categorisation of groups over the last two decades has been away from the focus on their organisational features, outlook and political behaviour, and towards studying their acceptance or otherwise in the corridors of power, as Grant and others prefer. In drawing attention to issues of status and relationship to government, his typology is a valuable tool in analysing the effectiveness of individual groups. Yet all of the classifications alluded to have been the subject of regular criticism, encouraging writers such as Rhodes[16] and others to place more emphasis on the way in which policy emerges rather than on the types of groups involved in its creation. He argues that past concentration on the Westminster model of politics is inadequate to describe how government operates in the present day. There has been 'a shift from government by a unitary state to governance by and through networks'. Those taking the Rhodesian view are more interested in the respective roles of government agencies, pressure groups and other players involved in policy consultations.

••••••••••••••••••••••••••••••••••••••••••••••••••••••••••••••

### ☑ What you should have learnt from reading this chapter

- There are difficulties in any classification of pressure groups.

- Various typologies have been advanced, each with its own merits and difficulties.

- The most usual divisions are those between protective and promotional groups which work for many countries and the insider and outsider groups which are useful in studying British politics.

- More emphasis of late has been placed on the relationship of groups to government than on their protective or promotional role.

- Some writers prefer to stress whether or not a group's primary purpose is political or otherwise.

- Such categorisations are a convenient means of handling the massive number and great diversity of groups.

## Glossary of key terms

**Insider groups** Groups regarded as legitimate by government and in regular consultation with it. They are regarded as responsible and authoritative, and their advice and experience are relied upon by policy-makers. Examples include the NFU, the Police Federation and the RSPB.

**NIMBY groups** Local-action groups whose members are self-interested in that they are concerned to protect their lifestyle, but whose campaigns may help to make people aware of the threat to the environment in which they and others live. Commonly, they campaign against developments which will impact adversely on the view from, and value of, their own house or land.

**Outsider groups** Groups that either do not wish to have, or cannot acquire, consultative status with policy-makers. They tend to shun the political mainstream. Examples are Compassion in World Farming and the various human rights bodies.

**Peak or umbrella groups** Organisations that coordinate and represent the broad activities and interests of business or labour, such as the CBI and TUC. Their members are not individuals, but other bodies such as firms, trade associations or labour unions.

**Promotional groups** Groups that promote a general cause or idea, members not being drawn from any particular occupation but from people with a wide variety of backgrounds who share a common concern. Examples include the RSPB and Women Against Rape.

**Protective groups** Pressure groups that represent the material interests of particular economic or occupational groups that have a stake or interest in society. They provide a range of services for their members. Examples include the BMA and NFU.

## Likely examination questions

Analyse the various approaches to classifying pressure groups. Which approach is the most appropriate?

## Helpful websites

For basic information on pressure groups and their characteristics consult:

www.historylearningsite.co.uk/pressure-groups.htm

Most individual pressure groups have their own sites, covering such aspects as the history, objectives and organisation of organisations. Some examples are listed below.

www.cbi.org.uk  Confederation of British Industry

www.tuc.org  Trades Union Congress

www.greenpeace.org.uk  Greenpeace

## Suggestions for further reading

*Useful articles:*

W. Grant, 'Outsider in! Insider groups under challenge', *Politics Review*, 11, 2001.

W. Grant, 'Insider groups to direct action?', *Parliamentary Affairs*, 54, 2001.

*Useful books:*

R. Baggott, *Pressure Groups Today*, Manchester University Press, 1995.

B. Coxall, *Pressure Groups in British Politics*, Pearson, 2001.

W. Grant, *Pressure Groups and British Politics*, Palgrave, 2000.

M. Moran, *Politics and Governance in the UK*, Palgrave, 2005.

D. Simpson, *Pressure Groups*, 'Access to Politics' series, Hodder & Stoughton, 1999.

## CHAPTER 2

# How Pressure Groups Operate

## Contents

## Overview

Pressure group modes of operation are largely shaped by the characteristics of the political system in which they operate. In Britain, it is generally accepted by many group lobbyists that, whichever party is in power, the most effective way of achieving their objects is to establish good links in Whitehall so that the group is consulted whenever ministers are contemplating action or legislation that may affect it. But, for many cause campaigners, Parliament and the public are more likely targets. Many activists increasingly find themselves drawn to direct action as a means of getting their message across.

In this chapter, we explore the types of approaches employed by protective and promotional, insider and outsider groups as they seek to achieve influence.

## Key issues to be covered in this chapter

- Access points groups targeted by pressure groups
- Why groups target the executive: the mutual advantages for either side
- Groups and the legislature
- How and why groups seek to influence public opinion
- Other outlets for group lobbyists and campaigners

## Groups and the access points they employ

In any free society there are **access points**, formal parts of the governmental structure that are accessible to group influence. Where the emphasis is placed will vary from democracy to democracy. In Britain, the most obvious ones are:

the executive (ministers and civil servants);
the legislature (MPs individually and as members of the party);
public opinion.

In Britain, the main fact which determines the nature of group activity is the inherent strength of any government created by: the high degree of centralisation of power; the acceptance of strict party discipline at Westminster; and the general agreement that ministers should have the authority to govern and not be unduly restricted from acting in the way they it deem appropriate. Decision-making is therefore concentrated in Whitehall, with key decisions being made in government departments. Large, powerful protective and insider groups understand this and recognise the importance of having close contacts there.

The approach adopted by lobbyists and campaigners otherwise depends on the type of group involved. Protective groups may also have contacts in Westminster and, in the case of the unions, close links with several MPs. By contrast, many promotional groups will have very infrequent contact and little influence in Whitehall unless they are insider groups, such as the RSPB. They may have some spasmodic support at Westminster but will try to persuade public opinion in their favour in the hope that the press and MPs will then take up the cause if it proves to be one of much concern. In addition, in recent years there have been new focuses on which lobbyists and campaigners can seek to exert influence and apply pressure, the devolved machinery and the European Union among them (see chapters 6 and 7 for detailed coverage of these areas). For some activists, direct action is an important campaigning tool, enabling them to exert and apply some leverage over those whom they seek to influence.

## The traditional outlets used by pressure groups

### The executive

In almost all countries, protective groups target the executive branch of government. Sometimes, they deal with ministers directly but elected politicians mainly set out what Hague and Harrop[1] refer to as the 'broad contours' of policy. More often, lobbyists – who are interested in the small print of policy – have contact with senior figures in the various departments of state. Groups require access to the seat of power, and it is in the departments that decisions are made and the details of legislation finalised. Matthews[2] explains why this is so: '. . . the bureaucracy's significance is reinforced by its policy-making and policy-implementing roles. Many routine, technical and "less important" decisions, which are nonetheless of vital concern to interest groups, are actually made by public servants.'

Most leading British protective groups have close contacts in Whitehall. It is the Higher Civil Service which offers advice to the secretary of state, the political head of a government department, and so it is very worthwhile to contact senior civil servants. Civil servants/ministers find relevant groups useful to them. Governing large, industrialised societies is a complex business in which there are many choices to be made and competing demands to reconcile. Governments therefore make a practice of consulting widely, dealing with representatives of all significant groups in society. Such consultation is valuable to them, because:

1.  It is a means of ascertaining the views of members of the group, in the case of protective groups, employers, employees and professionals among them. This may be valuable in helping ministers to formulate plans for legislation and monitoring the success of measures that have reached the statute book.
2.  They can get technical information and advice, based on the knowledge and practical experience of the issues that members possess.
3.  They may obtain assistance in carrying out policy. From the BMA, they may not only find out about the incidence of any infectious diseases that GPs are coming across but also gain the support of doctors in any programme of mass or localised vaccination. The same is true of farmers who are in a position to help ministers handle outbreaks, such as **BSE** and foot-and-mouth disease.

4. Finally, ministers can use such contacts as a means of passing information to the people who will be most interested so that groups become important avenues for communication between government and members of affected interests.

Consultation between government representatives and groups is a constant process, and the range of dialogue is immense. In some cases, it is statutory, a particular measure laying down the interests that ministers are obliged to consult. More often, it is discretionary although, once any group has been asked for its views, it tends to assume that this will be the forerunner of similar contacts in the future. If ministers feel that high-quality and specialist advice and assistance are available, that the leadership of the group is representative of its members, and that the organisation has wide support within the sector in which it operates, they are likely to want to see any initial consultation as a precedent for further consultation. Of course, groups benefit in return. They get to know about the department's current thinking, hope to influence its decisions, and get legislation drawn up in line with their recommendations.

In the case of insider promotional groups, such as the RSPB and the RSPCA, they are valued in Whitehall for the knowledge and expertise they can provide. Other campaigners may be contacted where their specialism might be useful to decision-makers in Whitehall, the more so if their cases are well argued and their methods of campaigning non-provocative and responsible.

Contact with the executive can be arranged via formal and informal links – government-established committees, the circulation of government documents and widespread consultation conducted in other ways. The National Farmers Union (NFU) and those employed at the lower end of senior policy grades in the Department of Farming and Rural Affairs (DEFRA) are in frequent contact. The NFU values its consultative status in Whitehall and likes to operate in a quiet, behind-the-scenes way which avoids too much publicity. Only when a row breaks out will it turn to open public methods. The BMA has similar regular, on-going contacts.

Insider groups, such as the BMA and NFU, are very important to government. So, too, are business groups whose leading figures also tend to be in regular contact. They have an advantage at this level.

## Box 2.1  Tripartism or neo-corporatism

The term used to describe the various forms of tripartite bargaining between governments and interest groups (representing business and labour) which have been common in Europe and were employed in a weaker form in the Britain of the 1960s and 1970s. The aim is to make the process of government more consensual and to avoid open conflict: and to foster harmony among the competitive interests in a market economy.

When this relatively weak form of corporatism was practised in Britain, peak organisations, such as the CBI and TUC, had an important role in planning and implementing certain key economic and social policies. In discussions with the government, the interests represented agreed to certain deals, making 'trade offs' which gave them some of what their members wanted. The underlying idea was that all those involved were seeking to elevate the national interests above purely sectional concerns. Union leaders were prepared to exhibit restraint in wage demands in return for employers doing their best to maintain employment and keep the prices of their goods down. The role of government was there to represent the national interest, doing its best to create a stable, benign economic climate which would encourage the other elements to pursue unselfish policies. Accorded such influence, the social partners were willing to seek and encourage the compliance of their members. Discussion of policy was effectively depoliticised, much of it being determined in meetings behind closed doors.

Since the 1980s, there has been a marked reduction in corporatist activity across Europe as governments have increasingly moved to free-market competition, with greater use of competition and deregulation. Margaret Thatcher was notoriously scathing about the influence of entrenched interests. She was unwilling to accept the power of organised labour and was unwilling to bargain with its leaders. Heads of 'big business' organisations also detected a change in their status, the CBI being placed at a greater distance from government. The Thatcher approach was based upon vigorous competition and more open markets, with government unwilling to step in and assist companies experiencing trading difficulties.

They play a pivotal role in the economy as producers and employers. In the 1960s and 1970s – the age of tripartism or **corporatism** (see Box 2.1 above) – it became fashionable for leading bodies, such as business/trade organisations and trade unions, to work with representatives of government in the management of the economy. Each side contributed its views, and ministers sought to get agreement about what the economy could afford by way of price rises and wage increases. Such corporatism has gone out of fashion in the last two decades although it is still practised in some European countries.

Today, almost all government departments are involved in the process of consultation and discussion which forms an important part of the workload of many officials. The Treasury does not consult in the run-up to the Budget because of the need for secrecy on sensitive information. It does, however, receive submissions from interested parties on what they would like to see in the annual statement. Once the Chancellor has revealed his or her proposals, then consultation can take place on their implementation. The Foreign Office is inevitably less in contact with domestic pressure groups because of the nature of its work. Civil rights groups, alarmed by human-rights-related issues, may lobby to reverse governmental decisions, however, as may the families and friends of British nationals held captive overseas.

Of course, consultation is not the same as influence. Many groups may be consulted on a particular area of policy (see the examples given on page 145 in the case of the Scottish Executive) but this does not mean that their views are necessarily highly regarded. Large groups, such as the CBI, TUC, BMA and others, may seem to be at an advantage. Promotional groups with a relatively small membership can achieve influence, however, if the public is thought to be in broad sympathy with their aims. If their standing with the public diminishes, then their views may seem less important. In the mid-1980s, the Lord's Day Observance Society still held a remarkable hold over governments of all colours, particularly in discussion of the issue of the Sunday trading laws. By the mid-1990s, that influence was dwindling as church attendances continued to decrease and society became more liberal. Whereas the Thatcher government was unable to pass its Shops Bill in 1986, the Major administration was able to pass a compromise measure allowing all retail outlets to open for six hours on Sunday.

Policy-making at any level of government tends to be sectoralised. Each sector has its own policy network involving decision-makers and group lobbyists working together to do something that may be of benefit to them both or at least prevent them from striking attitudes

## Box 2.2  Policy networks in modern democracies

The concept of policy networks has attracted much attention in recent years. They describe the different kinds of relationships between groups and government and the range of players (organised groups, national and European civil servants, regulators and academics) in any particular sector. The term is a generic one denoting a continuum from close and stable policy communities to looser, more open and discontinuous policy or issue networks.

**Policy communities**
For many years, there were particularly close links in America between interest groups, congressional committee chairmen and government departments, an arrangement often referred to as 'iron triangles'. In democracies such as Britain, there was more talk of 'policy communities'. Such communities involved a high degree of interdependence between insider groups and government, without the involvement of committee chairmen in the legislature. They were characterised by close, mutually supportive ties, based on a stable relationship between the participants and a high degree of contact. The idea of policy communities fitted in well with Grant's classification of insider and outsider groups, the former having close involvement in decision-taking. In Britain, policy communities were formed around subjects such as food and drink policy, technical education and water privatisation. In all cases, the interaction between the groups and government was close and continual, with both sides placing a premium on mutual and largely secret co-operation.

In the last two decades, the autonomy of such communities has given way to broader consultation and discussion in 'issue networks'. Issue networks are wider and looser and, in addition to the three elements above, describe other players involved in discussion of a policy area, including the research institutes and the media. Media scrutiny and the attentions of consumer protest groups have led to a more critical analysis of policy-making processes so that secret deals and mutual back-scratching are now less frequent or effective. As Hague and Harrop[3] have explained in relation to the United States, 'the iron has gone out of the triangle; now influence over decisions depends on what you know, as well as who you know'.

Policy communities have begun to decay in most democracies, and the trend is towards the more open style of policy-making which characterises issue networks. The impact of any particular group may vary from time to time or issue to issue, partly depending on the expertise it possesses. There are more participants in issue networks, relationships are not continuous or particularly close, and there is less interdependence.

and adopting policies that damage one side or the other. **Policy networks** is the name given to such sectoral groupings (see Box 2.2 above), with the relationship being either close and continual (policy communities) or loose and wide (issue networks).

### The legislature

In many countries, groups often voice their views via parliaments and assemblies although whether they place much emphasis at this level depends in part on how much influence the representative body can wield. In Britain, there is a strong system of party discipline, so that MPs are likely to be less responsive to group persuasion. Powerful protective British groups prefer contact with the executive but MPs are lobbied by them as well as by campaigning groups. So, too, on a more limited basis, is the House of Lords.

British groups rarely participate directly in a general election in order to secure the election to Parliament of a candidate representing their organisation. They may show preference for a particular candidate or party, however, either of which articulates their viewpoint on an issue such as the 2003 war in Iraq. Green groups were active in the build-up to the 2001 election, Friends of the Earth offering a comparison of party attitudes and performances. (See Box 2.3 on page 52).

Once elected, MPs can expect to receive contacts and be invited to attend social gatherings, taken on tours of factories or environmental sites by relevant groups, or expected to meet delegations. In one study of 253 organised interests,[5] 75 per cent of them claimed to be in regular or frequent contact with one or more MPs and more than half also maintained contact with the House of Lords (see Box 2.4 at the end of this section). They might rank its influence below that of the executive branch but the trend since the 1980s has been towards more lobbying of the legislature, for several reasons:

## Box 2.3  Green intervention in the electoral process

In 2001, as in the 1997 election campaign, some of the leading environmental pressure groups, including Greenpeace, FoE, the CPRE, the RSPB, the WWF, the Wildlife Trusts and the Green Alliance, campaigned together under an umbrella grouping entitled 'Vote Environment'. The basic objective was to increase their influence by producing a unified voice for the environmental movement. In so doing, they hoped to push environmental and transport issues higher up the election agenda. Their efforts were complemented by those of a large alliance of twenty-four charities that campaigned under the *Global View 2001* banner and focused on the themes of international development and globalisation.

Among other techniques, in 2001 the Green lobby:

- used the Internet and e-mail extensively, creating election websites as a key resource for influencing Green-inclined voters;
- arranged a rally and publicity exercise to generate interest in the last week of the campaign, coinciding with World Environment Day. Media coverage, however, was limited mainly to the broadsheets and BBC on-line;
- via its Green Cross Code Campaign, invited candidates to support five pledges on business accountability, climate change, genetically modified food, transport and waste. Just under a third of candidates from the main parties responded, with Liberal Democrat candidates showing high rates of support for green positions;
- provided a wide range of information on the parties' environmental positions, passing judgements on their manifestos.

In a press release, *How Green Are The Parties?*,[4] FoE provided a detailed analysis of the party manifestos, measuring them against ten important environmental yardsticks, ranging from climate change, fuel poverty and energy production at the top, to global issues and sustainable development.

1.  The improved sophistication of the resources available to campaigners makes contact with parliamentarians more easy. Technology allows the use of e-mail which enables group organisers to circulate the majority of MPs (and peers) at the touch of a button.

2. The growth and development of the select committee system since the 1980s has created new targets for influence, providing campaigners with a clear focus for their lobbying. By giving oral and, more often, written evidence, they have a chance to place the views of their members in the public domain and, they hope, determine the character of committee recommendations. The increasing importance attached to pre-legislative scrutiny by the House serves to make the input of groups even more worthwhile.

3. The attitudes of governments. The Thatcher and Major administrations were unenthusiastic about the corporatist approach to policy-making which had reached its peak of influence in the previous decade. In general, they were less receptive to many group campaigners, encouraging lobbyists to turn to MPs. Moreover, the existence of governments with large majorities since 1979 means that it can be more productive for groups to work on backbenchers in the hope of persuading them to oppose what ministers are trying to steamroller through the House.

Elected representatives have often worked as business people, lawyers, teachers or trade unionists in their earlier life so that there are likely to be members more than willing to speak up for the interests of various groups in the community. They may be willing to champion individual causes or even put forward a private member's bill. MPs who draw a high position in the annual ballot to introduce such a bill soon find themselves contacted by campaigners who hope to persuade them to introduce a measure relating to their cause. They may have a draft bill ready or else provide assistance in devising one; for example, pro-life groups are keen to find someone willing to introduce legislation restrictive of the circumstances under which abortions can be carried out.

Groups like to have members sympathetic to their aims and seek out such members. They will supply them with information and arguments, and employ various methods to retain contact. They may appoint MPs to honorary positions within the group, form a parliamentary panel of sympathetic members, encourage the formation of an all-party grouping to represent causes such as **temperance** or support for Israel, advise members to sit on appropriate party committees or, in the case of ex-MPs, perhaps employ their services as a professional lobbyist.

Interested members can assist or promote the cause of groups in various ways:

1. When new legislation is produced, they may sponsor amendments suggested by pressure groups.
2. They may ask a parliamentary question on their behalf, in order to ferret out information, clarify an ambiguous position, goad ministers into action or protest against some policy or occurrence on behalf of the group.
3. Advance group concerns in a general debate.
4. Initiate legislation on behalf of the group.

Influence at the parliamentary level includes elected representatives, committees or even a particular party. Prominent British pressure groups often claim to be non-political though some have clear party leanings. CBI attitudes on 'free enterprise' broadly coincide with Conservative ones, and the unions have historic links with the Labour Party and some are affiliated to it. The TUC is not formally linked and plays no part in the Labour organisation though there is regular contact between the two bodies and they share a common desire to change society for the benefit of working people.

In lobbying Parliament, groups hope to:

• amend or sponsor legislation in a direction favourable to them;
• influence the climate of discussion on relevant issues of public interes;
• gain parliamentary backing for causes they may have first raised outside the chamber.

**The appeal to the public**
Groups try to influence the public who, after all, are the voters in the next election. American groups have long gone in for this style of pressure in the anticipation that any demonstration of popular backing will inspire the legislature and the executive to respond favourably.

Some groups are held in high regard and any campaigning they

## Box 2.4  Group activity and the House of Lords

When Finer wrote the first edition of his landmark study of the lobby in Britain in the late 1950s, he did not see fit to include a mention of group activity in relation to the House of Lords. Fifty years later, such an omission would be negligent.

According to the findings of the Study of Parliament Group,[6] 70 per cent of group representatives interviewed claimed to have had contact with the House of Lords, 59 per cent of them 'regular' or 'frequent' communication. The vast majority found the dialogue with peers 'useful' or 'very useful'. Other studies[7] have confirmed that lobbying of the second chamber has increased and that on balance groups find it beneficial and effective. Baggott[8] points out that peers are 'more independently minded than MPs and less fearful of the whips', hence the number of defeats inflicted on the Thatcher and Blair administrations. Of course, like members of the lower house they are liable to be swayed by interests and causes with which they have connections. They are expected to declare any pecuniary interests and not promote or oppose legislation in areas where they are receiving a fee or reward.

At the time Finer was writing his book, the composition of the Lords was unreformed. The **Life Peerages Act** was passed in the year of its publication. At the time, it was widely condemned for its hereditary composition, its overwhelmingly conservative (and Conservative) bias and the absenteeism of a large proportion of its members. From the 1980s onwards, it has undergone a renaissance, its contribution to the working of Parliament being much more highly rated. The arrival of the television cameras before they appeared in the House of Commons; the growing influence of the life peers and the change their arrival brought to the character of the second chamber; the near removal of the hereditaries in 1999; the sense of responsibility felt by members to provide an effective opposition to governments with a huge majority: all are credited with creating a new spirit of professionalism.

Given their new-found respectability, peers have been more assertive in forcing governments to justify their policies. This increased willingness to challenge the decisions of the elected chamber has not found favour with some government ministers. But peers are now widely accepted by many commentators as performing their duties conscientiously and effectively. Because of this, as Grant[9] explains: 'The House of Lords offers fruitful ground for inserting relatively technical amendments which may be important to a pressure group's members.'

In its campaign against the abolition of fox hunting (see Chapter 8), the Countryside Allliance made extensive use of contacts in the Lords where a large number of peers shared its broad approach. Its spokespersons had detected a significant improvement in the quality of its performance since the 1999 reform and felt that it could be helpful to their cause. They made use of circulars to, and meetings with, peers of sympathetic persuasion. Peter Jenkins of the British Consumers Association[10] has explained why his group has also found the second chamber helpful: 'Because the present government has such a large majority in the House of Commons, we have found it easier to work in the Lords. It's a case of lobbying sympathetic peers, explaining what the impact of the legislation will be if it is unchanged, and persuading them to table amendments.' Contact may be with individual or sympathetically inclined peers or with an all-party committee. It ranges from letter-writing and e-mailing to the submission of briefs, newsletters and magazines. On occasion, there may be an accompanying request that peers ask questions or raise points in debate.

Over the last few decades, groups have come to see the benefits to be gained from lobbying the upper house which has become a new focus of group activity. Its role in scrutinising legislation has sometimes created considerable difficulties for the party in power, whether it be the Conservatives under Margaret Thatcher or Labour under Tony Blair. In the discussion of controversial bills involving civil liberties (e.g. the legislation on freedom of information, the detention of alleged terrorists, asylum seekers and ID cards), campaigners have been active in contacting peers to fortify their resolve in thwarting or improving Blairite proposals. Similarly, in the case of disadvantaged groups, varying from the disabled to students threatened with the prospect of payment of tuition fees, campaigners have been willing to work with cross-bench and opposition peers in a bid to defeat ministers. The amendments that the Lords can make to bills are more likely to be accepted by the Commons when they are constructive, of a technical character and designed to improve legislation which peers recognise that ministers have the mandate to introduce.

*See also chapter 8, for coverage of the involvement of the House of Lords in the moves to ban hunting with dogs.*

undertake is likely to arouse strong support. The BMA benefits from the generally positive feelings people have about the medical profession and health service. Groups looking after child and animal welfare evoke a warm response. Groups that advocate less popular causes (such as **Outrage!**) or whose views are considered extreme (for example, CND) are, by comparison, handicapped.

There are two broad types of public campaign. **Background** campaigns are intended to create a favourable impression for a cause over a period of time. In Britain, Aims for Freedom and Enterprise, a long-time crusading organisation against nationalisation and in favour of privatisation, keeps up a steady flow of information and becomes more prominent at election time. A more dramatic **fire brigade** campaign may quickly rally support and get MPs and government ministers to take notice. The Snowdrop campaign in 1996–7 used this blitz approach.

Whereas the public level seemed to be the least influential a few years ago, in the last couple of decades it has become more common. Campaigns are often expensive, time consuming to organise and unpredictable in their outcome, but the development of modern mail-shots, advertising and marketing techniques has made them more appealing. In addition, television provides opportunities for publicity (see page 59) and some organisations now campaign via the medium. By persuading voters to take an issue on board, they hope to generate public interest and raise awareness. Environmental groups, which have flourished in the last two decades, have consciously sought to mobilise support through the use of television images and discussions.

For those groups which employ direct action, television can provide a means of gaining valuable publicity. The prolonged Greenham Common anti-Cruise missile protest of the early 1980s attracted some attention. So, too, the campaigns against the M3 extension at Twyford Down (see page 133) and against the Newbury bypass a decade or so later gained extensive coverage. More recently, so have the campaigning activities of Fathers 4 Justice.

## Alternative outlets

### The legal route
As yet, British groups have made only limited use of the legal route, recognising that it can be a costly process and not deliver the outcome required. Some of the most well-known legal cases brought by groups in the 1980s and 1990s were decided in the European Union's Court of Justice in Luxembourg and in the Council of Europe's Court of

Human Rights in Strasbourg, over issues such as equal pay and the abolition of corporal punishment in schools, respectively. The method has become increasingly popular in recent years as a means of ensuring that local and national government carry out their responsibilities and as part of any campaign to effect changes in the law. Even where a legal challenge fails, it can be useful as a means of politicising an issue and generating publicity.

Bodies, such as the Equal Opportunities Commission and Greenpeace, have won considerable victories in the courts. Greenpeace has been particularly active in the courts, sometimes bringing its own case (for example, the unsuccessful challenge in 1997 to the DTI over its granting of licences for oil exploration on the Atlantic Frontier, as part of an attempt to slow down oil exploration west of Shetland) sometimes defending itself (for example, when BP responded to the 1997 challenge and sought a court order freezing Greenpeace's assets). Friends of the Earth withdrew from its protest at Twyford Down in 1998 after learning that it faced sequestration of its assets if it did not do so.

More recently, the Countryside Alliance used the judicial route in an attempt to delay the implementation of the ban on fox hunting, claiming that it was a denial of members' rights under the European Convention. Britain is a much less litigious society than the United States where civil rights' and other groups have made extensive use of the courts. The passage of the **Human Rights Act** (1998), however, has paved the way for challenges by groups opposed to governmental legislation on asylum seeking and other issues where there appears to be a threat to individual or group liberty.

**Other outlets**

Groups can be effective in other ways: by working with political parties, lobbying other pressure groups and companies; and using the mass media to create a favourable climate of opinion for their action. There are also other layers of government which provide access, at the local, devolved and European levels. The last two of these are fully discussed in chapters 6 and 7, respectively.

Most groups adopt a neutral attitude towards the political parties. They understand that too close an identification with one party may jeopardise prospects for influence should another assume the reins of power. The tendency is to rely less on party connections and more on consultation with government, whichever party is in office. Of course, there are exceptions. We have already noted the bonds between Labour and the unions, and the broad similarity of approach to private enterprise of the Conservatives and several business interests. But in neither case can the organisation count on the support of the party with whose outlook it is broadly aligned.

Another trend has been the growth in lobbying of other pressure groups and companies. Some years ago, the National Trust became an important arena for conflict between pro- and anti-hunting with dogs campaigners, an argument won by those who wanted a ban in 1997. Private companies have also been targeted by campaigners. It may be the supermarket that sells bananas produced by an exploited labour force; the sportswear store that sells trainers or footballs produced by cheap child labour; large corporations like Shell Oil, whose activities in Africa and elsewhere have been seen as the cause of environmental degradation; the financial-service institutions who fail to promote an 'ethical' option for would-be purchasers of unit trusts; or the moneylenders who trade on people's desperation by charging exorbitant and exploitative rates of interests.

Most groups like to use the media in their campaigning for they recognise its potency as a means of influencing opinion (see Box 2.5 overleaf on the Save the Valley campaign). The importance of the media for lobbyists was highlighted in the 1990 findings of the Study of Parliament group[11] which found that groups ranked this outlet third as a means of influencing public policy, after ministers and civil servants and before MPs. The media have become a central focus for promotional groups seeking to steer popular attitudes, providing as they do the opportunity to address a mass public. In particular, those directing protest activities recognise the value of free publicity that their stunts can attract. As Grant Jordan[12] points out: 'Protest without media coverage is like a mime performance in the dark: possible, but fairly pointless.' If the activities of protesters can generate striking images, editors and journalists will be especially willing to cover them. Jordan notes that those involved in direct action recognise the value of staging 'events': 'An implicit contract exists whereby if protesters can give the media stories and pictures, then opportunities to air concerns are available.'

On occasion, newspapers, television and radio stations, and advertising bodies are themselves the target for group activity. They have the capacity to help set the political and social agenda so that those who wish to see a cause obtain a higher or lower profile are naturally attracted to the broadcasting authorities. Grant[13] refers to the interesting example of the popular BBC Radio Four serial, *The Archers*, whose writers and producers have regularly been the object of

---

### Box 2.5  Skilful use of the media in the Save the Valley campaign

In the 1980s, the media were used by campaigners seeking to save the Valley as the football ground of Charlton Athletic FC. After serious financial problems, the club no longer owned its ground which needed substantial renovation. Its decision to share facilities with Crystal Palace at Selhurst Park, however, never won the backing of many supporters who disliked the idea of driving 10 miles across London to see a home game. For two seasons they maintained a weekly chant: 'We should have stayed at the Valley'. In 1987 the directors decided to return to their home area and repurchased the Valley, with a view to building a new ground there. They even formed a political party, the Valley Party, which fought a full-scale election campaign through the ballot box at the local elections.

Canvassers used door-stepping and leaflets to publicise the cause. Above all, what the campaigners needed in order to persuade the Labour-controlled council to back their return, was attention from the broadcast media and national newspapers. The local paper was fully behind the venture. An extensive poster campaign was undertaken, thirty-five sites being booked for most of the month before the April 1990 election.

Media coverage was an important part of the success. Although funds were limited, the Valley Party was able to attract national coverage of what was a local issue, both at the press conference to launch the campaign and in items on *Thames News*, *Newsnight,* and LBC and Capital Radio. Articles in *The Guardian*, too, were seen as helpful. Above all, however, advertising was 'at the heart of an effective campaign. It was the advertising which generated the powerful media coverage and helped to recruit sixty citizens who, in the space of a couple of months, became a potential political force in the Borough [Greenwich].

campaigners concerned about alleged moral decline and farming practices in the village of Ambridge.

Lobbying of local government has been another growth area in recent years. Here the term is widely used to include not only elected local councils and elected mayors but other bodies that operate locally, including health authorities. Groups are active at the local level in spite of the broad decline of local democracy. Council and other bodies still have substantial decision-making powers and are, at times, on the receiving end of lobbying from a wide range of bodies. Many of these organisations are not primarily political but, on occasion, their wishes may conflict with those of councillors. A football club may find its facilities threatened by proposed development, or a

### Table 2.1  Access points available to British groups: a summary

| International | UK national government |
|---|---|
| United Nations | The executive |
| UN-related bodies such as World Bank | Parliament (both chambers) |
| G8 | **UK sub-national government** |
| Overseas governments | Local authorities/devolved machinery |
| **European Union (see chapter 7): main targets** | **Miscellaneous** |
| Council of Ministers | Other pressure groups |
| European Commission | Private companies |
| European Parliament | Public corporations |
| European Court of Justice | The media |

Adapted from R. Baggott, *Pressure Groups and the Policy Process*, Politics Association, 2000.

supermarket may feel that a new local policy banning the driving of cars through the main street is detrimental to its profitability. Other groups are long running and more often involved in local controversy. The Campaign to Protect Rural England has local branches around the country. These and other amenity groups, such as the Victorian Society, are often active insider groups that have to be consulted before any decisions with serious planning implications are taken. This may be the case before there can be any demolition of locally listed buildings.

In particular, the proliferation of local action, NIMBY-type groups has made grass-roots decision-makers an obvious target for group activists. The decision of many middle class urban dwellers to move into rural areas has increased group activity for such people are more unwilling to ignore planning infringements, tolerate the use of chemical sprays or accept the denial of the rights of ramblers than those who have long been used to them. In some cases, they are willing to defend a 'rural ideal' that they have long possessed, even when others in the countryside are willing to embrace new technologies and approaches.

## Summary

As we have seen, the methods open to pressure-group campaigners are numerous. The choice of access points to target will be determined by the character of group they represent, its ability and willingness to provide government with something it needs, and the resources available.

There are more outlets for lobbyists than there were in the 1970s. The European Union and local authorities have been significant new additions, as has the devolved machinery created by the Blair government. For many groups the focus remains at the national level, be it in England, Scotland or Wales, but for the protective groups representing big business, labour and professional interests, Brussels and Strasbourg have become important locations. Some campaigning groups, operating in the environmental and aid arenas, have seen the benefits of combining lobbying of the British government with attempts to influence international machinery such as G8 Summits.

In chapter 1, we examined the characteristics of protective and promotional groups. We have now analysed the access points they are likely to target. The findings about the nature of groups and the access points to which they direct their lobbying are summarised below.

| Table 2.2 British protective and promotional groups: their characteristics and approaches | | |
|---|---|---|
| **Characteristics** | **Protective groups** | **Promotional groups** |
| Aims | Defend interests of membership. | Advance an idea or cause. |
| Focus | Executive (Whitehall) and legislature (House of Commons especially), and EU institutions. | Legislators, public opinion and international bodies, such as EU, G8 etc. |
| Membership | Restricted to those in trade or profession. | Open to all. |

## What you should have learnt from this chapter

- There are many points of access at which pressure-group lobbyists and campaigners can direct their persuasive efforts.

- Traditionally, activity focused on the executive, the legislature and the public, the last mainly the target of those denied influence in Whitehall where decision-makers are located.

- More recently, new focuses have been identified, the role of the courts, the European Union, local and devolved authorities, and the media becoming ever more significant.

- The choice of target will be much influenced by the nature of the group and the resources at its disposal.

## Glossary of key terms

**Background campaigns** Campaigns which seek to create a favourite image for a cause after a long period of time.
**BSE** The abbreviation for bovine spongiform encephalopathy, a slow-developing viral disease of cattle which affects the nervous system and

turns a cow's brain into a spongy jelly. There was an outbreak of BSE at the time of the Major administration, made the more alarming because of the fears that it could be passed on to humans in the form of CJD.

**Corporatism**  A relationship between the state and major interest groups in which decisions on domestic economic and social policy are taken in regular meetings of representatives from the three sides (often known as the social partners) – government, business and labour. Via such an approach, governments gain acquiescence of the other social partners in the implementation of policy. A strong feature of the highly consensual Austrian and Scandinavian democracies.

**Fire brigade campaigns**  Dramatic campaigns designed to rally support quickly.

**Human Rights Act 1998**  The measure that incorporated the European Convention on Human Rights into British law and provided for the first time a written list of rights available to British people.

**Life Peerages Act 1958**  The statute passed by the Macmillan (Conservative) government that provided for the appointment of peers for the duration of their life (as opposed to peerages that can be handed down by inheritance). It was brought in to diversify membership of the second chamber, thereby allowing for the inclusion of people from different backgrounds.

**Outrage!**  A radical direct-action campaigning group formed to fight for the rights of lesbian, gay and bisexual people.

**Policy networks**  The relationships between senior civil servants, group leaders, academics, think tanks and other players in particular economic and social sectors. They may be close, excessively cosy and limited to few players (the interest group and governmental officials in policy communities) or more flexible and inclusive (the range of voices represented in issue networks).

**Temperance**  Moderation in, more usually interpreted as abstinence from, the consumption of alcoholic liquor.

## ? Some Likely examination questions

In what ways and to what extent do pressure groups influence policy in the United Kingdom?

In what ways do pressure groups seek to influence **1.** the executive and **2.** Parliament in Britain?

It used to be said of British pressure groups that 'least noise equals most success'. Does a study of developments in group activity over recent decades confirm or counter this view?

To what extent does the concept of policy networks further our understanding of pressure-group politics and the policy process?

## Helpful websites

The websites of leading groups often have sections on 'campaigns' and 'lobbying': for example, see www.outrage.co.uk/ Outrage!

## Suggestions for further reading

W. Grant, *Pressure Groups and British Politics*, Macmillan, 2000.

D. Marsh and R Rhodes (eds), *Policy networks in British Government*, Clarendon Press, 1992

M. Read, 'Policy networks and issue networks in the politics of smoking', in D. Marsh and R. Rhodes, as above.

## CHAPTER 3

# Pressure Group Resources and Success

## Contents

## Overview

Pressure groups operate at key access points in the political system. Some have good channels of communication with decision-makers, others operate more at the public level. Their degree of effectiveness does not solely depend on whether they have insider status or not. It is influenced by a range of factors.

In this chapter, we analyse three broad factors that, together, determine the efficacy of group activity, their resources, their access to focuses of power and the political climate against which they operate.

## Key issues to be covered in this chapter

- The factors that determine the extent of group influence in different countries
- The difficulties in assessing group influence and effectiveness
- The importance for a group of being well resourced
- The importance of access in Whitehall and why some groups possess this
- The need for public support
- The varying fortunes of groups according to the climate of the times

## Determinants of group influence across the world

Group activity flourishes more in economically advanced, industrialised societies with a high level of educational provision and attainment than in traditional agrarian ones lacking an educated populace. But the degree of influence exerted varies significantly between even the most advanced Western states.

Principal determinants of group influence include:

- the **political culture**;
- the institutional arrangements;
- the nature of the party system;
- the level of governmental intervention in social and economic life.

Pluralist societies recognise the right of groups to advance their opinions and play a role in influencing the formation, development and implementation of policy. They encourage, and in some cases require, the involvement of groups with government bodies. **Semi-democracies** are less willing to encourage group engagement with the political process, and one-party regimes often try to stamp out any factional activity. American groups operate in a relatively open society in which there is well-established freedom of information legislation and a culture which is open to lobbying. Lobbyists have the protection of the First Amendment which guarantees their rights of expression, of assembly and to petition government. American pressure groups are known for the influence they wield. Some European democracies lack such openness and have been more suspicious of sectional activity.

In unitary countries which are highly centralised – such as Britain and France – the focus of attention for lobbyists tends to be the executive so that insider (often interest) groups may be powerful. In France, too, there is much direct consultation between lobbyists and administrators. By contrast, the decentralised, federal United States disperses political power so that there is a different and wider range of access points for lobbyists. Moreover, its separation of powers makes Congress an important target although battles lost there can be fought out in the courts.

The nature of the party system, too, can be a relevant factor. Where there exists a multi-party system, there is fertile scope for lobbyists, as so many parties may feature in a coalition government. Where there is a one party dominance – Japan under Liberal Democrat rule – influence tends to have a narrow focus on the ruling party. In addition, where parties are less organised and lack cohesion in the legislature, there are usually good opportunities for group spokespersons to maximise their influence. The business lobby was able to enjoy significant influence under the Fourth French Republic. In the United States, the president is unable to count on party loyalty to see the policy through. Bill Clinton's health proposals were given a rough ride by the American Medical Association and various business interests. British parties are more tightly disciplined, with MPs being more likely to support the party line than listen to campaigning-group activists.

Finally, in countries with a commitment to state intervention – and particularly those that adopt a corporatist approach to decision-making – there is much consultation with business and labour interests. Peak associations are essential partners and play an integral role in the political system. Hague and Harrop[1] quote the Swedish system as one in which there are close, but not institutional, links between the trade unions and the Social Democratic Labour Party and in which the legislative process in the Riksdag is geared to close consultation with affected interests. Of course, by no means all groups are involved in, and benefit from, such consultative status.

In a pluralist democracy, such as Britain, groups have extensive opportunities to make political demands and engage in political actions.

## The determinants of group effectiveness in Britain

Group influence not only varies from state to state but even within the same country. Groups experience varying degrees of success at different times. For our purposes, success may be interpreted as gaining access to a centre of decision-making and exerting influence over the development of policy.

Inevitably, some groups exert more influence than others. In part, this may reflect their ability to exploit opportunities for influence available to them, but a more likely explanation must lie in the nature and underlying strength of the groups themselves. Little academic analysis of the effectiveness of groups and their campaigning has been conducted, for several reasons:

- There are different ways of approaching the task. One is to examine the decision-making process and the way it functions in a policy area. This will involve looking at the groups involved and the policy outcome and deciding to what extent governmental policies are influenced by group campaigning. As Grant[2] points out, there is a problem: 'How does one compare a substantial impact on a policy which is basically unfavourable to a group with some small adjustments to a policy which is more in line with a group's thinking?' He illustrates the point by referring to the influence of the CBI in the 1970s and 1980s. It had considerable influence on the Labour administrations of Wilson and Callaghan, although Labour policies were often not in line with its own outlook. It had less influence on the preceding and following Conservative governments whose views on free enterprise were more attuned to its own. Another is to invite the views of players in the consultative process, asking them about the impact that campaigning had. But lobbyists will probably tend to overstate their impact, taking the view that their contributions were taken seriously and highly regarded. Those charged with responsibility for making decisions are more likely to play down group influence and to stress that they were acting in the general good.
- It is difficult to distinguish and measure the ingredients of success for individual groups or the particular factors affecting the outcome of group campaigns. In many cases, a variety of circumstances combines to achieve the desired outcome. For instance, in securing gains in environmental policy, a group might justifiably draw attention to its prominent role in persuading the public, legislators and policy-makers of the need for action. But pressure from the European Union or adverse media publicity may have been more significant in galvanising ministers into action.
- **Single-issue groups** have clear goals and their success can be assessed according to whether or not ministers have acted on their demands. The Campaign for Lead-free Petrol and Snowdrop both had a straightforward objective which was achieved. But most groups, although they operate in a particular area of policy,

have more than one aim. In the case of protective groups, they may place more emphasis upon the achievement of some policies than of others, perhaps because of their relevance at a particular time. This makes them willing to compromise over the full attainment of all of their legislative aspirations.

- Even in the case of a group which has consultative status in Whitehall, this is no guarantee that its views are accorded much weight. As we have seen in chapter 1, there are more than 200 groups consulted on policy issues relating to motorcycles but, in many cases, their influence is modest.

## Key factors in group influence

Whatever the difficulties in reaching a judgement about group influence and success, there are certain general factors that can be isolated, such as those affecting the broad decline of union influence (see pages 31, 95–7). This is a more fruitful means of examining group impact and effectiveness than trying to specify the influence of groups on a particular governmental action or piece of legislation.

Three general considerations merit further consideration:

- The resources of the pressure group.
- The access of group campaigners to those who have the power of decision or who themselves might influence it.
- The political circumstances and the climate of the times in which the group is operating.

## Group resources

A group's political resources are those elements, in many cases largely under the control of the group, that can influence the decisions and actions of those on whom they seek to have an impact. Various pressure groups have dramatically different levels of resources, their behaviour in particular circumstances often depending on the ones that it has available and its calculations of the costs and benefits associated with employing a particular mix of them. The ones that are significant can, therefore, differ according to the situation but they include such things as membership, leadership and staffing, esteem, funding, organisation, public support, and the capacity for social disruption.

## Membership

The extent of a group's membership and, more especially, the size of its activist base are important. Large groups are often more successful than small ones although too large an organisation can lack cohesiveness and unity. What matters is the cohesion, commitment and determination of those involved, rather than a sprawling membership, some of whom belong to more than one organisation and lack dedication and other valuable qualities. When a group lacks unity, its influence on the policy-making process may fall considerably even if the group is large. Internal disagreements often work against a group's interests; they make it difficult to achieve a consensus around which everyone can unite.

Many large groups are well supported financially, having the capacity to collect more money via subscriptions and contributions. Apart form financial resources, they also have the potential to mobilise time and energy in the service of an issue, and carry out research. The RSPB (see Box 3.1 below) gets a substantial income from its extensive membership, enabling it to employ a large full-time staff, control a massive annual budget and seek out specialist information.

### Box 3.1  Three influential pressure groups: reasons for their effectiveness

**The British Medical Association**

The British Medical Association represents doctors from all branches of medicine in the United Kingdom. It is a voluntary association with about 130,000 members, some 80 per cent of practising doctors. It speaks up for the interests of doctors at home and abroad, provides a range of services for its members and engages in scientific research. These involve lobbying not only the British government but also the European Union as well.

The BMA is one of the most influential and effective protective, insider groups. In addition to protecting the professional and financial interests of its members, its staff and members take many actions to influence the policies of the British government regarding the health care system in matters such as the pay and training of doctors, the work of GPs and hospitals, and the quality and quantity of medical facilities. On these and other issues, members use their expertise to provide valuable professional and technical information. They serve on committees of enquiry in Britain and the European Union and engage in regular and continuing dialogue with ministers and officials. They also assist in implementing health policy, advising government of outbreaks of infectious conditions in the community and co-operating in policies of vaccination. This is perhaps their greatest leverage, their capacity to help in provision of the National Health Service or withdraw their services and thereby deny assistance. The relationship of the Department of Health and the BMA is therefore necessarily close. In the modern state, ministers rely on the assistance of the relevant professionals.

Given the wealth of its members, the BMA can contribute substantial amounts of money to influence policy-makers directly or to finance public information campaigns. Its members command respect from political actors because of the doctors' high status and standing.

Status, size and density of membership, expertise, financial resources, contacts with government and the media, and the inherent importance of, and public interest in, the provision of good health – these are the ingredients of the group's success.

### The National Farmers Union

The National Farmers Union represents around three quarters of the full-time commercial farmers and growers of England and Wales. It protects the interests of its members and provides them with services in return for payment of a subscription. In addition to defending the farming community, its 'central campaigning objective is to promote successful and socially responsible agriculture and horticulture, whilst ensuring the long term viability of rural communities' (www.nfu.org.uk).

The National Farmers Union is one of the leading protective and insider groups. It likes to operate in a way that avoids too much publicity. It concentrates its attention on Whitehall where it long enjoyed a close relationship with the Ministry of Agriculture, Fisheries and Food, now renamed as the Department of the Environment, Food and Rural Affairs (DEFRA).

DEFRA consults the NFU on various initiatives, indeed, it has a statutory obligation to do so. It values its advice and technical expertise. It knows that the NFU speaks for a large percentage of the farming industry so that, in speaking to its representatives, it is likely to get its message across to much of the agrarian community. Much of this contact is formalised but much also is informal, with frequent phone calls being made by those working for both organisations. The NFU values its consultative status in Whitehall. Only when a row breaks out will it turn to open public methods. For this reason, the NFU uses the media less than many groups.

Over the last three decades, the NFU has been active in lobbying the institutions of the European Union. It has its own office in Brussels and is active in the euro-group, the Committee of Professional Agricultural Organisations of the European Community (COPA). Its personnel spend much time on European policy, for many agricultural matters are decided by the European Union via the Common Agricultural Policy.

As the main voice of farming interests, the NFU carries great weight in Whitehall and has often been able to extract concessions to its viewpoint, particularly under Conservative administrations. The size and density of membership, financial resources, organisational strength, contacts in Whitehall and Brussels, professional expertise and ability to assist ministers and officials in the implementation of policy on often high-profile issues such as outbreaks of foot-and-mouth disease – these are the main factors making the NFU such an effective behind-the-scenes group.

**The Royal Society for the Protection of Birds**
The Royal Society for the Protection of Birds has developed into Europe's largest wildlife conservation charity, with more than a million members – some ten times more than thirty years ago. Membership is open to anyone with an interest and who is willing to pay the annual subscription. From its initial stance against the trade in wild birds' plumage, the issues which the Society tackles have grown hugely in number and size.

The RSPB is a promotional group with insider status. Apart from working with ministers and officials in Whitehall, advising on government policy in its sector, it has been an effective campaigning organisation. It has marketed its cause with great skill and success, using methods such as direct mailing and catalogue trading, and taking opportunities to convey its views via press advertising and other media. As part of its mode of operation, it sometimes works in alliance with the RSPCA – as when they co-operated in tackling the problems of international trade in rare birds. It lobbies the European Union, working directly with the Commission in formulating the directive on the conservation of wild birds.

The RSPB, along with other animal-welfare and environmental organisations, arouse public sympathy. It deals with an issue about which people feel warmly. Its effectiveness derives from its size, its ample resources and organisational strength, its professional expertise and sophistication, and growing public sympathy in recent years for the type of issues with which it deals.

More significant than the sheer weight of numbers is the satura-
tion and **density** of those involved. If a group can speak for the vast
majority of those who work in a sector or can justly claim to be
echoing widely held concerns, its bargaining position with government will be all the stronger. An all-encompassing membership provides a group with greater authority and a stronger bargaining
position with government. The declining density of union memberships (as outlined on page 95) weakened labour's bargaining power in
the closing decades of the twentieth century, in Britain and elsewhere.

The problem of low density may indicate that there are several
groups that claim to represent an industry or profession. In the United
States, those engaged in agriculture are represented by three major
organisations which collectively have a lower percentage of membership than the National Farmers Union (see Box 3.1 on pages 72–3).
The teaching profession in Britain is widely thought to have suffered
reduced influence because of the differences over priorities and
tactics between the various organisations representing teachers. The
authority of the National Union of Mineworkers diminished in the
mid-1980s after a large group of its members seceded and formed the
breakaway Union of Democratic Mineworkers. It could no longer
claim to voice the views of the majority of those who worked in
demanding conditions underground.

Hague and Harrop[3] note that, in the European Union, breadth of
membership is regarded as especially important for lobbying organisations: 'Groups which can demonstrate their support from national
associations in most member states receive a more cordial reception
from policy-makers in Brussels.' In Britain and elsewhere, high levels
of penetration often arise because – as in the case of professional
bodies such as the British Medical Association (see Box 3.1 on pages
71–2 for a study of its strengths as a protective group) and Law
Society – membership is a condition of practice.

### Leadership and staffing

Organisations that lack the large memberships and generous funding
of major economic interest groups can, nonetheless, achieve success
if they have good leadership. Charisma, creative sense, energy, enterprise, flair, ideas and strategic sense are definite assets in a leader. In
the past, organisations such as Friends of the Earth and Shelter have

often been well led, most notably in the days of Jonathan Porritt and Des Wilson, respectively. Both commanded respect, having the capacity to communicate their group's agenda and advance a strong intellectual case to the wider public and decision-makers. Both had a sound understanding of the media and how it works and were able to use it effectively for the benefit of their cause. In Wilson's case, the flair for publicity was deployed with other organisations, in his campaigning zeal for lead-free petrol, freedom of information and other causes. Others who have been strongly identified with well-known causes include David Bellamy in the animal welfare and environmental fields and, more questionably because of the methods adopted (see page 64), the high-profile Peter Tatchell of Outrage!, the movement for homosexual equality.

If effective leadership is backed by a committed, efficient staff and a solidly united membership, then the group has two very considerable assets.

## Esteem

Groups enjoying high prestige are more likely to carry more weight in negotiations and exercise influence. Professional groups have a high social status even though they can, on occasion, be militant and restrictive in their working practices. Doctors are much less criticised than trade unionists, even if they do threaten to employ coercive tactics. Many trade unions lack such respectability, as do groups such as NACRO (representing ex-offenders) and Release (representing drug addicts).

## Funding

In general, money, perhaps even more than numbers and intensity, is decisive to successful group operation. Hrebenar and Scott[4] have observed that 'quality leadership, access to political decision-makers, a favourable public image, a hard-working and knowledgeable staff are just some of the resources that can be purchased with the careful expenditure of adequate amounts of money'. Money helps groups organise internally and exercise influence externally.

Mounting campaigns, running a British headquarters (and perhaps operating an office in Brussels, or perhaps in Belfast, Cardiff or Edinburgh) employing permanent staff, conducting research, producing literature and attending meetings make pressure-group activity an expensive enterprise. If there is a perceived need to employ a professional lobbying agency, then this is something that large groups might wish to finance.

One of the problems of group activity is often said to be that some groups are more influential than others (see pages 209–10). Wealth is a key factor in accounting for the discrepancy. Generally speaking, umbrella organisations on either side of manufacturing industry, businesses, unions and leading professions are able to mobilise vast resources. They are able to attract funds and can afford to adopt a high-profile and bold strategy of self-advertisement.

As we have seen, larger membership often equates with greater income. If the group comprises a broadly wealthy section of the community, as does the NFU with its 150,000 farmers, it has the resources to spend well on organisation and research. So, too, in the case of the RSPB, its income enables it to employ a costly marketing strategy, based on regular, high-profile advertising and direct mailing. This assists it in seeking to arouse the enthusiasm of large numbers of people, some of whom will join and/or purchase goods through its trading section, thereby adding to its annual income.

In the case of many promotional groups, such resources and strategies are far beyond their capability. Several are small bodies and – even if they are nationally known – operate on a shoestring, relying on the goodwill and commitment of a small number of paid staff and voluntary workers.

## Organisation

Closely related to finance is organisation, for a sound financial base enables a group to fund the necessary offices and staff. Protective groups are generally well endowed. Unions were traditionally able to organise their members who were concentrated in large workplaces; employees could be rallied in support of the threat or use of industrial action. Some of these advantages have been dissipated in an age of union mergers, as groups in many different sectors have been brought under the orbit of larger, general unions.

The members of some cause groups are scattered and difficult to identify and organise. They include some of the most vulnerable sections of society, such as the disabled, the unemployed and single mothers. But as we have seen with the RSPB, promotional groups can be well organised. Moreover, even some much less well-resourced bodies nonetheless operate effectively on the basis of a small, highly centralised and highly professionalised command structure. In particular, they have the advantage of being able to respond quickly to new developments.

'Good organisation' implies a coherent structure, a clear strategy, a united membership, a committed staff, and able, inspirational leadership. As such, it is an asset for any group with aspirations to political influence.

## Public support

Groups whose campaigns are in tune with the popular mood have a considerable advantage. **Public opinion** changes over time, and causes that once lacked popular support may, ten years later, gel with the outlook of many potential electors. Governments are sensitive to the views of the electorate, particularly near election time, and some politicians have particularly well-developed antennae enabling them to detect the way opinion is shifting.

Smoking is an issue in which there has been a movement in public opinion. Today, surveys show much greater numbers in favour of a total or partial ban on smoking in enclosed public places and, in promising to introduce a ban (albeit with exemptions), the Blair government knows that it has not only the support of groups operating in the health sector (primarily the BMA) and Action on Smoking and Health (ASH), but of many voters as well. In legislating for the introduction of identity cards, ministers seemed to have strong public support although, as details of the costs and viability of the scheme unfolded, the level of popular backing diminished. If the policy runs into problems in the House of Lords, then ministers might decide that the cause is not worth the difficulties involved.

Any group with a large membership has an advantage, for this suggests that its goals are widely supported. Because the BMA is the voice of all doctors and the NFU represents the wishes of many farmers, their views command respect. On the other hand, although the TUC has nearly 7 million affiliated members (more than 10 per cent of the population) it does not have the density of support that the other two organisations possess. Many groups of workers are not strongly unionised, enabling ministers to portray unions as a significant but, nonetheless, self-interested, sectional interest.

Promotional groups, in particular, are actively committed to winning the backing of the public. If they can successfully demonstrate that they have popular support, they have a valuable resource. Health and welfare groups are in a strong position, and so increasingly are environmental ones when they take up farming and food issues. Groups representing asylum seekers or ex-prisoners, or however that find themselves facing opposition from others with a differing viewpoint (as in the case of pro- and anti-abortion campaigners) find it less easy to show that they have the public behind them.

**The ability to make strategic alliances**
Some groups are able to supplement their own resources by forming strategic alliances. Consumer groups may on some issues be able to boost their influence by co-ordinating their activities with civil rights groups, environmentalists and organised labour. In the battle against the introduction of identity cards, libertarian campaigners co-operate with activists from groups representing asylum seekers and immigrants who fear that they will be the victims of endless requests to prove that they have a right to be in Britain. In attacking symptoms of alleged moral decline, Care for Scotland works with other groups as part of the Scottish Evangelical Alliance to fight against aspects of the 'permissive society' such as gay sex, quickie divorces and cohabiting couples. In the same way, the **Christian Right** in America works with right-to life groups, groups professing taxpayers' rights and conservative think tanks such as the Heritage Foundation.

## Group access to and contacts with decision-makers

### Expertise and information
Many groups have strong connections with the executive. Insider groups – business, labour and professions among them – are in a better position than outsider groups to claim decisive or exclusive expertise. Decision-makers and legislators may have their own views on issues of broad community benefit (such as rights for lone parents and gay people) but, on matters involving technical understanding

and perhaps help in the implementation of policy, they are reliant on the advice and assistance of well-resourced groups. They may receive detailed assistance in drafting legislation from a well-informed group; Shelter was actively involved in drawing up the Homelessness Act (2002).

The BMA, the NFU and the RSPB all command an audience among decision-makers because of their specialist knowledge. They offer policy-makers in Whitehall valuable information which is helpful because ministers and officials cannot be familiar with all the technical detail in business, professional and environmental practices; they offer consent, for officials know that it is prudent to be seen to have consulted affected interests; and finally they may on occasion offer active help in administering decisions.

MPs, too, are receptive to lobbyists' influence. There are emotional and historical, as well as institutional, links with Labour MPs. A substantial number were once sponsored by a trade union, and though today the arrangements are rather different, many members on the Labour side of the House still have strong union links. The New Labour government may exhibit some coolness to unions, and there are serious differences over issues such as the **Private Finance Initiative**, but this does not prevent trade unions from seeking support from members of the parliamentary party.

Many pressure-group campaigners in the anti-poverty and civil-liberties arena have a close connection with individual Labour or Liberal Democrat MPs. A *Study of Parliament Group*[5] survey found that three-quarters of groups had regular or frequent contact with MPs of one party or another, 66 per cent had given evidence to select committees, and 47 per cent had contact with all party groups.

MPs are a good conduit to influence parliamentary opinion. Groups use them selectively, sometimes making personal approaches, at others resorting to mass mailing. Ideally, the 'blanket' approach needs to be accompanied by a direct appeal to a member, particularly one active or interested in the lobbyist's area of policy.

Some groups with technical expertise operate more or less on their own in their chosen field, especially if they are concerned with highly specialised matters. In this case, they face little opposition from other lobbyists, and ministers and MPs regard them favourably. Key policy issues are often more contentious, however, and they receive representations from several other bodies who have deeply held and often conflicting views. This was particularly the case with issues such as Sunday shopping, smoking and blood sports. In these cases, ministers tend to weigh carefully the electoral consequences of taking action that may offend an important section of the electorate. One of the reasons that made Tony Blair reluctant to ban fox hunting with hounds outright was the knowledge that this would be offensive to many rural interests and would divide the urban and rural communities. For a 'big-tent' politician seeking the broadest appeal, this was a barrier to action.

Contacts with the executive and with Parliament are invaluable but, in recent years, many groups have been concerned also to influence public opinion. In attempting to do so, they increasingly rely on the media.

## Use of the media

Over recent decades, the media have become an acknowledged part of group activity in all democracies. Many British promotional groups have taken up public campaigns – sometimes involving direct action – in the knowledge that the media can provide information and publicity for the cause, and help to create a more favourable climate of opinion. Insider groups have also used the media. Well-resourced bodies, such as the BMA, may be able to fund poster campaigns and press advertising. For most groups of whatever type, these would be an enormous drain on finances. But there are other opportunities to convey their work and achievements. If they can attract the curiosity of journalists by the inherent interest of their campaign and the vivid images it conveys, the cause may receive much coverage. Make Poverty History was able to draw attention to the plight of the world's poor, and the African continent in particular, in its crusade in 2004–05. The ability to use the mass media and arouse public indignation has at various times been particularly significant over emotive issues such as the export of live animals, GM foods, hunting, and the war over Iraq.

Baggott[6] quotes an interesting example of use of the media, that concerning Surfers Against Sewage. The group has been successful in 'highlighting the pollution of beaches and coastal waters by attracting media attention'. He notes its use of strong visuals, with activists clad in wetsuits and gas masks surfing in sewage-ridden waters and riding in brown inflatable dinghies: 'The spectacle has attracted the attention of the media and even resulted in a television documentary about the issue of sewage pollution which examined the activities of the group.'

New technologies have increased the reach of pressure groups, particularly the development of computerised and personalised mass mailing. Targeting has been used to contact people likely to share a common concern, such as members of environmental groups. Key figures in Friends of the Earth have had a close association with the media, some having at one time worked in television or the newspaper industry.

## The political circumstances and climate

The demands that groups can make and the actions in which they can engage depend on the boundaries of acceptable political action within the particular political environment. In democratic systems, groups have extensive rights, lobbyists being widely accepted as legitimate players.

### Government response

The attitude of ministers is crucial to any group and is a key factor. Some groups have goals that are compatible with the aims and outlook of the ruling party for example, the way that a Labour administration was expected to be sympathetic to union pressure and a Conservative one to approaches from big business. As we have seen on page 48, the CBI and TUC lost some of their former influence in the Thatcher and Major years. The non-corporatist, free-market Institute of Directors and the Freedom Association, however, shared a broad philosophy and approach to policy with the Conservative governments. In the case of the unions, their impact has been reduced since their heyday in the 1970s. They find Labour ministers more willing to consult and listen but Blairite policies often do not accord with their own priorities.

The governmental response may also be affected by the size of the parliamentary majority. Governments in the 1970s – especially the Labour ones from 1974 to 1979 – lacked the dominance of subsequent administrations. Two out of three of each of the Thatcher and Blair

election victories left ministers in an overwhelmingly dominant position in the House of Commons, so that ministers were able to pass
much of their legislation through the lower chamber with little
difficulty. This may have made them less interested in consultation
although, arguably, it was the broad attitude of ministers to the role
and value of pressure groups which made it hard for some groups to
achieve the degree of influence they wanted. In both cases, there was
what Baggott[7] describes as an 'antigroup philosophy' within the government, as illustrated by the Blair observation relating to anti-GM
campaigners: 'we should resist the tyranny of pressure groups'.

In the case of any group, timing is all-important. Governments are
more willing to take tough decisions and ride roughshod over opposition to their policies in the period after an election victory. In the last
year or so in office and with an election looming, ministers are likely
to be more sensitive to group and public pressure and more susceptible to influence. This is especially true if the cause seems to have
popular support. Having delayed taking decisive action over the abolition of hunting with dogs in the first few years in power, ministers –
and certainly Labour MPs – seemed more willing to resolve the issue
in 2004–05. They understood the need to enthuse their demoralised
supporters by giving them some 'good red meat' on which to campaign.

Some groups, that once had a very powerful position in the
economy, find that the tide has moved against them. Miners were in
a very strong bargaining position in the 1970s when oil supplies were
in short demand following the quintupling of prices by the OPEC
countries. A decade later, when the Thatcher government confronted
them in the Miners' Strike of 1984–5, ministers had ensured that
the groundwork was carefully prepared and stocks were ample. This
seriously weakened the position of the NUM and its leaders. Their
industrial action posed less of a threat to power supplies.

### Sanctions implied or applied

Ministers can afford to ignore the views of some groups that can bring
little pressure to bear in support of their campaigning goals. The
homeless cannot withdraw co-operation or go on strike, neither can
lone parents. A union can embark upon a campaign of industrial
action, a multinational company can move its investments elsewhere,

and a group such as the BMA can refuse to co-operate with the government in forming and administering a policy. At worst, doctors can be organised into threatening a withdrawal from the National Health Service, as they have done on occasion. The mere threat of such an action is likely to galvanise ministers into making a concession for major disruption in the NHS – with stories of sick patients not being treated – would reflect badly upon them.

Some groups have the power to cause major inconvenience and disruption in society, so that they can effectively 'hold the nation to ransom' by persisting with their demands. This now happens far less than it did in the pre-Thatcher years. Several unions find ministers much more willing to resist their threats than happened a generation ago. Ministers are more resistant to pressure. If the fire workers adopt

## Table 3.1  Factors in determining group success: a summary

Traditionally, protective groups are thought to have possessed more power in Whitehall than promotional ones, but their success may vary according to these specific factors:
1. The degree of government support for the aims and ideas of the group;
2. The government's need for co-operation and support;
3. The bargaining power of a group within the economy;
4. Good timing is all-important;
5. The representativeness of the group. Does an organisation speak for the vast majority of those who operate within the sector?

Generally, promotional groups are viewed as less powerful than groups which consult with Whitehall though, as we have seen, organisations such as the RSPB are insider ones. Lacking such access, most operate more with the public. Factors of relevance here include:
1. The attitude of the government;
2. Proximity to an election;
3. Parliamentary support from all parties;
4. A good case, well informed and well argued, and not too partisan;
5. Sound leadership, organisation and funding;
6. A favourable climate of opinion;
7. Media attention.

a militant approach and go on strike, the army will be brought in to provide emergency cover. Other groups, such as the nurses, are always inhibited from taking industrial action by the knowledge that, to do so, might imperil the well-being or lives of their sick patients. In the case of teachers, they have the capacity to bring about disruption in the classroom but, to do so, reflects adversely upon their professional status. The time when strike action might be really effective is during public examinations but withdrawal of labour at that time would be widely regarded as reckless and unfair to great numbers of children.

## ✓ What you should have learnt from reading this chapter

It is difficult to ascertain what makes some groups more influential than others, not least because it is difficult to isolate the factors that cause decision-makers to make their decisions. Nonetheless, certain factors can be identified:

- Group influence varies from country to country.

- Within a country, some groups are more effective than others, some are winners and others losers.

- Groups need to possess a wide range of resources: inspired leadership, professionalism, sound funding and popular sympathy being major assets.

- They need to possess access to the focuses of decision-making and/or to be able to convey their views in the media and win popular approval for their cause.

- They benefit if the political environment is conducive to their work.

## 🔎 Glossary of key terms

**Christian (or Religious) Right** The term covers a broad movement of American conservatives who advance moral and social values. First known as the Moral Majority, it later evolved into the Christian Coalition. Highly active in the Republican Party, it wants to see the United States return to its 'true heritage' and restore the godly principles that made the country great. Members are fundamentalist in doctrine (in that they accept the literal truth of the Bible) and disapprove strongly of abortion, euthanasia and same sex liaisons and marriages.

**Organisation of Petroleum Exporting Countries (OPEC)** A permanent intergovernmental organisation created in 1960 with the aim of co-ordinating the policy of the production and distribution of petroleum of its members and ensuring stability of prices.

**Political culture** The widely held underlying political beliefs and values which most citizens of a country share about the conduct of government, the relationship of citizens to those who rule over them and to one another.

**Private Finance Initiative (PFI)** The contracting out of large public sector capital projects such as hospital and school building to the private sector; the facilities may be leased back to the public sector.

**Public opinion** The cluster of attitudes and beliefs held by people about a variety of issues, in our case those concerning politics and policy issues. There can be no single public opinion, but rather a range of several opinions held by members of the public.

**Semi-democracies** Sometimes known as authoritarian or façade democracies these newer forms blend several traditional features of a Western-style democracy with more authoritarian impulses. Countries such as Russia or Singapore have competitive elections and the trappings of a representative democracy but there may be some attempt at manipulation of the outcome of elections, the media may be muzzled and policies can be implemented with little regard for human rights.

**Single-issue groups** Groups that deal with a specific issue of popular interest. Many operate in areas such as birth control, civil liberties, environmental protection and the sale of firearms. Snowdrop was a single-issue group that lobbied hard and successfully for a ban on handguns. In the United States, the pro- and anti-abortion groups are of a similar type.

## Likely examination questions

'The most important resource a pressure group can have is public support.' Discuss.

'In pressure-group politics, organisation is all.' Discuss.

Why are some pressure groups more successful than others?

What factors make pressure groups effective in influencing political debate and outcomes?

## Helpful websites

The individual websites of influential groups may be worth consulting. These give an idea of the strength of individual organisations and the contacts they possess.

## Suggestions for further reading

*Useful books:*

B. Coxall, *Pressure Groups in British Politics*, Pearson, 2001.

W. Grant, *Pressure Groups and British Politics*, Palgrave, 2000.

## CHAPTER 4

# Trends in Group Activity since 1979

## Contents

## Overview

The pressure-group scene has undergone several changes over the last generation. There has been a proliferation of group activity and more targets for the growing number of groups to lobby. Approaches used by campaigners have in many cases become more professional. Others have been more willing to resort to direct action, much deployed by those engaged in the politics of protest.

In this chapter, we briefly review how the world of group representation is changing. In particular, we examine the trends in group activity, most of which are covered in more detail elsewhere in the book, before examining the fate of various types of group during the Conservative and Labour governments since 1979, with particular reference to declining position of the trade unions. We briefly assess whether the overall influence of pressure groups is increasing or decreasing before moving on to a case study concerning the growing impact of environmental politics.

## Key issues to be covered in this chapter

- Increasing group activity and in the popularity and influence of popular movements
- Developments in the approach to lobbying and in the institutions targeted by lobbyists
- The growth of professional lobbying
- The fortunes of pressure groups in the Conservative years and under New Labour
- The decline of union influence
- Assessment of trends in group activity and influence
- A case study: the growth in and assessment of environmental campaigning

# The explosion of group activity

Since the 1960s there has been what Heywood[1] refers to as 'an explosion of pressure-group activity'. There are myriads of British groups, covering the whole spectrum of policy issues. Some 34,000 organisations are recognised by the *Directory of British Associations*,[2] but there are many more that operate at the local level. In particular, there has been a surge of interest in single-issue campaigning, on subjects from gay rights to the export of live animals to the Continent, from gun control to the siting of a motorway or other public amenity. Over the last two or three decades, the number of these and other pressure groups has soared.

There are also additional outlets at which they can target their propaganda (the devolved bodies, the European Union) and there is also a growing willingness to lobby local authorities and the courts. New techniques of putting across ideas and information have emerged, in particular the growth of **professional lobbying** (see Box 4.1 overleaf) and the increased use of direct action as part of the politics of protest.

Many groups have become increasingly sophisticated in their understanding of the appropriate outlets for their campaigning. The well-resourced RSPCA has become familiar with the new world of **multi-level governance**, its main British operations being complemented by the activities of Scottish SPCA and its European department (see pages 149–51 and 181–2). Its campaigners and lobbyists ensure that European legislation is implemented by British ministers, they are active in the home countries, and they employ a wide range of tactics to put their message across.

There has been a dramatic increase in nationwide popular movements. More single-issue groups have emerged and, via television, have achieved enormous publicity and demonstrated the extent of popular feeling in favour of their campaign. So, too, have certain causes, such as the countryside and environment, gained popular backing. On the one hand, there is the success of the Countryside Alliance whose march on London in 1997 showed ministers the scale of unrest in country areas about trends in governmental policy in recent years. More typical of the situation in most European countries are the new social movements about which we have written. As

## Box 4.1  The increasing use of professional lobbyists

Over recent decades, pressure groups have developed a more sophisticated approach to the ways by which they seek to influence 'pressure points' in the political process. Some turned to the use of the new commercial 'lobbying industry', an American-style import. Multi-client 'professional lobbyists' began to make an impact in the 1980s. These were defined in a House of Commons report as those who are 'professionally employed to lobby on behalf of clients or who advise clients on how to lobby on their own behalf'. Such agencies trade their political knowledge and expertise to clients in return for considerable financial reward. They are hired for their inside knowledge of the workings of government and their contacts. There are some sixty of them, and they have at times represented groups as diverse as British Airways and Tottenham Hotspur FC. Some groups are small specialist ones, such as Political Planning Services. Others have a much larger client base. Most major pressure groups may have a specialist lobbying department, employ the services of one of the professionals, or operate via both routes.

In the 1980s there were some spectacular successes for paid lobbyists, as well as a number of less apparent ones. In the passage of the Financial Services Act, many 'City' interests lobbied the Standing Committee considering the bill, and secured several technical amendments favourable to their cause.

Concern has often been raised over the activities of these professional groups, especially their close relationships with certain MPs. The act of representing a consultancy for professional lobbyists was regarded by many as legitimate, as long as it was acknowledged. It was hoped that party loyalty and discipline would be sufficient to ensure that MPs behaved properly and did not allow themselves to be unduly influence by those who paid them.

What do lobbying companies expect for paying MPs to act as consultants? Most MPs provide not very much in return, reporting back to the group monthly on relevant political developments of interest to the company, acting as its 'eyes and ears'. From the lobbyist's point of view, they are pleased to be able to use the MP's name on the top of their notepaper as an adviser. It creates the impression that the group has access to, and influence in, the 'right places'. The fear is that, in some cases, that connection might be misused and that companies are buying influence over legislation, influence which is denied to smaller, less well-funded groups within the community. Some MPs have been less than open in disclosing their connections and, in the last few years, a few highly publicised examples have arisen.

In the 1987–92 Parliament, thirty-five MPs received payment from such agencies for representing their interests, and this led to doubts as to whose interests the member was most concerned with, his paymaster's or his constituents'. Some critics alleged that the close ties were a 'corrupting' influence. Members were supposed to declare their 'interest' before they spoke in Parliament but often they failed to do so.

The number of cases of allegedly improper behaviour grew in the 1990s, disquiet focusing particularly on the behaviour of some MPs who were accused of taking money and favour without proper acknowledgement. Most notably, in the 'cash for questions' allegations, two junior Conservative ministers were forced to resign their posts after it was found that they had performed services on behalf of Ian Greer Associates, the then agent of Mohamed Al Fayed, in his campaign to prevent the tycoon Tiny Rowlands from regaining control of Harrods, without declaring their interest or the payments they received for the services rendered. The issue raised the questions of who should police MPs to ensure that they did not exert undue influence on behalf of those who funded them and whether MPs should be allowed to work for political consultancy firms and receive money for political services, even if these services and payments were publicly declared.

Such cases led to calls for a strengthening of the Register of Members' Interests to ensure that more information was provided, including the amount a member receives in annual payment from his backer. In 1994, Lord Nolan was asked to chair a new Committee on Standards in Public Life. His report led to calls for a revision of the rules governing the relationship between MPs and lobbyists. In response, Parliament established a new Committee of Standards and Privileges to regulate members' behaviour, the formulation of a Code of Conduct and the establishment of a Standards Commissioner who was handed an investigatory role. As part of the new arrangements, restrictions were imposed on the ability of MPs to raise or promote a cause or issue in return for payment (the advocacy rule). Later, this was extended to prevent an MP who has been funded by an organisation from introducing a delegation of its employees to a minister or civil servant. The register of interests is now more carefully monitored for discrepancies.

we have seen, New Left politics, are characterised by the involvement of younger and better-educated people within society who take up issues such as minority rights, anti-nuclear protest, international peace, anti-globalisation, Third World concerns and the environment in general. Using tactics ranging from boycotts to passive resistance, and engaging in activities such as protests or more violent demonstrations, these unconventional forms are no longer new, having become an accepted feature of group activity in Western societies.

## Pressure groups under the Conservatives, 1979–97: a changing scene

In the 1980s, Tory governments were not well disposed to group activity. In 1986 the then Home Secretary, Douglas Hurd,[3] issued a sharp rebuke to groups which he attacked as 'strangling serpents' which created unnecessary work for ministers and made it difficult for them to reach decisions in the public interest. He argued that they distorted the proper constitutional relationship between the executive, Parliament and the electorate. Along with some other senior Tories, he seemed to be casting doubt on the right of groups to have their say in the formulation of policy. This was particularly the case in relation to the unions, for ministers were wary of any corporatist arrangements through which unions and big business would develop a close relationship with government. Margaret Thatcher was especially hostile to the idea of negotiating with groups which she viewed as essentially self-interested.

### Winners and losers in the Conservative years

The Conservative reaction to lobbyists differed according to the type of group they represented. If unions and many welfare groups aroused suspicion, others, which were more sympathetic to Conservative attitudes and policy, received a different response. Some had views which were music to the ears of ministers, such as the Adam Smith Institute with its espousal of free-market economics.

The Freedom Association also benefited from ministerial approval. It stressed the rights of individual working men rather than union-organised labour and was opposed to excessive governmental intervention in our daily lives. It achieved success by adhering to its traditional approach of addressing Conservative fringe meetings rather than by direct lobbying of ministers. Leading members felt they had more influence by operating indirectly, encouraging Conservative activists and voters to write in to ministers to express their fears. The Association was also willing to take up individual cases at industrial tribunals and in the European Court of Human Rights for, by focusing on a few individual cases, they could achieve changes they wanted in employment law. On several issues, ministers agreed with the views of the Association; in others, it needed their assistance.

The British Medical Association was at variance with ministers on several aspects of health policy. It opposed ministerial efforts to reform the NHS in the late 1980s, particularly the idea of creating an internal market. Yet its co-operation was needed in the implementation of the proposals. The government was helped by the fact that there were members of the organisation who wanted to see an accommodation with the government which was willing to make some concessions to allay the fears of the profession.

Generally, the environmental lobby fared well. As we see on pages 102–7, its lobbyists found that their views were listened to in Downing Street and Whitehall to an extent not previously experienced. In part, this greater receptivity owed much to the increase in public interest on, and media attention to, environmental issues in the late 1980s, at a time when the Green Party was gaining impressive indications of popular support – most obviously, in the European elections of 1989.

A widely held view among pressure-group activists was that, in the Tory years, more was achieved by quiet diplomacy than by displays of public outrage on the media which tended to make ministers dig in their heels. Work with Tory backbenchers was often more effective than going public, resort to which was a clear sign that the argument was being lost. Commentators noted some improvement in the opportunities for consultation after John Major took over. He seemed more willing to consult with the TUC and union leaders, and did arrange their first meeting in Downing Street for several years.

The new prime minister's policies could still provoke controversy, however, especially over the closure of pits. It was announced in late 1992 that thirty-one pits were to close and this led to a determined campaign by the unions and others who were sympathetic to the miners' cause. Some Tory MPs were willing to rebel to protest at the way in which the future of mining areas was being put in jeopardy. Members of the moderate Union of Democratic Mineworkers particularly resented that some of the pits where they were the dominant union were singled out for closure. After all, they had helped the government in 1984 at the time of the Miners' Strike and felt that they were entitled to more favourable consideration.

In the 1980s the situation for a number of pressure groups was difficult. Campaigners for social groups had policy ideas and attitudes that were often at variance with those of ministers. In the Major years, the party was still pursuing a programme largely inherited from its predecessor, involving privatisation, welfare-state reform, trade-union reform and deregulation. This brought it into conflict with many group activists who fundamentally disliked the nature and tone of ministerial approaches. Teachers were at variance on the issue of school testing. Although some concessions were made to their objections, they found ministers generally confrontational on the issue and successfully boycotted the tests in 1993.

From 1979 to 1997, groups were operating in a hostile environment, with a government that did not like to listen. The boundaries of the achievable were radically different from these in times past. Many groups are in business to change what they dislike about society; they are likely to find the *status quo* unpalatable, for there are always injustices to put right and causes to take up. Especially in the case of promotional groups, they often wish to see radical solutions on matters of social concern, emphasising what still needs to be done rather than resting on past achievement. By their nature, they were often unlikely to be attracted by Tory philosophy, particularly that of a right-wing set of ministers.

## The 1997 Labour government and group activity

From the beginning, Labour ministers were committed to the case for more consultation with interested groups. It was outlined in a document produced in 1998: 'It is important to build consultation with outside interests into plans for policy development, both on specific proposals and services and more generally. Consultation will help lead to more realistic and robust policy, better reflecting peoples' needs and wishes.'[4] The early years of the new government suggested that consultation with experts and outside was, indeed, taking place, there being much discussion with a variety of task forces and advisory groups reviewing broad areas of policy. Many green papers and other consultative documents were produced, in part a reflection of how many new policy initiatives were under consideration. Moreover, more generous time was allowed for thought and comment than in the Conservative years. Yet, within a relatively short period, there were suggestions that many of the government's new task forces were not always consulting an adequate range of groups; that they did not always operate with the desirable degree of openness; that there was insufficient consultation over new initiatives in education and health; and – among welfare groups involved with single families – the suggestion that advice deriving from consultation was being ignored.

The rhetoric of some ministers suggested a similarity of approach with Conservative predecessors. For Hurd's allusion to 'strangling serpents', read Home Secretary Jack Straw's[5] warning to elected politicians against becoming 'agents of sectional interests'. He went on to say that 'the link between local communities and their elected representatives is worth a thousand pressure groups. It is the basis of democratic accountability.' A few months later, the Prime Minister[6] was – in relation to GM crops – referring to 'the tyranny of pressure groups'.

Yet there were reasons for optimism. The Labour Party is in the business of seeking to change society, as are members and supporters of many socially oriented promotional groups. Even if Labour governments frequently disappoint them, groups in the social field will often find that their staffs, supporters and objectives sit more easily with a Labour administration, which at least shares some of their values and priorities, than with a Conservative one. Campaigning groups, such as Shelter, Stonewall and the Low Pay Unit, found that they received recognition, for the reason given by one writer:[7] 'Labour likes people on the inside of the tent'.

The initial enthusiasm for the government was tempered by the rigid adherence of the Chancellor to the spending limits laid down by his Conservative predecessor. This tight rein on expenditure made it impossible to tackle some serious problems in educational and health provision, in the way that activists would have liked to see happen. They awaited a relaxation of spending curbs, and relied on the fact that the priorities of Labour – even at a time when higher taxation was not being contemplated – would reflect their own values. When the restrictions on spending were eased and the Chancellor began to release more money for education and health, group activists welcomed the burst of social spending.

With the arrival of a Labour government in May 1997, the unions were in a different position from the one they had been in for many years. They desperately wanted a Labour government, even though there were some reservations about the Blairite creation, New Labour. They found themselves consulted more and offered a more inclusive approach to policy-making. But key spokespersons for New Labour made it clear that there would be 'no special favours'[8] for the unions, and that they would listen to and consult with any body whose views they wished to hear. In that spirit, ministers proceeded to meet business as well as union leaders frequently. Some businesspeople played a prominent role in government, to the extent of actually serving in office at a high level.

If there were grounds for trade-union regret that the traditional bonds between the industrial and political wings of the Labour movement had been much loosened, nonetheless, union leaders were aware that they had achieved certain policy goals that mattered to them, including action on a minimum wage, youth unemployment, the signing of the Social Chapter and the recognition of unions at GCHQ and in other places of work. But most of these gains were in the early years and, since then, New Labour has been a disappointment to many core supporters of the party. The long-term decline of union influence has been a key feature of the last twenty-five years (see Box 4.2 on pages 95–7), covering the terms of both Conservative and Labour administrations.

Within a few years, a range of group activists covering several areas of policy became increasingly critical of Labour in office, most obviously union leaders, education, health and welfare campaigners, and groups concerned with civil liberty. The last found aspects of Blairite New Labour policy distinctly unpalatable; inroads into trial by jury; ministerial interference with sentencing; the 'tough' line taken on asylum seekers; the limited nature of, and delay in, implementing freedom-of-information legislation; and the proposed introduction of identity cards.

## Box 4.2  The general decline in the influence of trade unions as interest groups

Trade unions have in most countries suffered from a shrinking membership partly as a result of the decline of manufacturing in countries such as Britain and the United States in both of which new, less-unionised service industries have become ever more significant. As a general trend, unions have failed to cater for the growing number of office workers and those in services (often small scale and harder to motivate) but membership has suffered from other factors such as:

- unemployment, which has hit workers in traditional industries;
- public attitudes to unions which were influenced by the hostile approach adopted by conservative governments across the Continent and in the United States in the 1980s and 1990s;
- the increase in the amount of part-time working, especially by women, which made union activity difficult to organise;
- the increased diversity of workforces in terms of qualifications and working conditions.

The decline has not been universal, or at the same rate, because of differing economic and social conditions prevailing in different countries. Some unions have been skilful in making adjustments in their attitudes and appeal.

### Union membership in selected countries, 2000: percentage belonging to a union

| 80% or above | 70% or above | 40% or above | 30% or above | 20% or less |
| --- | --- | --- | --- | --- |
| Denmark | Norway | South Africa | Australia | France |
| Sweden | | | Germany | USA |
| | | | Italy | |
| | | | UK | |

Figures adapted from those provided by International Labour Office

### Trade union power in Britain: a contentious issue

You don't get me, I'm part of the union . . . till I die . . .
It's out brothers out, out, out, out.

Extract from the refrain from the
Strawbs' hit record, *Part of the Union*, 1972.

Britain's trade unions have always been prone to allegations that they have excessive power but, by the 1960s, their role in the political and economic system was being identified as a major problem. Governments were said to under growing challenge from the unions. A consensus developed that their leaders – often referred to as barons – were often politically motivated and only too willing to hold the country to ransom. Concern was made all the stronger because of the widespread belief that there was no adequate framework of law in existence to regulate union activity. If there was one incident that finally convinced the public that the unions were 'out of control', it was the 'Winter of Discontent', a label applied to the spate of strikes and ensuing disruption which occurred between January and February 1979. It reduced union popularity to an all-time low and fatally damaged the reputation of the Labour government whose ministers seemed unable to exercise control over the industrial wing of the movement. The events highlighted disquiet about the role of the unions within the party and enabled the Conservative opposition to focus attention on the need to 'tame' the unions.

When the Conservatives entered office in May 1979, ministers made tackling the issue of union organisation and power a priority although they had only a few relatively modest proposals for legislation. Subsequent Thatcher governments, however embarked upon an incremental and systematic programme of 'reform'. They introduced six main statutes to tame the unions by altering the law relating to their organisation and practices. Among other legislative changes:

- Secondary picketing was made unlawful.
- Ballots were required for the election of union executives and before official strike action could be taken.
- New rights were granted to employers.
- Controls were introduced over the way unions raised and spent money for political purposes.

In addition, the long and exhausting struggle between the government and the miners in 1984–5 was won by ministers whose hand in the battle to weaken the unions was also assisted by the sharp growth in unemployment.

Much of the anti-union legislation introduced in the Conservative years has been accepted by New Labour. The Blair government has distanced the party from the unions while introducing some pro-union changes, such as workplace ballots. There has been much dissent in the union movement and sporadic talk of disaffiliation by some individual unions; others have made a cut in their funding of the party. The growing sense of detachment between Labour's two

wings has been increased by the retirement of some stalwart supporters of Labour ministers and their replacement by a new breed of
more militant left-wing leaders.

Since the 1980s, union power has been in overall decline, the result
of several different factors:

- The legal controls introduced by the Conservatives;
- Marked changes in the labour market, reflecting the broad economic shift involved in the decline of heavily unionised manufacturing industry and the rise of new, less-unionised and often
  hi-tech firms and of the service sector;
- The weakening position of the unions in its relationship with its
  major political ally, the Labour Party. In recent years, the party has
  revised its institutional links with the unions, changing sponsor-
  ship arrangements, reducing the representation of unions at the
  annual conference and their role in choosing parliamentary candidates and the party leader, and seeking new sources of funding
  from the business world.

Given its reduced influence in British politics, union leaders began
in the 1980s to show a new interest in the European Union, membership of which many of them had previously opposed. There was
a new interest in seeking to influence policy in Brussels, partly
through alliances made with other European unions via euro-groups
(see page 184). In addition, there were opportunities to expand
workers' rights by testing the European law as embodied in the
Human Rights Act.

Many members of environmental groups, who had welcomed
Labour's victory in 1997 and its promise to 'put the environment at the
heart of government', also became more critical in their approach.
Friends of the Earth and other groups recognised that there were some
gains but found the overall performance of the government disappoint-
ing. In a press release, *How Green Are The Parties?*,[9] issued for the 2001 election, FoE provided a detailed analysis of the party manifestos, measuring
them against ten important environmental yardsticks, ranging from
climate change, fuel poverty and energy production at the top, to global
issues and sustainable development. It assigned ministers a modest score
of 23 out of 50. Labour fared well on agriculture and the countryside,
and on promises on green taxation and public expenditure, but badly on
transport (for promising to build a hundred new roads), pollution and

public health, and corporations and businesses. Thereafter, many greens became more disenchanted and, by 2004, were at odds with ministers over GM crops, progress on climate change, transport policy, and the Iraq war which aroused the passions of many Greenpeace activists as well as many other groups. (For further information on the character, size and impact of the environmental movement, see the case study below.)

As Labour ran into policy difficulties and became mired in controversy over the preoccupation with spin rather than with substance, and the alleged lack of frankness of ministerial statements over Iraq, there was frustration and disappointment in many groups with a government that had enjoyed an unusually easy ride in its first few years in office. According to its critics, Labour in office was variously described as being 'too willing to placate big business' and the Americans; embrace Conservative solutions to policy issues; speak and act harshly on asylum seekers and crime; and too unwilling to challenge the readership of the *Sun* and the *Daily Mail* as part of the bid to retain popular support. Themes often voiced concerned the lack of meaningful consultation, the short time allowed for it, and the failure to heed advice when solicited. Critics found the Blair government guilty of the arrogance of power that is often associated with a party long in office.

To some extent, the criticisms of campaigning organisations are unsurprising. Labour governments in office tend to pursue policies that are more right wing than those favoured by their supporters. Compromises are always unpopular for idealists in groups tend to want to see ministers move quickly and decisively in their direction. The path of progress – indeed, the Blairite approach – is to move with public opinion rather than to get too far ahead of it. The pace and nature of ministerial changes were therefore inevitably going to disappoint those activists who wanted and expected more concessions to their viewpoint and swifter progress towards the achievement of common goals.

## Developments and trends in the British Green Movement since 1979: a case study

### The nature of the Green Movement

In the eyes of the outside world, there is one broad environmental movement in each region, country or continent but two types can often be distinguished:

1. Those which are traditional nature-**conservation** movements. The main thrust of the nature-conservation movements is to protect species in danger of extinction in a modernising world. They are often in the forefront of the fight against pollution. They are content to operate within the existing economic order by proposing moderate reforms and ensuring that politics has a 'green tinge'.

2. Those more radical ones concerned with political **ecology** and anti-nuclear issues, often referred to as New Left movements. They seek dramatic change in which ecological and social needs are seen as more important than the economic concerns of the existing pattern of society, in particular, the obsession with economic growth. The anti-nuclear movement is an offshoot of the political ecology one, members often sharing similar membership and a common outlook. Its main preoccupation is with the danger posed by nuclear power stations and the search for alternative energy sources. Within its orbit, the emphasis has been on decentralisation and individual or small-group activity, sometimes of a more radical and unconventional kind. (See also chapter 5 on protest politics for a discussion of radical environmental protest.)

**Categories of green pressure groups**

There are many green pressure groups. Few fall into the protective or interest category, if only because people who support the environment tend to be altruistic in their concerns rather than self-interested. The Country Land and Business Association, however, has an obvious interest in the protection of the countryside though their perspective is very different from that of the many green activists who abhor modern farming techniques. By contrast, there are several promotional groups seeking to advance policies of general benefit, ranging from Friends of the Earth and Greenpeace to less well-known and often more localised radical, direct-action groups.

In the environmental field, several of the better-known cause groups are also – by Grant's analysis – insider ones as well. The Campaign to Protect Rural England and the Royal Society for the Protection of Birds are in frequent touch with representatives of government. He notes that the RSPB has been the best-resourced

British group. As an indication of its insider status, it 'was closely involved with the European Commission in the formulation of the EC Directive on the conservation of wild birds'. Garner[10] portrays the World Wide Fund for Nature (WWF) as the 'classic example of an insider group that uses its conservation expertise as a means of gaining access to governments throughout the world'.

## The growth and size of green groups

The foundations of the environmental lobby were laid in the late nineteenth century, with subsequent bursts of growth in the late 1920s, late 1950s, early 1970s and late 1980s. It was in the 1970s that new groups were formed, such as Friends of the Earth and Greenpeace, both committed to adopting vigorous high-profile campaigns to draw attention to environmental dangers. Such groups have been the main source of opposition to government policies and have done much to raise the profile of the environment as a political issue.

British environmental groups and movements have experienced an impressive rate of growth over the last generation. Many groups experienced a substantial increase in membership in the 1980s and 1990s. Whereas Lloyd and Goyder[11] identified nearly a hundred national environmental groups and several thousand local ones with a combined membership approaching 3 million in 1980, more recent estimates place the figure well over 6 million.

Increased income from rising membership enables groups to afford more staffing and to engage in more active and widespread campaigning. It has also allowed for more extensive research. Some of the best-resourced groups, such as the RSPB and the WWF, have increasingly widened their interests from their specific concerns, so that they now place them in a wider ecological context. They have a better understanding of the interdependence of environmental problems. For instance, the RSPB looks beyond its narrow remit to examine how bird life can be affected by various other issues such as intensive agriculture and urban encroachment.

Prominent within the developing Green Movement of recent decades has been the animal rights lobby. Having its roots in the animal-protection movement of the nineteenth century, when various forms of animal cruelty were practised, it has gone through several subsequent phases. Some groups are preoccupied with species preservation, whereas others – including many more radical bodies – are concerned with issues relating to animal rights and animal liberation (see pages 8–9 and 126).

In several cases, environmental groups have made effective use of the media to advance discussion of green issues and, via the European Union, have acquired a new channel through which to seek political influence. Their importance is all the greater because of the failure of the Green Party to make significant electoral headway. Group activity and direct action seem to provide a more productive

### Table 4.1  The growth in membership of the largest environmental groups, 1981–2006

| Group | 1981 | 1995 | 2006 |
| --- | --- | --- | --- |
| National Trust | 1,050,000 | 2,300,000 | 3,400,000 |
| Royal Society for the Protection of Birds (RSPB) | 440,000 | 890,000 | 1,049,000 |
| Wildlife Trust | 140,000 | 260,000 | 600,000 |
| World Wide Fund for Nature | 60,000 | 210,000 | 430,000 |
| Greenpeace | 30,000 | 410,000 | 221,000 |
| Friends of the Earth | 18,000 | 230,000 | 102,000 |
| Ramblers Association | 37,000 | 94,000 | 140,000 |
| Woodland Trust | 20,000 | 150,000 | 130,000 |
| Campaign to Protect Rural England (CPRE) | 29,000 | 45,000 | 60,000 |

NB These rounded figures have been adapted from those provided by R. Garner, *Environmental Politics*, Macmillan, 2000 and brought up to date via relevant home web pages/direct contact.

area of activity. Several new and more radical organisations have flourished, often loosely affiliated to some larger body but operating at a local level.

Within the environmental lobby, many group campaigners have seen the wisdom of working in coalition with members of other groups. Alliances may be formed in pursuit of a particular campaign, such as the ban on fox hunting (see Chapter 8), or may become a permanent feature. The Council for Environmental Conservation was an unsuccessful early attempt at co-ordination in the field of conservation but, since the 1980s, working under the title of the Environment Council, it has developed a series of committees. In particular, Wildlife Link has been useful in enabling various agencies to exchange information and make a united representation to government. Several environmental groups and their members belong to the Green Alliance that was formed in 1985 as an umbrella organisation representing the non-party political aspirations of the Green Movement. It has a membership including individuals, campaigning groups, community groups and green businesses. As a non-party alliance, it seeks to bring about change by motivating people to take charge of their lives, rather than to effect these changes via political candidates and the ballot box.

One of the best-known umbrella bodies is Transport 2000 which has a membership comprising not just groups such as Greenpeace and FoE but also a range of interested organisations, such as the rail unions and public transport user groups. The Real World Coalition is also a high-profile agency that was formed in the mid-1990s to bring together a range of groups concerned with sustainable development – Christian Aid, Oxfam and the Save the Children Fund, among them.

### The impact of green campaigning under the Thatcher and Major administrations

After what was widely seen as some initial hostility to environmental matters, **Margaret Thatcher** underwent a rare change of mind in the late 1980s. She addressed the Royal Society in 1988 and spoke of the importance of sustainable development and of the need to nurture the environment. A year later, the party conference heard that the Conservatives were 'not merely Friends of the Earth' but also 'its guardians and trustees for generations to come'. Her new-found commitment and the actions which followed gave the topic a greater priority in government thinking and helped to promote a response from the other parties. Her 'conversion' and the increased interest of other parties reflected to some degree the pressure of external opinion as environmental matters became the theme of media discussion, particularly after the success of the Green Party in the 1989 European elections; activists were interviewed and featured in various political programmes.

Many commentators questioned the genuineness of the Thatcherite commitment to the environmentalists' agenda. They felt that scenes of her bending over to pick up litter and making speeches about green politics being synonymous with conservation, heritage and English values, amounted to little of practical benefit. Deep greens were scathing about the way the Thatcherite administrations could live with leaky atomic submarines, cracked nuclear power stations, new motorways, and a thriving arms-export industry. Nonetheless, some members of Friends of the Earth and other organisations found a receptive ear for their ideas.

In the administration of **John Major**, Environment Secretary John Gummer, was keen to display strong green credentials. An organic farmer himself, he soon earned respect from many green lobbyists for his initiatives. They had doubts, however, about the nature and pace of the action plan on sustainable development published two years after the Rio de Janeiro conference. Although they praised Gummer for his willingness to bring environmental issues to the centre of policy-making, they felt that the documents on sustainable development, climate change, biodiversity and forestry failed to reflect much of their input. Green lobbyists questioned whether the consultation process with ministers was really making any difference for, rather than clear targets and strategies, they were offered the promise of more discussion. As Jonathan Porritt[12] pointed out, [without these] 'in all honesty, it is possible to imagine a sequence of these meetings stretching from here to eternity without delivering the goods'.

The overall picture of pressure group activity under the Conservatives was a mixed one. Certain groups operated with little change in their fortunes, being seen as fairly neutral in ministerial eyes. Generally, those which straddled the political Centre Right were more likely to gain attention. If anything, there tended to be a preponderance of Conservatives in the CPRE and, in rural areas, they often had the support of their local Tory MP. They secured successes, such as in their campaign to make the government rethink its plans to downgrade 'green belts'.

## New Labour and the green lobby since 1997

The environmental lobby has been sharply critical of ministers over a number of issues, ranging from the slowness with which they moved on the issue of renewable energy to their timidity in relation to policy on fox hunting. They feel that the government has been unwilling to do enough to improve the provision of public transport and to tackle the issue of car dependence. In their view, ministers have not had the political courage to speak the truth and say publicly that it is the demand for driving that needs to be curbed, perhaps by making motorists pay as they drive via congestion charges. Meanwhile, motoring costs continue to fall and public transport becomes more expensive.

Greenpeace, along with FoE and some other campaigning groups, has maintained relentless pressure over GM crops. It was scathing about the so-called public debate on the issue, suggesting that ministers failed to create sufficient opportunities for people to get involved and that the public's views as expressed in local meetings were not sufficiently heeded. Greenpeace activists have been highly critical of ministers over the war with Iraq and played a key part in organising public demonstrations.

Jonathan Porritt, former exponent of ecological thinking and FoE activist, and now chair of the British Sustainable Development Commission, has echoed some recent green doubts. Although he is seen by some environmentalists as having 'gone native', too willing to work with the present administration, Porritt[13] has not felt barred from offering public criticism of the performance of ministers, including the Prime Minister. Lack of firm direction and leadership and a marked inclination (indeed, a 'naive adulation') towards the business community were among the alleged Blairite offences, as was the lack of a coherent strategy for tackling green issues.

Past and present members of the green lobby suspect that the enticing promises New Labour made in opposition and at the 1997 election were designed to keep the greens on board and suggest these have been watered down or ignored ever since. A *Guardian* leader[14] has portrayed the environment as 'Labour's blind spot', concluding that:

> The truth is that New Labour has never been interested in the environmental agenda . . . It regarded it as being anti-business, and feared a collision with Middle England's love of cars and consumerism. The matter has been left to drift; environmentalists describe an alarming degree of ignorance and indifference in Number Ten.

### An assessment of green campaigners and campaigning in recent decades

As we have seen, the membership of environmental groups has expanded rapidly over the last three decades, a period when party membership has been declining. Promotional groups may often be less favourably resourced than the protective variety but, even if they have less money, they benefit from the support of enthusiastic activists willing to devote time and energy to their cause. This is particularly true of the newer and more radical bodies.

McCormick[15] has described Britain as having 'the oldest, strongest, best-organised and most widely supported environmental lobby in the world'. But Robin Grove-White[16] of the Centre for Environmental Change at Lancaster University has detected a change in the traditional environmental movement. In particular, he has written of 'a growing proliferation of new, frequently fragile, but vibrant social networks developing around issues like health, food, gender, personal growth, leisure, animals and vegetarianism'.

One of the successes of the Green Movement has been its ability to promote the environmental agenda in British politics by skilful use of the media. But at election time, when other concerns seem more pressing to many voters, its effects seem more marginal. Charles Secrett,[17] The Director of FoE, criticised the media for under-reporting green issues during the 2001 campaign. Drawing on a survey conducted at Loughborough University, he found that environmental coverage made up only 0.8 per cent of all news stories. He concluded: 'Environmental issues have been under-reported throughout this election campaign. The mainstream parties have let the public down by ignoring the environment. And too much of the media has collaborated with this betrayal.'

Environmental groups have experienced some difficulties. They are prone to internal divisions over the approach to lobbying and contentious matters of policy. Within the RSPCA, a section of the membership prefers to adopt a high profile and engage in direct campaigning whereas the majority prefers to seek to influence those in authority by quieter discussion and consultation. There are also divisions over individual policies. Fox hunting has been a difficult issue to handle. Within the National Trust, a number of its members have both supported and practised the sport, whereas others have taken the view that hunting is an antisocial and unacceptable form of behaviour.

Because of lack of funds, some groups have been forced to concentrate on one issue, for many of them lacked the resources to pursue all the objectives that they would have liked to tackle. Moreover, research carried out by Jordan[18] and others indicates a high level of membership turnover among cause groups. Some years ago, he pointed out that only 35 per cent of those who joined Friends of the Earth in 1991 rejoined a year later.

Groups have also faced a difficulty in deciding how best to advance their position. As Rawcliffe[19] points out, the question of 'natural limits' to greening policy within the prevailing power structures is unavoidable for them because it is 'through existing power structures that environmental pressure is both expressed and constrained'. Thus, there is both danger and opportunity in moving closer to the existing centres of power. The balance between these is always a matter of judgement. In as much as groups adopt more moderate and even institutionalised stances, working with government and seeking to raise the profile of environmental issues at election times, they run the risk of being outflanked by more radical groups such as Earth First! whose members are prepared to take direct action.

With so many people belonging or sympathetic to environmental organisations in the United Kingdom, there ought to be a significant part of the electorate that could be mobilised around green issues. Some environmental pressure groups, however, have been wary of being too overtly political because of their charitable status. They also realise that they have to work with and lobby any incoming government.

With the exception of FoE and Greenpeace, which have tended to adopt a critical outlook on aspects of Labour's performance in office, group activists have tended to be cautious in their criticisms of the leading parties.

. . . . . . . . . . . . . . . . . . . . . . . . . . . . . . . . . . . . . . . . . . . . . . . . . . . . . . . . . . . . .

## ✔ What you should have learnt from reading this chapter

* There have been substantial changes in pressure-group activity over the last generation.

* The number of groups has expanded and the range of access points has increased.

* New techniques of pressure have been applied, including professional lobbying and direct action.

* Under the Conservative governments, there was a general distrust of pressure groups, and unions and social groups fared badly.

* Under New Labour, campaigning groups have been more widely consulted but have often felt disappointed with the outcome – especially those concerned with human rights, civil liberties and the environment.

* Overall, groups have experienced less influence than they did a generation ago.

* Environmental groups have grown rapidly, their approaches, methods and success varying significantly. The green lobby is now a substantial element in group activity.

## 🔎 Glossary of key terms

**Conservation** The protection, preservation and careful management of the world's resources. Conservationists are those who argue for husbanding the available resources. The term is also applied to organisations such as the National Trust which wishes to preserve fine buildings as well as areas of outstanding natural beauty.
**Ecology** The study of the relationships between living organisms and their environment. As a political doctrine, ecologists espouse a more radical creed than environmentalists who are also alarmed by the damage and destruction caused by the nature and pace of economic development. Ecologists have a more deep-green, anti-materialist and anti-technological stance. They wish to change society's present direction for they fundamentally question its values.
**Multi-level governance** The multiple layering of government. A description of the way in which the British political system operates today.

It is no longer the Westminster system of the past, with institutions and powers concentrated in London. There are various tiers of government, with the European Union at the top, then the British government, the devolved bodies and local administration, plus a number of unelected **quangos** that also exercise considerable power.

**Professional lobbying**  Lobbying carried out by specialist organisations that offer to influence policy and effect high-level contracts in exchange for payment. Often, the lobbyists are using contacts made during an earlier career in Parliament or ministerial office as a bait with which to attract business. Many companies and large, well-resourced groups may employ a professional lobbying firm in addition to conducting their own campaigning.

**Quangos**  An unelected quasi non-governmental organisation is one created and funded by government but which has operational independence.

## ? Likely examination questions

Examine the changing nature of pressure-group activity over the last twenty-five years.

'Many important pressure groups have had les access to government since 1979 than was previously the case.' Discuss.

Examine the impact of the Blair government on the fortunes of pressure groups.

Discuss the view that pressure groups now have less influence than they did a generation ago.

How successful have environmental pressure groups been in influencing government policy in Britain over the last two decades?

Which environmental groups are most effective at popularising their cause and influencing governmental action?

Assess the impact of the green lobby in British politics.

## Helpful websites

Several of these tend to be covered in other chapters – e.g. Chapter 7 on lobbying the European Union. But see also:

www.appc.org.uk Association of Professional Political Consultants, the regulatory body for lobbyists

The sites of well-known environmental groups, including those involved in direct action, illustrate their priorities:

www.earthfirst.org.uk/ Earth First!

www.foe.co.uk/ Friends of the Earth

www.greenpeace.org.uk/ Greenpeace

## Suggestions for further reading

*Articles:*

A. Denham and M. Garnett, 'Influence without responsibility? Think tanks in Britain' in *Parliamentary Affairs* 52:1, 1999.

B. Doherty, 'Paving the way: The rise of direct action against road-building and the changing character of British environmentalism', *Political Studies*, 47, 1999.

S. Thomson, I. Stancich and L. Dickson, 'Gun Control and Snowdrop', *Parliamentary Affairs*, 5:3, 1998.

D. Toke, 'Power and environmental pressure groups' in *Talking Politics*, 9:2, winter 1996.

*Books:*

B. Coxall, *Pressure Groups in British Politics*, Pearson, 2001.

W. Grant, *Pressure Groups and British Politics*, Palgrave, 2000.

G. Jordan (ed) *The Commercial Lobbyists: Politics for Profit in Britain*, Aberdeen University Press, 1991.

## CHAPTER 5

# Protest Politics and Direct Action

## Contents

## Overview

Over the last few decades, there has been an escalation of protest politics. Individuals and groups have been willing to resort to various forms of non-violent direct action as a means of drawing attention to their demands. Such direct action has been a particular feature of the environmental movement in Britain and overseas but it has been used by others who recognise that it is a powerful publicity tool.

In this chapter, we examine the meaning and extent of direct action and assess examples of the politics of protest.

## Key issues to be covered in this chapter

- The meaning of direct action and its various forms
- The growing popularity of such action and explanations for its increased use
- The environmental movement and direct action
- Examples of popular protest in recent years and their common characteristics
- The legitimacy of direct action by individuals, groups and popular movements in a democracy

# The meaning of direct action

Direct action is not a new phenomenon. Over many centuries, marches and demonstrations have been used by those who wished to protest against their living and working conditions. Over the last two hundred years or more, trade unions have employed action as a weapon with which to persuade reluctant employers to meet their demands. But, in the last few decades, there has been a marked upsurge in the growth of forms of direct action by individuals and groups. These range from demonstrations and 'sit-in' protests, to squatting and striking, from interrupting televised events and non-payment of taxation to the invasion of institutions in which the activities conducted cause offence. Groups committed to opposing hunting or other forms of alleged mistreatment of animals have often been willing to resort to forms of direct action to voice their protest.

By direct action we mean doing for oneself what the government has refused to do. This may mean that homeless people find a home by occupying unoccupied property. By extension, the term has been used more widely to allude to any attempt to coerce those in authority into changing their viewpoint – as when the homeless might occupy a council office until they are housed. These activities invariably involve law-breaking which may be passive (such as obstruction or trespass) or violent, if the furniture is broken up or a person threatened. Today, the usual meaning of the term is 'action taken outside the constitutional and legal framework'. In Baggott's[1] words, it describes a situation when a group 'takes matters into its own hands, rather than relying on established methods of decision-making, to resolve a problem'.

Direct action does not have to be violent. It can be militant without being violent and, if violence is used, it may be against property rather than against a person. Non-payment of a portion of taxation by Quakers who disapprove of any defence policy based on the willingness to use force is non-violent but illegal. So was the willingness of those seeking the vote for women at the beginning of the century who organised themselves into the Tax Resistance League (their cry was 'no taxation without representation').

Campaigns of direct action may start off as peaceful protests but can easily become violent. Many people might choose to engage in an orderly demonstration against some motorway development or the export of live animals to the Continent. They might find that, as passions become inflamed, so disorder creeps in. Protest marches have often turned out to be occasions in which violence erupts, and the demonstrators become locked into confrontation with the police who are seeking to maintain law and order. Of course, this does not necessarily happen, and the right to peaceful protest is one which civil libertarians would wish strongly to defend.

## Box 5.1  Forms of direct-action protest politics distinguished

### Non-violent and legal

Many forms of organised protest by members of pressure groups or broader popular movements fall into this category. It may involve boy-cotting goods sold by companies whose products are produced under conditions using an exploited workforce, signing a petition, distributing literature, attending a meeting, joining a march or demonstration. The Make Poverty History march on and through Edinburgh (see page 118) was an overwhelmingly peaceful attempt to persuade those international leaders attending the G8 Summit at Gleneagles of the need to act decisively to alleviate conditions on the African continent.

### Non-violent and illegal

A more coercive gradation of protest politics involves forms of obstruction and disruption. Although they are intended to be peaceful, they may – but not necessarily so – spill over into violence, if only by a small section of those protesting. At the peaceful end of the spectrum might be the withholding of tax payments by those who oppose the spending of money on national defence; a trespass to demonstrate that ramblers have a right to open access on footpaths; or the blocking of a main road by worried mothers who feel that there should be a pedestrian crossing to help their offspring cross safely. Other examples of varying degrees of gravity might include the release of mink from a mink farm or of animals from a laboratory by animal rights activists; the digging up of graves by anti-hunt saboteurs; and the destruction of GM crops by Greenpeace or other environmental activists.

The protest is not intended to harm people physically but rather to draw attention to the 'unacceptable' nature of what is being done and to the unacceptable behaviour of those who perpetrate it. Most involved recognise that the use of violence might be counter-productive and intend to keep their protest peaceful. But when enthusiastic activists (particularly when gathered en masse) encounter resistance, some of them may become involved in physical struggle.

**Violent and illegal**
At the more extreme end are those forms of direct action that are not only illegal but violent, intended to do harm to those held responsible for the ill about which campaigners are registering their protest. An attack by opponents of abortion on those who carry out the operation; the use of incendiary devices against laboratories involved in experimentation on animals or stores selling fur coats; and the use of letter- or car-bombs are examples of these fortunately rarer methods of protesting.

## The growing popularity of direct action

In recent years, some promotional groups have seen more point in using direct action as an additional means of persuading government into following their ideas. By so doing, they achieve publicity, for the television cameras are likely to be present at some mass protest or demonstration. Of course, noise and publicity are not the same as influence, and it is still true that, for some organisations, resorting to various forms of demonstration is an indication of weakness rather than strength. When the TUC called a 'Day of Action' in 1982, this was a reflection of its limited access to Whitehall in the Thatcher years. Many local-action and promotional groups have used direct action as an additional tool, however. Members of NIMBY groups have often used this approach in their bid to block moves to build a housing estate on green-belt land, or stop the felling of some ancient tree in the name of progress.

In recent years, groups have used direct action when they have campaigned against the use of fur for clothing, hunting foxes, or the Miss World contest. Animal rights activists and anti-motorway protesters have been in the forefront of such campaigning and have often been adept in arranging for the television cameras to be present at their demonstrations. A reading of the local papers on any day will probably reveal the activities of groups who seek to gain publicity by some dramatic gesture.

Hijackers and terrorists among others have shown how effective techniques of law-breaking can be, but few groups are willing to resort to such extremist tactics to attain their desired objectives. Many groups are willing to employ forms of direct action, however, most of which are illegal.

Among the reasons for the growth in direct action over the lasts twenty years or so has been the rise of causes and movements associated with the environment (see below). This has triggered a mass of activity, local, national and international. Another factor was that, in the Conservative years (1979–97), there were often limited opportunities for consultation with previously powerful groups such as trade unions finding themselves out in the cold. Beyond these factors, however, there is the more recent ease with which protest can be organised via the World Wide Web, e-mail and mobile phones. Technology has not only assisted protesters, but also journalists who have become ever more alive to the opportunities for identifying themselves with causes, the publicising of which might help establish their own careers.

## Environmental groups and direct action

Much of the increase in protest politics has been related to the causes of the environment and social justice. The journalist John Vidal[2] has drawn attention to the explosion of such grass-roots protest, pointing out that:

> The modern phenomenon of 'direct action' started with anti-nuclear protests and moved, via Greenpeace and Friends of the Earth, to environmental, animal welfare and road protesting. Today, it is spreading into almost every area of life and becoming the ultimate expression of political, environmental, corporate or social disquiet.

According to a survey[3] in 1996, Britain was thought to have 'more grass-roots direct-action environmental and social justice groups than ever before'. It found that of a dozen groups analysed, their members had been involved in more than five hundred separate 'actions' in one year. In particular, there was:

- a proliferation in protest by city-based groups with no formal membership or constitution;
- a situation in which many local groups were operating in partnership with similar bodies elsewhere;
- a trend towards the use of greater illegality.

Other findings[4] have suggested that there is now a more wide-spread acceptance of the view that obedience to the law is not always appropriate and that law-breaking in exceptional circumstances and for reasons of conscience is acceptable (support up from 46 per cent to 55 per cent between 1983 and 1996). Vidal has offered a range of explanations for such an increase in grass-roots protest at the very end of the twentieth century; among them:

- developing disillusion on the part of many campaigners with the performance of the Labour government; public campaigning may even have actually increased since 1997 because of the wide-spread expectations that had been unleashed by the arrival in office of a 'progressive government' and the subsequent disap-pointment when it failed to carry out the policies favoured by protest campaigners;
- the growing recognition that protest is an effective means of getting concerns placed on the national agenda;
- the help and training given to concerned individuals and groups by organisations such as Friends of the Earth.

The more zealous environmentalists have on occasion resorted to violence, which they regard as a necessary and effective way of com-bating official obstinacy and structural force. In their view, the time for bargaining is over given the magnitude of the issues and the impli-cations of the decisions which they are confronting and challenging. Hoad[5] points out that, in their eyes, the issues of 'destruction of natural habitat and species depletion' and many others are so serious in their implications that 'only by taking a pro-active stance will any-thing be accomplished'.

Of course, not all environmental protesters have been willing to be obstructive. Moderates among them see the regular, even persis-tent, use of illegal and violent direct action as giving the cause a bad name. They are prepared to boycott goods, block roads and impede the movement of goods at dockyards, even to the point of inviting arrest, but methods such as syringing cans of food, releasing mink or digging up the graves of former hunt leaders are seen as beyond the pale.

What is significant, however, is the way in which the environmen-tal movement has managed on several occasions to unite moderates and radicals in the same campaign. Baggott[6] quotes *The Campaigning Handbook* to illustrate the point: The **Twyford Down protest** for example, was strengthened by informal alliances with local conservatives and the radical–traditional axis has become a feature of protests since.

---

## Box 5.2  Attitudes to environmental campaigners: élitists and tree-huggers?

As we have seen in the main text, individuals and groups within the environmental movement have often been involved in protest politics. Their activities have sometimes been derided, perhaps most conspicuously by the late Labour cabinet minister, Tony Crosland, who referred to the conservation lobby as being 'hostile to growth and indifferent to the needs of ordinary people. It has manifestly a class bias and reflects a set of middle and upper class value judgements.'

Dunion[7] makes the point that environmentalists have regularly been caricatured as tree-huggers 'sentimentally more concerned with nature than people'. In his view, this image of middle-class idealists concerned to protect nature while others get on with making ends meet – although very wide of the mark – still lingers. A *Daily Mail* columnist[8] has referred disparagingly to environmental campaigners, with 'their woolly jumpers and their occasional public display of affection for trees'. In Scotland, a fisherman's leader[9] in the Shetland Islands has noted the distinction between 'school-educated fishermen . . . and university-educated tree-huggers'.

The original tree-huggers were anything but middle class. Peasant women in northern India were alarmed at the commercial loggers and sports goods manufacturers who felled trees on the mountain slopes, activities that made flooding more likely and denied them fodder for animal feed, fuel for cooking and fruit for their consumption. Banding together, they encircled tree-trunks with their arms, challenging the loggers to attack or seek to remove them in the face of occasional beatings and much abuse. They were nicknamed *chipko* (meaning 'tree-huggers').

*Chipko* protesters were ordinary villagers who found themselves transformed into 'troublemakers'. They were a poor and marginalised people 'galvanised into action by the implementation of decisions which were made without their voice being heard'.[10]

**Direct action at an international level**

The 1990s saw the emergence of a widespread movement of opposition to globalisation (see Table 5.1 for examples of major demonstrations). It is not an easy movement to characterise, but three broad points can be emphasised:

1. The anti-globalisation movement is diffuse. There are self-appointed spokespersons, such as Ralph Nader, Naomi Klein and Anita Roddick, rather than accredited leaders, and there is little in the way of formal organisation. Anti-globalisation is best thought of as an umbrella term covering a wide range of groups – environmentalists, campaigners for debt relief, human rights activists and so on – which have a wide range of beliefs and concerns.

2. It is economic rather than technological or cultural globalisation that has aroused the deepest feelings of opposition. Opponents of globalisation see American-style capitalism as the root cause of world poverty, the debt crisis and environmental pollution. Thus, to a large extent, anti-globalisation equates with anti-capitalism. Anti-globalisation activists have made business centres and conferences of global financial institutions the targets of their demonstrations. Although a number of these demonstrations have ended in violence it would be quite wrong to conclude that most anti-globalisation activists support violent protest.

3. There is a strong thread of anti-Americanism running through the anti-globalisation movement. The United States is seen as the architect of the existing international economic order, as the lair of the most powerful multinationals, and as the world's worst polluter. Otherwise disparate groups can make common cause in viewing the United States as the enemy – particularly when its president is a right-wing Republican whose administration has close links with leading multinational corporations.

As part of the Gleneagles protests in the Make Poverty History campaign (see below, pages 118–19), 225,000 joined a protest march through Edinburgh, making a symbolic ring around the castle in an overwhelmingly peaceful demonstration. Two days later, the much smaller demonstration of some three hundred hard-core protesters – an assortment of anarchists and anti-capitalists from France, Italy and Spain, as well as Britain – led to violence which brought the city

## Table 5.1  Major anti-globalisation demonstrations

| 1999 | London | May Day demonstration in the City, London's financial district: extensive damage to property. |
|---|---|---|
| 1999 | Seattle | 50,000 demonstrators protested at a World Trade Organization conference: turned into the 'battle of Seattle', with 600 arrests made. |
| 2000 | Davos | Demonstration at the annual meeting of the World Economic Forum at the Swiss resort of Davos. Dozens of injuries and hundreds of arrests. |
| 2001 | Quebec | 30,000 protestors took to the streets at the Summit of the Americas. Over 400 people arrested as police clashed with demonstrators. |
| 2001 | Genoa | 100,000 demonstrators took part in protests at the G8 Summit, a conference of leaders of the world's eight most powerful economies. One protestor shot dead: dozens injured. |

centre to a standstill and led to five times more arrests. Larger protests around the city were also violent, with missiles such as cobbles and paving stones being thrown at the police.

**Make poverty history**

The Make Poverty History coalition – part of the Global Campaign Against Poverty (GCAP) – was created in 2004 to galvanise the Western World into action on the issue of world poverty. It co-ordinated a series of events and marches around the country over several months, culminating in the G8 Summit at Gleneagles. The timing was designed to coincide with the British presidency of the G8 and of the European Union, as well as with the twentieth anniversary of Live Aid. Its organisers wanted to see urgent action by world leaders, as part of a moral crusade 'to tackle the greatest evil of our times'. They argued that poverty was not caused primarily by nature but by factors such as global trade, debt and insufficient and inefficient aid, exacerbated by the pursuit by governments of inappropriate economic policies. Coalition backers included many churches, faith and charitable bodies, ranging from Advantage Africa to Afghan Poverty Relief, from the Movement for the Abolition of War to Traidcraft, and from Time for God to Tzedek (Jewish Action for a Just World), supported by well-known clergy, entertainers (most prominently, Bob Geldof) and politicians among many others.

At Gleneagles, the assembled delegates took decisions that went some way towards satisfying the demands of campaign organisers and the many people who supported the cause in Britain and around the world. Debt cancellation worth £25billion and increases in aid were agreed, deals on trade and curbing the arms trade were referred for further discussion, and on climate change a compromise was reached. Perhaps inevitably, those involved were disappointed that more had not been achieved but recognised that real gains were made.

## Direct action in practice: some case studies

### Case study 1: peaceful protest at Greengairs, 1996

Greengairs is a traditional working-class and former mining community in north Lanarkshire, Scotland. The excavation of opencast coal over many years created a vast hole long since used as a landfill site for depositing waste material from all over Scotland. Debris ranging from asbestos removed from offices and schools to decomposing dead fish was regularly dumped, much to the chagrin of local inhabitants who were alarmed by the flies, rats and smell, as well as by the foul emissions.

In 1996, news leaked that a lorry-load of contaminated soil was being delivered to Greengairs by Shanks & McEwan, a leading British waste-disposal company. This was too much for the newly formed Greengairs Action Group who saw it as a massive environmental injustice that contaminated English waste was fit for burial north of the border. Members took to the streets, blockaded the site and carried placards warning against 'the toxic time bomb' among other peaceful forms of protest.

The situation was ultimately defused when Shanks & McEwan agreed to an independent assessment of the site and accepted its findings. The contents of the site were to be left undisturbed but there was to be regular monitoring to check for any health and safety hazards.

There was to be no more dumping in Greengairs. A substantial victory had been achieved, the company being conscious both of its responsibilities and of the potential damage to its reputation. The protest was the launch pad for the subsequent campaign for environmental justice for Scotland. In 2002, the First Minister of the Scottish Executive paid a symbolic visit to the community and made a speech in which he declared that:

> . . . too often the environment is dismissed as the concern of those who are not confronted with bread and butter issues. But the reality is the people who have the most urgent environmental concerns in Scotland are those who cope daily with the consequences of a poor quality of life, and live in a rotten environment, close to industrial pollution, plagued by vehicle emissions, streets filled by litter and walls covered in graffiti. This is true for Scotland and also true elsewhere in the world.

### Case study 2: the case of Earth First!

According to its website, the general principles behind Earth First! are 'non-hierarchical organisation and the use of direct action to confront, stop and eventually reverse the forces that are responsible for the destruction of the Earth and its inhabitants. EF! Is not a cohesive group or campaign, but a convenient banner for people who share similar philosophies to work under.'

#### *South Pacific Solidarity!*

Serious sabotage and damage committed during an invasion of New Tribal Missions HQ in the UK.

On 11 October more than fifty people took direct action against the New Tribes Mission (NTM) UK Headquarters in Grimsby, in solidarity with resistant indigenous people of the Philippines, West Papua and Bougainville. NTM have stated that they intend to preach to every tribe on the planet by 2025, such as the Agta of Northern Luzon and tribes in Mindanao.

NTM build airstrips in jungles, have their own planes to ferry first missionaries and then businessmen, Coca-Cola and the military. First comes Christianity and then corporations. The indigenous people of West Papua have declared missionaries one of their 4 biggest threats: they are as responsible as mining or logging companies for ecological and cultural destruction.

The activists visited NTM wearing West Papuan masks, invaded and occupied the offices. They severely outnumbered the missionaries working there. Essential information and equipment was [*SIC*] removed which will prove valuable to research for resistance to NTM. Other people sabotaged and damaged essential computer hardware, software and other office equipment. Others argued with workers. Others demonstrated outside or in the village nearby with banners. A timing device was planted in a toilet that later opened a valve on the cold water supply leading to flood damage during Friday night/Saturday morning. All the protestors [*SIC*] left the scene without arrest, although missionaries attempted – and failed – to stop people leaving.

> Extract from environmental protest website in November 2002:
> www.eco-action.org

## Case study 3: Fathers 4 Justice

Fathers 4 Justice (F4J) is a civil rights, direct-action group formed in 2002. It campaigns on behalf of fathers who claim to have suffered injustices in the quagmire of divorce proceedings and feel that the legal system is stacked against them. In its literature, it talks of the rights of both parents and grandparents. It comprises fathers, mothers, teachers, doctors, barristers, police officers and many others supportive of the view that Britain is needlessly creating a nation of children without parents and parents without children.

F4J has adopted a twin-track strategy based around publicity and pressure: raising awareness through publicity, 'making injustice visible', and mobilising a 'dads' army' on the one hand, and seeking influence through the political system, and especially MPs, to bring about meaningful change on the other.

As part of its bid for publicity, it supports peaceful, non-violent direct action based on the Greenpeace model, sometimes – in its view – 'with a dash of humour thrown in for good measure'.[11] It has engaged in various high-profile stunts, sometimes raising awareness in unique and even provocative ways. In May 2004, two members of Fathers 4 Justice caused a security alarm at Westminster when they hurled purple powder at Tony Blair. There were immediate fears that it might be a chemical or biological toxin but later it was proved to be harmless flour. The two protesters had managed to evade the newly installed glass screen, for they were seated in the front three rows of the gallery outside the security fitting. On other occasions, they have climbed public buildings, once scaling a gantry at 7.45 a.m. and causing disruption to one of London's main railway lines. At Christmas, also in 2004, members processed as Fathers Christmas, employing the slogan 'Put the fathers back into Christmas'. In September 2005, while Tony Blair was addressing the Labour conference, one of the demonstrators from the May 2004 incident scaled the roof of the Houses of Parliament to continue his protest, unfurling a banner which read 'Does Blair care?'.

The leadership announced that it was disbanding in January 2006, following negative publicity surrounding an alleged plot to kidnap the son of the Prime Minister. Some members continued operations as the 'Real F4J', gaining much publicity by interrupting the live Lottery draw on BBC1, shouting and running in front of the cameras. The protestors portrayed the event as marking the dramatic return of their campaign and pledged to stage further stunts as opportunities arise.

### Case study 4: the fuel protesters of September 2000 and September 2005

Prior to every budget, the Treasury is advised by various interest groups, ranging from the CBI, the NFU and the Road Hauliers Association (RHA) to lower or at least not increase fuel duties on petrol and diesel, often without success. Well after the 2000 budget, small businesses in the road-haulage and other industries, dependent on using petrol and diesel (such as farmers and fishermen), had kept up sustained pressure over the high level of fuel tax. The crisis in 2000 centred on the willingness of these discontented groups to use direct action against the Labour government in order to force the Chancellor, Gordon Brown, to lower the price of fuel. The events that followed were more reminiscent of French than of British politics, the past behaviour of French farmers providing the inspiration for some of the tactics involved.

The direct action began on 7 September when a number of protesters started to picket the entrance to an oil refinery in Cheshire. Many of the pickets involved in protesting were from the small-business sector. Within a few days, hardly any petrol was being delivered to petrol stations throughout Britain. Motorists engaged in panic

## Box 5.3  The fuel protest: main players

**Who was involved?**
*On the one side:* a coalition of small business-people, farmers, fishing workers and others whose livelihoods were affected by the price of fuel (plus sympathetic motorists and politically motivated antagonists of the Government).

*On the other side:* ministers of the Labour government elected in 1997, many anti-private-transport campaigners in the environmentalist movement.

**Who was caught in the crossfire?**
Oil companies, tanker drivers, the police, trade unions and the public.

buying and shortages of fuel developed. The events highlighted the vulnerability to disruptive action of even an advanced, modern economy.

By 11 September, the problem was escalating as petrol supplies were not getting out of the refineries, either because the petrol-tanker drivers would not cross picket lines out of sympathy for the aggrieved protesters or because of fear of intimidation and reprisals.

In his study of the episode, McNaughton[12] notes how a feature of the fuel protests was the success of the activists in organising picketing:

> Groups of activists were able to move rapidly from one hot spot to another and small bands of truck drivers formed slow-moving convoys to disrupt traffic flows. The use of the Internet and mobile phones was the key to their organisation, demonstrating the potential for technological advances in communications for the activities of pressure groups.

The government could not be seen to yield to the threat of force for to do so would be portrayed as weak and indecisive. Moreover, other groups would see that ministers could be pushed around. On the other hand, not to make any move would be to allow essential groups, such as ambulance crews and those working in the blood-transfusion service, to be deprived of vital fuel, causing havoc in essential services; supermarkets would run out of food (panic buying of food soon became an issue); individuals going to work would be affected; and the public would become increasingly dismayed. Many motorists, long aggrieved by the high costs of fuel, were already becoming sympathetic to those engaged in direct action. There was a case for concessions but they had to be handled sensitively and without undue haste or panic.

Ministers were only too aware of how the issue was inevitably seized upon by journalists who were on to a good story. Protests were reported sympathetically, with stories of hardship faced by victims of an uncaring government that did not seem to understand popular concerns. Scenes of blockades, motorway turmoil, and motorists tooting their horns in a gesture of support were regularly on television news. But ministers had allies in the trade-union movement. Unusually, on this occasion, the union leaders were supportive of tanker drivers crossing picket lines. This was because they saw the protest as being right wing in origin, backed as it was by small businesses and groups such as the Countryside Alliance that were keen to embarrass the government. For the TUC, the crisis was not the media portrayal of popular, spontaneous demonstrations by a hard-hit section of the community supported by public opinion, against an unpopular administration.

The Prime Minister called in to Downing Street the bosses of the oil companies and made it clear that they should get tanker drivers to co-operate and, if necessary, cross picket lines and make deliveries. They pointed out that many drivers were not employers but rather self-employed owners of their tankers who could not be easily persuaded into so doing. After a week, however, pickets had withdrawn and tankers were supplying petrol stations. It was not the threatened use of troops that ministers had contemplated, nor any governmental climb-down on reductions in duties that swung the outcome (though ministers helpfully hinted at the prospect of a concession in the near future). Ultimately, it was the change in the public mood. This was reflected in press headlines in the *Mirror* and other newspapers that called for a cessation of action. Leading protesters soon realised they would rapidly lose sympathy if essential services were imperilled, supermarkets ran out of food, and people could not get to work.

In November, the Chancellor felt able to make a concession, freezing the fuel duties until the following budget and making other changes that effectively reduced the prices of petrol and diesel. Direct action had highlighted the issue of high fuel prices and, in a sense, had the desired effect. The protesters eventually got some of what they wanted. But, on the other hand, the government did not back down. The rise and fall of the issue illustrated the importance of public support if action is to succeed. At first, there was plenty of popular and media sympathy. It began to melt away as the consequences of the confrontation became apparent.

Five years later in 2005, the fuel protests were of a very different order. In September 2005, the organisers of the demonstrations were the same collection of farmers, hauliers and business people who had drawn spontaneous support from the public previously. They were organised in the People's Fuel Lobby and joined by a newly formed Welsh Hauliers and Public Less Tax on Fuel Campaign. They came from all parts of the country and claimed that their businesses were struggling as fuel prices breached the £1 a litre mark in some areas. Their methods were the same, with communications being conducted by e-mails, mobile phone texts and Internet blogs to draw together like-minded individuals in a bid for public support. Even in the best-supported pickets of refineries, however, the demonstrators were outnumbered by journalists and, at several terminals, there was no one at all to be seen. Tankers came and went as usual. So, too, the disruption of motorway traffic by a large convoy of lorries, coaches and taxis on the M4 and M60 made much less impact than in 2000, with fewer getting involved – in part because it was felt that the authorities were too well prepared to allow the protests to achieve the drama of the previous occasion.

This time, scarred by their experiences in 2000, ministers were better prepared than ever before. Senior police officers had sufficient powers to break blockades at any of the nine major oil refineries. If necessary, the Civil Contingencies Act, brought in after the earlier protests, could be invoked; once the emergency laws were in operation, police powers would become infinitely greater and, in a worst case scenario, there was provision to call in the troops. Moreover, there were other differences which minimised the efficacy of the 2005 protests. This time around they did not have the support of the biggest haulage organisation in Britain, the Road Hauliers

Association, which represented 10,000 truckers. Their leaders and many members of the public were more willing to accept the ministerial line that consumers were the victims of global forces which were beyond Britain's control.

The fuel protests in 2000 and 2005, and other spasmodic ones between, have been typical of the new breed of popular movements. They possess a loose and decentralised organisational structure, and communication was conducted via the latest means of technology. They also show us how the rise of single-issue group activity has to some extent blurred the original Grantian distinction between insider and outsider groups in Britain. As in the case of those who campaigned against **genetically modified (GM) crops**, the traditional insider groups were peripheral players, leading some members of bodies, such as the NFU and RHA, to question the influence that their traditional methods gave them. The doubters were taken aback by the methods and approach of the new social movements and the tactics of the supporters of direct action. Today, some so-called insider groups employ multi-arena strategies in which they target a range of access points and employ a range of methods.

## Recent trends reviewed

That there has been an increase in the amount of direct action is indisputable. There has been a continuum of forms of pressure that begins with peaceful protest and then escalates to boycotts, demonstrations, strikes, riots and widespread revolt. Media interest has focused on the behaviour and lifestyles of prominent individuals involved and the causes they espouse. Those in authority have often been forced to reassess their actions and policies.

Environmentalists have been particularly willing to challenge government, and there have been some striking examples of **ecotage**. Much of the activity has been associated with members of new social movements who have been loosely organised around some central idea or issue. As Garner[13] points out, animal rights protest has been an important element among the wider environmental conservation movement. It adopts

> a wide range of direct-action strategies . . . This has most notably included breaking into factory farms and laboratories where the

animals may be released, equipment destroyed and evidence of ill-treatment compiled . . . The Animal Liberation Front . . . consists of autonomous cells of activists and, for obvious reasons, has no hierarchical organisational structure.

Much of the protest of recent years has not been carried out by individuals and groups operating on their own. The trend has been towards their involvement in wider populist movements which have benefited from communications technology and careful use of the media. In some cases, these movements plan a programme of activities over many months (Make Poverty History and the Countryside Alliance), but often they erupt on to the political scene, as in the case of the fuel protests. In this last case and in many others, a single issue captures the public imagination and galvanises people into action. This was the case with Snowdrop.

There are common factors in the outlook and behaviour of some of the recent popular movements. They tend to:

- emerge abruptly, perhaps ignited by a spark (e.g. the Dunblane massacre) which make a sudden and dramatic impact;
- be based on issues which arouse an emotional response, perhaps fuelled by a tabloid campaign and accompanying television coverage;
- use direct action to draw attention to their demands;
- get a swift – if carefully managed – governmental response, to head off the escalating revolt.

Rather than relying on persuasion and rational argument and operating through the conventional pressure-group methods of lobbying the executive and the legislature, and participating in enquiries and so on, popular movements rely on the implied threat of a mass revolt at the ballot box. Such activity does not fall easily into the classic typologies of pressure-group activity. Movements cannot easily be described as protective or promotional. They have features of both sectional and cause groups, for they represent the private interests of those whose lifestyle or livelihood has been threatened or damaged (rural interests and parents in the case of the Countryside March and Snowdrop) but their campaigning quickly develops into a wider crusade for action supported by many people not immediately involved and with no personal interest at stake. Of the fuel-tax protesters, McNaughton[14] notes how:

[they] managed to tie their case to a general concern with high levels of taxation and the poor state of public transport in general'. Their activity illustrates that outsider groups can achieve success, if they can create a high level of public response.

Opinions vary about the contribution such popular movements make to democracy. It can be viewed as positive, in that they mobilise the interest and encourage the participation of many people who would otherwise remain uninvolved in the political process. They illustrate that ordinary people can have an impact on government and force those who govern to be responsive to public concerns. Yet, on the other hand, their behaviour is coercive in that, there is an implied threat that, if their grievances are not addressed, there will be serious consequences for those in authority, possibly mass punishment at the ballot box.

The danger is that ministers may feel so threatened by the sudden eruption of hostility that they consider they must concede to demands even though they may be the demands of a vociferous minority. The media can generate such interest that the issue becomes immediately pressing. As McNaughton goes on to observe: 'The fuel tax protesters did not have to take into account the environmental consequences of lower petrol prices. The Snowdrop Campaign did not have to consider the civil liberties of those gun owners who wished to pursue a private pastime for peaceful purposes.' In other words, governments have to govern for the general good and cannot allow themselves to be held to ransom by vocal, but in many cases, self-interested campaigners – even if those campaigners succeed in arousing widespread popular sympathy for their cause.

## Is direct action legitimate in a democracy?

In a perfect democracy, decisions would be made in the light of the best available information and those who make them would show compassion and reasonableness. Everyone would be equally free to secure consideration of his/her interests and would accept the fairness of the result. This may be a desirable scenario but the reality is that many individuals and groups feel that the traditional political processes fail to respond to their wishes. Whole communities often feel neglected, their inhabitants treated without consideration. They feel that their voice is not heard or expressed and that the narrow sectional interests of political parties and traditional interest groups have not engaged with their thinking and needs.

In particular, many members of the environmental movement feel that they operate under a system that is skewed against them. Their sense of alienation has therefore led them to see direct action as a normal, acceptable and necessary mode of operation. Dobson[15] sees it as a radical expression of this viewpoint, and notes the tendency to do-it-yourself politics: 'groups of (mostly) young people organise around a squat, a sound system, a drug, a piece of land and try to live a self-reliant life'. He regards their approach as a reaction to their 'disillusionment with mainstream political parties and [the] agendas they promote'.

Activists feel that their interests have not been fairly considered, and that no one in authority has read/listened to their case. They have gone through the usual democratic routes, or they may not have bothered. Direct action may seem to be the only worthwhile outlet available. Bureaucracy can be very slow to respond, and the temptation to force its hand is considerable.

Yet if everyone broke the law when they disliked some particular aspect of it, chaos would result. Law-breaking is a serious matter and should, in a democracy, be the course of last resort. Those who campaign on a law-and-order platform, especially on the political Right, will be particularly condemnatory of selective obedience to the law, in which people pick and choose the bits of it that they are prepared to accept. They will see this as a 'slippery slope' which can have dangerous consequences, and are likely to disapprove of the activities of campaigners who are prepared to break the law to press their claims.

Many people on the Centre-Left would more easily accept that, when those in authority are being totally unresponsive, direct action – even law-breaking – may be justifiable. They see it as being a most effective means of protest, for it has an advantage noted by Peter Melchett[16] of Greenpeace: 'Direct action doesn't just highlight issues; it simplifies highly complex subjects. It cuts through the jargon, mystery and bureaucracy, and it demands a straight answer.' Another enthusiast, however, Brian Martin,[17] an Australian 'Friends of the Earth' activist, has distinguished between the legitimacy of using peaceful direct action and violent protest. He finds the latter unacceptable for these reasons:

> Violence as a means for obtaining social change has several flaws: it often causes suffering; it abdicates moral superiority and alienates potential support. It requires secrecy and hence leads to undemocratic decision-making; and, if successful, it tends to lead towards a violent and authoritarian new ruling élite. Non-violent action as a policy and as a technique avoids these problems; its means reflect its ends. With non-violent action, energy is aimed at policies or structures, and not their supporters.

Des Wilson,[18] who has also worked as an activist in the pursuit of environmentalist causes, endorses Martin's view, while stressing that direct action should be used sparingly; the more it is used, the less effective it becomes. It should follow every possible effort to persuade by reason and reflect 'total frustration at the obstinacy, unfairness, and possibly the brutality of "the system", rather than be "a self-indulgent expression of the impatience of protesters"'.

History confirms that direct action often works. It has often been the case that those who have made trouble have made progress. Many of the great social and political reforms owe something to the use of force, when aggrieved and obstinate people manned the barricades – the extension of the vote in 1832, and the recognition of the female right to vote, both followed such forms of campaigning. Today, ministers are aware of the strength of protest on issues, such as new roads schemes and airport runways, to an extent that would never have happened without the media portrayal of direct action.

## Conclusion

From pro-hunt rallies to fuel blockades, from action on GM crops to anti-Iraq war demonstrations, examples of single-issue protest have been a regular feature of British politics in recent years. Such actions suggest that far from being apathetic, as figures for electoral turnout in general elections might suggest, many potential voters are willing to involve themselves in political activity. They have preoccupations that do not neatly fit into the programmes advanced by mainstream political parties, however, and are seeking some other form of expression.

The politics of protest has a long history in Britain. In the nineteenth century, members of the anti-slavery movement, the Chartist societies and the Anti-Corn Law League, all used forms of direct action within and beyond the law. In the twentieth century, the suffragettes and the **Jarrow marchers** of the hungry unemployed used similar methods. But, in the late twentieth century, protests have become markedly more widespread and more people are willing to take part, whether by signing a petition, forming an action group or attending a demonstration. Some are willing to use more dramatic methods. These activists attract more media attention than ever before, for editors and journalists are keen to seize on issues and actions that make a good story and provide strong visuals (see Table 5.2 below).

Among the direct-action campaigners that have, from time to time, captured the political agenda in the Blairite years, some are bracketed with the political Left – as many protesters of the past have often been. But, with the absence of an effective parliamentary opposition, the right-wing press has seized on particular themes as the basis for an attack on ministers. As Kirsty Milne[19] points out, 'what is new is the congruence of protest, a partisan press in search of causes and an electorate whose anxieties are not being represented'. The fuel protesters, **Section 28** campaigners and Countryside Alliance have all championed causes usually associated with the political Right. As

**Table 5.2  Protest and press reactions in Blairite Britain: some examples**

| Cause | Press support |
|---|---|
| Countryside Alliance/ pro-hunting | *Daily Telegraph*, *Daily Mail,* both pro-Conservative |
| Opposition to repeal of Section 28/promotion of single-sex relationships | Scottish *Daily Record*, a traditionally left-wing paper |
| Fuel protests/high petrol prices | The *Daily Mail* and the *Sun*, the latter generally Blairite |
| GM crops/anxieties about trials and effects of their use | *The Guardian*, *The Independent* and the *Daily Mail* |
| Iraq war/doubts over war and criticisms of subsequent conduct | *The Guardian*,*The Independent* and the *Daily Mirror*, all traditionally Centre-Left/Left |

Milne puts it: 'Protest has been reclaimed by anyone who feels their identity under threat, be they fox-hunting polo players or villagers with gypsies on their doorstep.'

They are the types of issues to which parties and ministers have on occasion been slow to respond, with those in government sometimes caught unawares or incomprehending of the scale of public disaffection.

...........................................................................

☑ **What you should have learnt from reading this chapter**

- Sometimes, consultation through the conventional channels may not give groups what they want from government.

- Persuasion and rational argument backed by some public demonstration may be a more effective mode of campaigning.

- There are many forms of direct action, all of which are intended to apply pressure on those in authority; sometimes, that pressure can be illegal or even violent.

- Direct action has become more common in recent decades, an accepted means of conveying views.

- Some outsider groups deploy direct action as a means of first – rather than of last – resort, knowing that with media coverage they can generate valuable publicity for their cause.

- New means of technology have assisted groups in organising and co-ordinating their protest; this is especially the case with new popular movements.

- There are varying views about the appropriateness of direct action in a democracy.

🔍 **Glossary of key terms**

**Ecotage**  Direct action in the environmental field, including acts of sabotage on buildings and equipment; similar to eco-terrorism. An eco-terrorist is an extremist who is prepared to carry out terrorist acts against companies, industries and other workplaces if he or she feels that unnecessary damage to the environment is being caused.
**Genetically-modified (GM) crops**  Genetic modification is a special set of technologies that alter the genetic make-up of such living organisms as animals, plants or bacteria. GM products (current or in the pipeline) include medicines and vaccines, foods and food ingredients, feeds, and

fibres. A genetically modified food is a food product containing some quantity of any genetically modified organism as an ingredient. GM crops are mainly grown to increase the mass of food to feed more people. Their use is highly controversial.

**Jarrow marchers** Those who marched to London in 1936 to protest against massive unemployment in their town in the north-east; this was the best known of the several marches organised by local town councils troubled by the number out of work in their areas.

**Section 28** A notorious clause of the Local Government Act of 1986, which forbade the promotion of homosexuality in the classroom. Defended by many on the moral Right, it was strongly opposed by many on the Centre-Left. In Scotland and later England and Wales, the clause has provided the material for a political clash, prior to its removal by legislation.

**Twyford Down protest** A famous protest in the mid-1980s against a road-building scheme (involving the M3) that was said by campaigners to pose a threat to the environment. It began as a classic local protest by concerned residents who engaged in conventional campaigning tactics, working in tandem with Friends of the Earth. As legal avenues proved unsuccessful, it evolved into a non-violent direct-action campaign, using some of the methods of the original Earth First! campaigners in the United States. These included occupying a part of the road-building site known as the Dongas, hence their nickname – the 'Dongas Tribe'.

## Likely examination questions

'Protest is the last resort of a pressure group.' Is this any longer true?

Examine the approaches of environmental pressure groups in seeking to influence government policy in recent years.

## Helpful websites

The sites associated with some of the campaigns outlined carry useful information about how groups work, for example:

www.earthfirst.org.uk/  Earth First

www.makepovertyhistory.org/  Make Poverty History

www.countryside-alliance.org  The Countryside Alliance

 ## Suggestions for further reading

*Articles:*

A collection of articles on recent pressure-group issues especially concerned with protest politics – airport runways, animal rights, gun control, nuclear energy, road bypasses, and the environment, in *Parliamentary Affairs* 51:3, 1998.

W. Grant, 'Insider politics to direct action?' in Parliamentary Affairs 54, 2001.

R. Reeves, 'Inside the violent world of the global protesters', *The Observer*, 31.10.1999

*Books:*

K. Dunion, *Troublemakers: The Struggle for Environmental Justice in Scotland*, Edinburgh University Press, 2003.

G. Jordan and W. Maloney, *The Protest Business*, Manchester University Press, 1997.

H. Margetts, 'Political participation and protest' in P. Dunleavy et al., *Developments in British Politics*, 7, Palgrave, 2002.

D. Wilson, *Pressure: The A–Z of Campaigning in Britain*, Heinemann,1984.

## CHAPTER 6

# Pressure Groups and the Devolved Legislatures

## Contents

## Overview

The advent of **devolution** in the United Kingdom has created new opportunities for pressure-group activity. The devolved machinery in Scotland, Wales and Northern Ireland includes an assembly (in two cases with law-making powers) and an executive. Groups have developed contacts with both institutions, in each of the countries, although in the case of Northern Ireland their activity has been restricted by the reimposition of direct rule from Westminster. In all cases, devolution of governmental institutions has been followed by a decentralisation of pressure-group activity to reflect the extent to which power has shifted from Westminster to Edinburgh, Cardiff and Belfast.

In this chapter, much of the emphasis is on Scotland, for the Scottish machinery is more powerful than that in Wales, providing pressure groups with a real opportunity to influence decision-making. In Northern Ireland, the suspension of the assembly makes comment necessarily brief and tentative.

## Key issues to be covered in this chapter

- General considerations
- The nature of the devolved machinery in Scotland
- The access points available to Scottish pressure groups
- Why and to what extent groups lobby the devolved machinery
- The character and effectiveness of group activity in Scotland
- Group activity in Wales and Northern Ireland
- An assessment of early trends

## General considerations

As we have seen, pressure groups play an important part in the policy processes of the United Kingdom and elsewhere. Wherever power is exercised, decisions made or bills debated, there, too, will be groups seeking to express the social and political interests of their members and trying to see their ideas and preferences turned into legislation.

Before the introduction of devolved government in Scotland, Wales and Northern Ireland, decisions were taken at Westminster and carried out via the Scottish, Welsh and Northern Irish Offices, each headed by a secretary of state. Pressure groups that existed in each of the countries accordingly lobbied ministers and officials in those offices, their MPs or worked with other British pressure groups to offer advice, influence legislation and assist in monitoring its impact. As the amount of Scottish business and legislation handled at Westminster was relatively small and the relevant Scottish committees lacked substantial power, the role of groups was restricted. This applied to the other countries as well. Moreover, the relatively closed nature of established Westminster proceedings made it more difficult for lobbyists to achieve as much influence as they would have wished.

The introduction of devolution provided a more promising political environment, especially in Scotland where the rhetoric and intentions surrounding devolution placed a new emphasis upon pre-legislative consultation; a more open system of government; and the prospect of a more participatory democracy.

## The growth of group activity in Scotland since devolution

Following the introduction of devolved government in 1999, many British pressure groups have shifted their focus in response to the new arrangements. This is particularly true north of the border, for the Scottish bodies have greater powers and responsibilities than those created in Wales (see Box 6.1 opposite). Before the creation of the Scottish Parliament, there were exclusively Scottish interest groups. Since 1999, however, their range and number have significantly increased and they now concentrate much of their attention on the Scottish Parliament and Executive. Moreover, several British groups

## Box 6.1  A note on the devolved machinery in Scotland

The Scottish Parliament has primary legislative powers. It can legislate over the following areas:

Health
Education and training
Local government, social work and housing
Economic development and transport
Law and home affairs
Sport and the arts
Agriculture, fishing and forestry
Environment
Other matters

In all, there are forty-seven 'devolved matters'. Other matters are 'reserved' to the British Parliament at Westminster. These include the most vital functions of the modern state, such as the constitution, defence and national security, foreign affairs, macro-economic, monetary and fiscal affairs (other than Scotland's limited tax varying powers), employment, social security and transport safety and regulation. The Scotland Act (1998) assigns the Edinburgh chamber power over 'all matters which are not reserved', an open invitation to take up any issues or problems not falling into the matters reserved to the British Parliament.

**The institutions of government**
The Scottish Parliament has 129 members, elected by a mixture of two electoral systems. seventy-three are chosen by the First-Past-the-Post(FPTP) method and the other fifty-six on a 'list' basis in the eight existing Euro-constituencies. Members are known as MSPs, to avoid confusion with MPs. They serve for four years. Parliament's committee structure broadly parallels the structure of the Executive – for example, the Education, Culture and Sport committee deals with legislative proposals and administration relevant to the Education and Young People Department and the latter two aspects of the Tourism, Culture and Sport Department.

The leader of the largest party in the chamber becomes first minister in the Scottish Executive. Jack McConnell currently heads a coalition of Labour-LibDem colleagues who are chosen from, and accountable to, the Parliament.

have developed separate Scottish branches in order to lobby more effectively. Those groups that regularly come into contact with the Edinburgh machinery generally appear to have a positive view of the process.

From the beginning, the Executive has encouraged groups and individuals to become involved in the process of consultation. The presence of Labour and the Liberal Democrats in office may encourage a close relationship, for there is some movement of personnel between social-group activists and the two broadly progressive parties. So, too, MSPs have encouraged campaigners to petition Parliament and liaise with its committees. Committees engage in consultations, in a bid to discover public opinion on a wide range of issues prior to proposed legislation.

The resulting growth in activity has inspired the media to report on group demands, so that some issues have been extensively covered by journalists. The **Souter referendum** and the subsequent repeal of Section 28 (see Box 6.2 on pages 146–7) were-high-profile events that generated much discussion.

## A new style of Scottish government: consensus and consultation

In advance of the first devolved elections in Scotland (1999), several pressure groups were already reorganising themselves and mobilising their resources to focus on the new Parliament. Many campaigners had already developed high hopes of the new Scottish machinery

The theme of 'a new style of government' was often advanced in pre-devolution literature. The suggestion was made that, too often in the past, those who made decisions on Scotland's behalf were out of touch with the prevailing views of the Scottish people as expressed both individually and collectively via pressure groups. Many groups that had been excluded from the policy-making process during the 1980s and early 1990s felt that, once it was introduced, there would be a new age of consultation. As Grant Jordan[1] put it: 'Their business of social improvement was maybe not Thatcher's; they were Scottish based; they reflected the pro-Labour political majority in Scotland . . . for such groups change was very attractive. They assumed devolution would deliver for them.'

The final report of the Convention (the non-party body whose brief was to prepare a workable plan for Scottish devolution) declared that the new Scottish Parliament would 'differ from Westminster in a less procedural, and more radical, sense'. It was to be responsive to the wishes and values of the Scottish people by taking the 'views and advice of many specialist organisations and individuals'. It would provide 'a beacon of hope for a new and better politics'. In particular, one instrument towards a more consensual style of decision-making would be the introduction of an electoral system designed to produce greater proportionality among the elected. In itself considered to be a good thing, it would also 'frustrate any tendency towards an "elective dictatorship" by majoritarian governments resting on a minority of votes'.

Among other things, the proposed Standing Orders provided that:

• electors should be able directly to petition the Parliament;
• legislators should consult widely both before and during the legis- lative process;
• there should be facilities for the public and the media to meet MSPs easily;
• every effort should be made to encourage and promote construc- tive, rather than confrontational, debate and discussion.

**Consultative arrangements**
The Report of the Consultative Steering Group (CSG) on the Scottish Parliament (*Shaping Scotland's Parliament*) further raised expect- ations of a consultative future. Produced in 1999, it laid stress on con- sultation and suggested that: 'Draft Bills on Introduction should be accompanied by a memorandum explaining the consultative process undertaken and the degree of consensus reached, as well as . . . the consultative process undertaken.'

The Consultative Steering Group set consultation on a pedestal. It laid stress on the work of parliamentary committees as a channel for extra-parliamentary opinion; they would have the power to take oral and written evidence. It argued that pre-legislative involvement by committees would 'allow individuals and groups to influence the policy-making process . . . By making the system more participative, it is intended that better legislation should result.' It was argued that seeking comments on specific legislative proposals was not enough: 'What is desired is an earlier involvement of relevant bodies from the outset – identifying issues which need to be addressed, contributing to the policy-making process and the preparation of legislation.'

In urging this new era of consensus and consultation, there may have been a tendency to underestimate the volume of consultation that was typically conducted by the Scottish Office and Westminster departments in the pre-devolution days. But there could be no mistaking the fact that the intention was that the new machinery would operate in an altogether different way from what which had gone on before. The CSG was calling for a sharing of power between the people of Scotland, the legislators and the Scottish Executive. It invited comment about the arrangements for involving civic society, including women's groups, people from ethnic minority communities, people with disabilities, business and the general public.

The analysis of the responses to this invitation showed that there was widespread support for any mechanisms which could be found to involve the public, civic society and representative groups in the work of the Parliament. In particular, voluntary organisations and interest groups were particularly keen to see that formal systems were put in place to allow them to speak as representatives of their constituent groups. Many voluntary organisations (for example, Fair Play) suggested that the Parliament should set up a database of registered consultees who would automatically be approached on any relevant issues. Voluntary organisations were very keen to see that a distinctive role was given to those acting as a conduit between government and civic society. For example, the Royal Society for the Protection of Birds pointed out that non-governmental organisations involved a cross-section of people who felt that such groups more accurately reflected their concerns than the traditional political parties. It would therefore be sensible to build on their reputations and good works as a means of encouraging greater consultation with, and participation by, the public in the political process.

## The impact of devolution on group activity

Prior to the 1999 Scottish parliamentary elections, there were already Scottish groups with their own organisation, finance and membership. Examples of long-standing groups include the Convention of Scottish

Local Authorities (COSLA), the Scotch Whisky Association and the Scottish Wildlife Trust. Some were large and well-resourced, such as the Educational Institute for Scotland (EIS) representing primary and secondary teachers north of the border. Others were small bodies, sometimes heavily reliant on voluntary effort. There has always been a plethora of them because ever since the **Act of Union** (1707) Scotland had retained its distinctive educational, legal and religious structures, as well as its own form of local government. On these and other issues, there was a need for groups that dealt with specifically Scottish policies and concerns. As the Scottish Office began to acquire additional responsibilities, so, too, did this contributed to the number of groups operating in those areas.

Such groups did not need to transform their arrangements after the introduction of devolution but they needed to switch much of their attention to the devolved institutions. Much depended on the issue in question. Lynch[2] quotes the example of the Scotch Whisky Association, a solely Scottish-based organisation but one whose lob-bying still needs to be geared to Westminster (and, in some cases, the European Union): its policy concerns of alcohol duty, exchange rates, product standards, taxation and trade are functions still handled by the British government. The Scottish Trades Union Congress oper-ates in both arenas. Much of its members' work is concerned with education, health and local government but employment is a reserved British matter.

Since 1999, the number and range of groups operating in Scotland have significantly increased. In particular, several British groups have developed distinctive Scottish branches to lobby more effectively, examples including Age Concern Scotland, CBI Scotland, Friends of the Earth (Scotland) and NCH Action for Children Scotland. In some cases there was already an office in Scotland but the organisation of the pre-devolution arrangements needed to be strengthened. In others, the existing structure and staffing were sufficient to cope with the challenge of devolution. 'Situations vacant' advertisements in the press contained (and still contain) numerous advertisements for parliamentary liaison officers for public-, private- and voluntary-sector organisations desperate to ensure that they would not be left behind in the race for inclusion. Informal networks of organisations discussed how best they could work together to ensure that the apparent consensus in favour of group participation in the pre-legislative process would not fade once politicians and partisan interests became involved.

The prospects for groups in post-devolution Scotland looked promising. It offered a more open, accessible parliamentary system, with an Executive committed to pre-legislative consultation and several opportunities for lobbying of MSPs and committees. The political parties were receptive to receiving briefing parties and the expertise of lobbyists, lacking as they did the machinery and funding to organise and finance their own research. In addition, there was the Scottish Civic Forum (see the section below), an institution already organised.

Groups had to decide on how to allocate their resources. Whether they were already in existence or new Scottish divisions of existing British groups, campaigners and lobbyists needed to be clear in their understanding of where decisions on policy would in future be taken. In some cases, groups would need to operate at both Holyrood and Westminster, depending on precisely which powers had been devolved. In this case, they would need to allocate their staff accordingly.

### Table 6.1  Categories of selected Scottish groups at the time of preparations for devolution

| Types of group in Scotland, 1998 | Percentage |
| --- | --- |
| Scottish organisations | 22.3 |
| Scottish branch of UK | 50.4 |
| UK with no Scottish | 5.4 |
| Scottish regional groups | 18.8 |
| Private companies | 1.3 |
| Others | 1.8 |

Information taken from P. Cairney:
www.abdn.ac.uk/pir/notes/Level3/P13546/TheQuestionofAccess.doc

## The Scottish Civic Forum

The major development in the move towards wider participation was the emergence of the Scottish Civic Forum. This sought the involvement of religious and business organisations, trade unions, voluntary organisations and professional associations, but excluded from membership government agencies, statutory bodies, local authorities, for-profit organisations and political parties. The aims[3] restated those of the people who planned for the new style of inclusive politics:

> Our vision is that the Scottish Civic Forum will break the mould of old fashioned politics. It will increase participation, find new ways to open up dialogue, raise awareness and stimulate debate on the many challenges facing Scotland . . . [it will harness] the experience, practical expertise and capacity of Scottish *civic life* . . . It will be an avenue for finding new ways to increase dialogue and understanding between the people of Scotland and their Parliament . . . It will explore the prospects for consensus across civic life, but will also reflect and record disagreement and diversity where they exist. It will not contrive consensus where none can be agreed.

The Forum was clearly envisaged as an important, additional mechanism in the consultation process, providing an arena for the discussion of civic interests.

There was wide cross-party support for the Civic Forum's establishment, with calls for financial assistance from within the Parliament to encourage broad participation. Hopes were expressed that a Civic Forum: would promote participation, facilitate debate, and ensure social partnership; would be a 'gateway to the Parliament and its executive, not a gate-keeper'; would ensure that there was a Parliament for all Scotland; would permit dialogue to be conducted across the civic sector; would act as a complement to, rather than as a rival of, the new legislature. More than £300,000 was allocated by the Scottish Executive for a period of three years towards the running of the Forum; promises were made for further assistance in kind.

Given the new arrangements, it was hoped that groups with a social agenda and those representing minority interests would have a chance to flourish. The Civic Forum gave them an additional outlet so that their views could be expressed, reported, acknowledged and taken into account when decisions were made. In this way, the partnership between Parliament, the Executive and the people may be sustained.

Within a year of its creation in March 1999, 240 bodies – many of them small, voluntary associations – had registered their membership.

## Consultation with the Scottish Executive in practice

The Scottish Executive has enthusiastically embraced consultation with affected groups and publishes guidelines as to how these may be conducted: 'consultation exercises may involve seeking views in a number of different ways, such as written papers, public meetings, focus groups, questionnaire exercises or on-line discussion forums'. As the bodies consulted will vary between policy areas and the particular issues being consulted upon, the Executive publishes no registered list of bodies. Rather, it encourages ministerial teams to think widely about

---

### Table 6.2  Common approaches adopted by Scottish campaigning organisations

Pressure groups can effect change by using a variety of campaigning approaches:
- Highlighting the issue to raise awareness
- Attracting public support
- Influencing those with policy-making powers

To achieve these goals, they will undertake a range of actions that include
- Taking part in consultative exercises
- Lobbying Parliament, its members and committees
- Sending letters to the press
- Advertising campaigns
- Taking part in television debates
- Signing petitions
- Sending publicity material to members and supporters

In addition, some, of course, use direct action to highlight their causes, activities ranging from sit-down demonstrations or breaking into premises and releasing animals.

who may have an interest in responding to their particular exercise and to think afresh each time a consultation exercise is developed. The two examples in the table below provide an idea of the extent of consultation which has been the subject of much comment among some critics of the way in which the new system of government operates:

The consultation on a ban on smoking in public places is but one of around eight hundred conducted in the short life of the Executive. The Scottish Police Federation was consulted on 107 issues in the first five years and was pleased to be involved at the stage when important

## Table 6.3  Two consultation exercises under way in January 2005: categories of groups involved

| Smoking in public places | Paying for water services |
|---|---|
| Business organisations | Academic institutions |
| Local authorities | Age-related groups |
| Health organisations | Building industry organisations |
| Children and young people's organisations | Business organisations |
| Community organisations | Community councils |
| Old people's organisations | Environmental protection groups |
| Justice interests | Equality groups |
| Prison interests | Faith groups |
| Voluntary organisations | Libraries |
| Disability groups | Local authorities |
| Equality and ethnic groups | Poverty action groups |
| Religious organisations | Professional institutes |
| Rural organisations | Scottish Consumer Council |
| Trade unions | Scottish Water |
| Transport organisations | Water industry organisations |

**NB** In both cases, several groups were in discussion within each category. For instance, on smoking the children and young people's organisations included Children First, the Scottish Youth Parliament and Youthlink Scotland; the justice interests included The Association of Chief Police Officers in Scotland and the Law Society of Scotland; the voluntary organisations included the Scottish Council for Voluntary Organisations, the Scottish Human Rights Centre and ASH Scotland. Consultation on water services was a massive exercise, more than 5,000 initial consultation questionnaires being sent out.

decisions affecting its members were being taken. By contrast, there were some signs of consultation fatigue among members of bodies in the arts world who found themselves being regularly asked to think about a cultural strategy to be pursued in the future. In the words of one critic:[4] 'It's like a computer with a virus requiring continual self-assessment.'

The repeal of Section 28 and the Souter referendum on the subject comprised one issue in which groups were much involved in campaigning on either side of the debate, as is shown in the case study (see Box 6.2 below).

## Box 6.2  A case study of the repeal of Section 28

The Thatcher government prohibited the 'promotion of homosexuality in schools' in the contentious Section 28 (Clause 2A) of its 1988 Local Government Act. The clause was offensive to many sections of the community.

It was Labour policy on both sides of the border to repeal the measure but, under the terms of devolution, responsibility for effecting change fell upon the Scottish Executive and Parliament. Repeal was always going to be a divisive issue that required sensitive handling for it aroused strong feelings among many interested groups and individuals, particularly those with religious affiliations. Passage through Parliament was unlikely to be a problem, with all but the Conservatives in favour of change, but the opposing forces in the chamber and in the country outside were capable of stirring up strong feelings by their emotive appeal. They were likely to exploit the argument that legislation was anti-family, lacking due regard for the traditional family structure. Moreover, it could be portrayed as encouraging homosexuality and lesbianism. On the other side, the accusation could be made that the current status of the law was discriminatory against less conventional family forms and against gays. This was a lifestyle issue of deep moral concern to both sides.

In favour of change were the Labour, Liberal Democrat and SNP parties, supported by a variety of gay and lesbian groups who came together under the umbrella of the Equality Network. Those who organised the pro-repeal campaign were divided among themselves, some favouring statutory, mandatory guidelines and some wanting to compromise with their opponents in order to ease the passage of The Ethical Standards in Public Life Bill. By contrast, those against repeal were firm and united in their resolve. There were three main elements on this anti-repeal side, the *Daily Record*, religious leaders and the owner of the Stagecoach bus company, Brian Souter. He was willing to spend £1 million of his assets to finance the 'Keep the Clause' campaign in the private referendum which he organised on the issue. The anti-repealers were supported by the Scottish School Boards Association (SSBA). An important claim of the opponents of the Bill was that they had public backing, as indicated by the outcome of the referendum: 86 per cent wished to retain Section 28, on a low turnout of just over a third of the electorate.

The arguments continued throughout parliamentary debate on the Bill which, despite the strong opposition, was passed in 2000.

## The reactions of different categories of Scottish pressure groups

Inevitably, the willingness of groups to seek access to the agencies of devolved government is determined primarily by whether or not those institutions can decide, or at least help, to shape policy in their areas of operation:

*   **Manufacturing/commerce** Business and commercial groups will require access to the Scottish Executive and Parliament on issues such as the Business Rate which is determined in Scotland. On the other hand, regulation of banking is a '**reserved power**' so that London must be the target, not Edinburgh. Broadly, business groups were initially sceptical of devolution but have accepted that, for the good of their reputation in Scotland, they need to be seen to engage with the Executive and Parliament, especially in areas such as social exclusion and the devolved issues north of the border. CBI UK and IoD UK continue to handle European policy via their contacts with Whitehall and (in the case of the CBI) its office in Brussels. Another outlet for business groups is via the Gang of Five meetings which bring together the CBI, IoD and other organisations in order to apply collective pressure. Through this organisation, business leaders function as a watchdog over the Scottish Parliament. In the past, several of them have voiced fears about possible use of its tax-varying powers and feel that the activities of the Executive need to be carefully monitored. In their

publicity, members emphasise the importance of the business agenda in order to help create the money necessary to support funding for education, health and social policies.

With business and commercial groups there is more of a tendency to meet ministers and civil servants than MSPs and committees. The Gang of Five itself and its chief executives operate at the ministerial level, while the staff of larger groups, such as the CBI, will link up with civil servants at lower levels, that is, head of group or division. With trade groups, civil service contact is the most frequent.

- **Labour** Trade unions find many aspects of their work dealt with in Edinburgh, so that the Scottish TUC is heavily engaged with the devolved bodies. UNISON (see Table 6.3 below) has a very large Scottish presence,but, this is not typical of all unions. Of course, many labour issues, such as employment law and the

---

### Box 6.3 UNISON, Scotland's largest trade union

UNISON has approximately 145,000 members working in local authorities, health care, higher education, the voluntary sector and Scotland's utilities. It argues that there is a 'basic right to lobby' and that Parliament has made a good start, adopting open and clear procedures. It claims that the executive is less obviously accessible, with less clear procedures and openness.

Its lobbying techniques include:

- Responses to consultation papers
- Special briefings with MSPs
- Speaking to committees
- Talking to individual MSPs
- Discussions with ministers
- Cross-party groups
- Issues covering a vast range of issues

Some of UNISON's work is conducted as part of a broader campaign. It makes use of umbrella bodies such as the Scottish Trades Union Congress (STUC); engages in single-issue campaigns, such as Fuel Poverty (on which it works with Energy Action Scotland and Transco) and Housing Stock Transfers (in co-operation with it, STUC and other unions).

minimum wage are still reserved so that London continues to be the main seat of operations for many unions.

- **Farming/fishing** Agriculture is a devolved power but, as agrarian policy is largely determined under the Common Agricultural Policy by the European Commission, there is little point in lobbying extensively in Edinburgh. It is Britain, not specifically Scotland, that is represented in the European Union so, if the National Farmers Union or some other group wants to ensure a firm stand in the Council of Ministers, it is in Whitehall that the dialogue and persuasion need to take place. The Scottish Parliament has relatively little influence over fishing policy, so again there is only limited value in engagement
- **Social policy** There are several contentious British issues on which all policy is largely 'reserved' to Westminster, – e.g. responsibility for asylum seekers, social benefits, abortion and adoption more social than economic issues have been devolved, however encouraging campaigners to deal with the Executive and with Parliament. The fact that the coalition is of 'progressive' persuasion serves to encourage such engagement. Several British groups now have devolved offices responsible for handling Scottish policy. In some cases, aspects of an issue are devolved responsibilities, as with health care. Medical provision is devolved, but not issues surrounding medical training. The British Medical Association will shape its lobbying accordingly. The Royal Colleges of Surgeons and Physicians will find the Edinburgh administration less relevant to their work.

## Case studies: the experience of two influential Scottish pressure groups

### The Scottish SPCA and animal welfare

Animal welfare legislation in the Britain derives from many sources, the European Union, the British government and, following devolution, the Scottish Parliament. Today, most aspects of animal welfare have been devolved to Edinburgh although the issue of animal experimentation is a reserved matter controlled by Westminster.

Foremost among the organisations seeking to influence legislation is the Scottish Society for the Prevention of Cruelty to Animals

(Scottish SPCA). SSPCA involves itself in the formulation and improvement of new and existing animal-welfare legislation. It also works with the press and the media to keep animal welfare in the public eye. It believes in working within the law to achieve its aims and does not support the use of direct action. Violence for any reason is unacceptable to the leadership.

Some of SSPCA'S activities have traditionally involved working with local government. It worked with Edinburgh City Council to set up a training course for pet-shop owners, attendance at which was made a condition of obtaining a pet-shop licence. For several years, it has worked at the European level, as a member of the umbrella organisation, the Euro-group for Animal Welfare which co-ordinates campaigns in the European Union. Nationally, the Parliament now plays a key role in the Society's attempt to improve legislation in Scotland. It can exert influence via:

- a parliamentary officer who keeps MSPs up to date with current issues and promotes the work of the Society;
- its role as secretariat of an all-party animal-welfare committee which discusses and debates matters relating to animal welfare;
- consulting with the Executive: often it is asked to comment on draft legislation;
- lobbying MSPs on particular issues, hoping that this will influence the way they vote when legislation is introduced.

In common with many other cause groups, SSPCA often works in tandem with other bodies with similar approaches to particular issues. It works with farmers in support of the Quality Meat Scotland campaign, providing an opportunity to monitor the ways in which farm animals are kept and to urge best practice in welfare standards. It is a member of the Boyd Group, a discussion group comprising different sides of the animal-experiment debate. Recently it joined the Partnership for Action Against Wildlife Crime (PAW) which brings together agencies such as the Scottish Police Forces, the RSPB and Scottish National Heritage, in the battle to combat wildlife crime. By working together in this way, the organisation demonstrates the level of support for a campaign and can exercise greater influence. Changes to legislation are not usually carried out unless there is such evidence of a high level of public support.

SSPCA supported the Protection of Mammals (Scotland) Bill which prohibited fox hunting and, in recent years, has involved itself on a wide range of issues from intensive farming and cruel trapping to whaling and dog registration. The First Strike Scotland campaign highlighted the link between animal abuse and human violence.

### CARE, the Evangelical Alliance Scotland and religious/moral issues

Devolution has brought Scotland's churches close to the centre of power, allowing figures such as the late Cardinal Winning to be credited with diluting executive plans to repeal Section 28. Informed sources, however suggest that much was down to the lesser-known group, Christian Action Research and Education (CARE). Emulating the Christian Right in the United States, CARE has spent large sums on lobbyists to circumvent the electoral process and put morality firmly on the agenda in the Britain's parliaments and assemblies: in Edinburgh, London, Cardiff and Belfast. With an annual income of around £3 million, some six or so staff based in Scotland, England, Wales and Northern Ireland, and around 140,000 supporters, CARE has the ear of some of Britain's most senior MPS and MSPs.

CARE'S Public Policy Department acts as a think tank on ethical issues relating to the family, medical ethics, education, sexuality and medical standards. It has involved itself actively in a range of consultations and studies, particularly those concerned with the efforts of a Liberal Democrat MSP who has tried to introduce/amend legislation along the lines of the Oregon **Death with Dignity** law on euthanasia.

CARE wages a holy war against the so-called 'permissive society'. It has claimed the credit for ensuring that Scotland's Adults with Incapacity Bill did not allow back-door euthanasia and has been resisting executive plans to cut unwanted pregnancies by ensuring the 'morning-after pill' is made more widely available to schoolchildren. Working closely with a partner, the Evangelical Alliance Scotland, CARE has resisted the lowering of the age of homosexual consent, regarding gay sex as a mortal sin, and is fighting plans for 'quicky' divorces and new rights for cohabiting couples.

In Scotland, CARE has relieved the financial burden on a handful of MSPs by paying researchers or 'interns' to work in their private offices. At the height of the battle over Section 28, one such intern worked for the then schools minister. The minister denied that this relationship benefited CARE, but the organisation claimed responsibility on its website for ensuring that the law – as it finally emerged – did so in a form that laid down strict guidelines on how homosexuality should be discussed in schools.

Via CARE's auspices, a network of highly organised evangelical Christians spreads briefing papers to fellow travellers via the Internet. It meets discreetly with government ministers, leading one source[5] to suggest that their influence 'is rivalling the power of many of Scotland's elected representatives'.

CARE has also urged its 3,500 Scottish members to consider joining a political party to help give a moral lead in the Scottish Parliament. Some critics worry that falling membership of parties has left them vulnerable to entryism, a fear voiced by Tim Hopkins[6] of Scotland's Equality Network who notes how candidates can be selected by relatively small numbers of members. He fears that a takeover of small party branches and the selection of candidates with the narrow views of the Christian Right, might make the climate hostile for gay people.

CARE was much involved in the Review of Religious Observance in Scottish Secondary Schools. Those conducting the review found that out of 1473 submissions, 70 per cent came from individuals, 30 per cent from organisations. nine per cent, or 130, of all responses classed as 'individual' represented the views of CARE which has organised its members to bombard the committee with its arguments. As the similarity of the mail was detected, the committee treated this batch as one submission in order not to give undue weight to its opinions.

## Criticisms of group activity in Scotland

Some critics of the Christian Right feel that it poses a serious threat to the parliamentary process. Sociologist David Miller[7] of Sterling University's media research institute has voiced concerns about the activities of CARE and other like-minded lobbyists in front of a Holyrood standards enquiry. He says it is no longer enough that the Parliament regulates only commercial lobbyists and that such organisations should be subjected to greater scrutiny: 'We need to regulate the whole lot – groups like CARE and in-house corporate staff. The

## Box 6.4  The Lobbygate affair

In 1999, undercover reporters duped two lobbyists for Beattie Media (a public affairs and public relations company) into boasting that they could offer access to senior politicians, including then finance minister, Jack McConnell. One of Beattie's employees was Kevin Reid, son of the then Scottish Secretary, a link that served to heighten media speculation and public disquiet.

To the dismay of the Executive, which had decided upon an internal enquiry, Parliament's Standards Committee decided to hold its own full and open enquiry. Ministers had to swear an oath before giving evidence. The review cleared all within the Scottish Parliament of any impropriety.

system is open to abuse. Groups who can afford it gain undue influence in the parliamentary process. It's basically the buying of the Parliament.'

The more widespread concern is that, within the Executive some ministers have employed research staff representing outside organisations with vested interests in Executive policy. The suggestion is not that these employees have broken any rules, their interests having been registered in official parliamentary records, but some worry that it is unhealthy that they should have direct access to government ministers, access denied to representatives of other good causes.

### Registration

Tough new laws have been drawn up by the Standards Committee, demanding among other things that MSPs:

- disclose any share holdings in a single company worth more than £25,000;
- disclose any membership of a secret society such as the Freemasons.

The committee also wants Parliament to establish a register of commercial lobbying organisations seeking to influence MSPs, with the names of their staff and clients. They also want the executive to set up a similar scheme to ensure that lobbying of ministers and civil servants should be opened up to public scrutiny, with a more transparent system. Members will also be required to declared membership of all professional bodies, trade unions, pressure groups and cultural or sporting organisations to which they belong. The details of the code of conduct have yet to be established but it could extend to private dining clubs, such as the Speculative Society, which has been the subject of controversy surrounding the Scottish legal establishment.

## Assessment of group activity in Scotland

In an early assessment, Grant Jordan[8] concluded that for all the hype, a new form of politics had not emerged. There may have been plenty of consultation but there was little evidence that the views of group campaigners were having significantly greater influence than they had before. He adds an explanation:

> It does not seem that civic society is more prominent in Holyrood (Edinburgh) based politics than in the UK . . . Consistent with that vein of thinking would have been the emergence of a minority Administration negotiating ad hoc majorities on different policies. Arguably, the emergence of a stable majority coalition has frustrated the idea of Parliamentary majorities reworked anew on different topics. Such instability would have enhanced bargaining . . . To be blunt, once politics became a matter of for and against the secure executive, then the focus has to be on the civil servants and politicians in the executive, rather than on civil society and the Parliament.

Yet those groups contacted by the author (see Table 6.4 on pages 156–7) generally had a positive attitude to devolution and most felt that their input was being taken into consideration as decisions were made and were able to provide examples of their influence. Another positive aspect noted by campaigners is that they find it considerably more convenient to lobby in Edinburgh than it was in the days before devolution. They consider themselves to be engaged in the process, feel that they are in close proximity to the key political players and of course they also benefit from savings in time and travelling costs.

### Surveys of Scottish pressure groups

In early 2005, twelve prominent groups were contacted and ten of them filled in a questionnaires or spoke/wrote at length to the author. The interest groups that responded ranged from the large (e.g. BMA) to the relatively small, such as the promotional groups that covered areas and issues such as human rights, moral values, voluntary social work and the environment. The findings of those who provided a detailed response are outlined below.

Of the ten respondents:

• all claimed to be actively involved in regular, on-going lobbying of the devolved institutions;

• all felt that they were regularly consulted and had good access to the appropriate personnel, though two noted that sometimes things seem to be decided before consultations are ever printed/published and wondered how significant was the impact of their contributions;

• seven claimed that the emphasis of their lobbying had switched significantly from London to Edinburgh, the amount reflecting the extent to which the issues with which they deal are devolved or reserved ones;

• seven made frequent or fairly frequent tactical alliances with other campaigning bodies in order to present a more formidable case – for example, the BMA is part of a coalition, Scotland CAN (Cleaner Air Now), which campaigns for smoke-free public places and regularly liaises with other health unions such as ASH Scotland;

• six belonged to the Scottish Civic Forum. The general view was that in its favour, it holds public meetings on topics of widespread interest and helps to flag up relevant issues. It was seen, however as generally 'of little use' or mainly of use to 'small organisations and individuals, community groups etc' and 'those who are not regularly engaged in the consultation process'. The Scottish SPCA withdrew from the body within a short time, considering that 'it was not an essential – or even useful – tool for lobbying'.

In his early research on the impact of Scottish devolution on pressure groups, Cairney[9] has also found that most of them have a positive attitude to the decentralisation of power from Westminster; they feel that the policy process is more open and consultative than ever before; they believe their input is taken into consideration on the substance of policy as well as in the bargaining for resources; and they find the location of the Parliament more convenient because of time saved, reduced travelling expenses, and proximity to the political actors. In

## Table 6.4 Selected Scottish pressure groups and their experiences of devolution

| Group | Has devolution made a difference? | Is involvement in the devolved machinery regular? | Which are the key targets for lobbying? | Do you belong to the Civic Forum? Do you find it useful? |
|---|---|---|---|---|
| British Medical Association Scotland | Yes, because health is a devolved issue | Yes, active and ongoing | Executive ministers and officials, MSPs, written and oral evidence to parliamentary enquiries | No |
| Evangelical Alliance Scotland | Not really; no switch of emphasis. Lobby at any tier of government available | Yes, regular and ongoing | Executive ministers and officials, MSPs, parliamentary committees, Parliamentary enquiries | Yes No – 'little use' |
| Law Society of Scotland | Much of the work done in Scotland, but works closely with UK operation for many relevant issues still decided in London | Yes, regular and ongoing | Executive officials, MSPs, parliamentary committees, written and oral evidence to parliamentary enquiries | No |
| Royal Society for the Protection of Birds Scotland | Yes, because environment is a devolved issue. UK | Yes, regular, ongoing and increasing | Executive ministers and officials, MSPs, Parliamentary enquiries. | Yes Not very useful, little focus on |

| Group | | | Useful work done | | |
|---|---|---|---|---|---|
| | headquarters targets Westminster on issues affecting four home countries | | Useful work done through umbrella group Scottish Environment Link | environment | |
| Scottish Human Rights Centre | Campaigned actively for a Scottish parliament and does most of its work there, though sometimes campaigns at Westminster too | Yes, regular | Executive ministers and officials, MSPs, especially, parliamentary committee chairs and members | Yes | Not especially |
| Scottish Society for the Prevention of Cruelty to Animals | Yes, most animal-welfare issues devolved. Most of work done in Scotland | Yes, regular, much involved in pre-legislative scrutiny: 'viewed by executive as a key stakeholder' | Executive ministers and officials, MSPs, party and Parliamentary committees, Written and oral evidence to parliamentary enquiries | Joined at inception; left, seen as not a useful tool | |
| UNISON Scotland | Edinburgh now more important than London | Yes, active and regular | Ministers in early stages of legislation, MSPs when policies in practice. Work with parliamentary committees. Effective through STUC | Yes | No – large enough to do own lobbying |

**NB** Of course, surveys of group lobbyists may overstate their impact in the consultative process, for campaigners tend to assume that their contributions are taken seriously and highly regarded. They may have less impact than they think they do.

his review, however, Cairney found that spokespersons for the Bank of Scotland were less enthusiastic than most others consulted. They argued that, pre-devolution, they had important contacts with the Scottish Office and enjoyed a close relationship with the secretary of state for Scotland which gave the bank direct access to the Cabinet. Cairney makes two other cautionary observations. Some campaigners are worried that, as the institutions mature, they will come to rely on groups less. Others question whether the massive exercises in consultation make any real difference to what emerges as final policy.

These are early days in which to come to anything other than a tentative judgement about the efficacy of groups in the consultative process. But there is no doubt that an important new dimension to group activity has been created by the passage of the Scotland Act.

NB See also the case study on the abolition of hunting with dogs in Scotland in chapter 8 for further insights into how and with what effect groups lobby the new Scottish machinery.

## Pressure groups and the Welsh National Assembly

Wales was granted devolved government at the same time as Scotland although, as Box 6.5 opposite indicates, the powers of the Welsh machinery are significantly less than those of the Scottish Parliament. On a matter of primary legislation such as the ban on fox hunting, there is no scope for modification by the Welsh Assembly government. In the days prior to devolution, however, there were Welsh pressure groups that lobbied the Welsh Office and, since 1999, a number of UK groups has established a base in Wales from which to lobby the new bodies.

The Welsh machinery has been active in pressing for greater powers and some pressure groups such as UNISON Wales, have offered support for this aim. Meanwhile, UNISON lobbies in Cardiff rather than in Westminster/Whitehall on issues of particular concern to the principality. It is in regular contact with ministers, special advisers, senior civil servants and Assembly Members (AMs) and their staff, preferring to arrange face-to-face meetings but also making use of e-mails and telephone calls. As an influential protective group, it is consulted by the Executive, serves on working groups and gives evidence to Assembly committees. Sometimes, it works in conjunction with other campaigning bodies, forming tactical alliances to strengthen the case presented.

Issues affecting Wales are dealt with in primary legislation passed by the British Parliament, but:

- in several cases, the legislation might provide for consultation with Welsh bodies over the means of implementation in Wales (as in the case of an early Labour Local Government Act which allowed Wales to deviate from the Best Value provisions applicable in England and operate under distinctive regulations in the establishment of conditions of contracts).
- on occasion Westminster has passed a separate piece of legislation for Wales, such as the Health Wales Act. Groups involved in lobbying on this measure lobbied the Welsh Assembly government, rather than the Department of Health in London;
- [as the representative of UNISON in Wales, Howard Marshall[10] has explained] even on issues where decisions are taken in

---

### Box 6.5  A note on the devolved machinery in Wales

Under the terms of the Wales Act 1998, Wales has a sixty member National Assembly from which an Executive – led by a first minister – is formed. The Assembly has significantly weaker powers that the Scottish Parliament, possessing no taxation or primary law-making responsibilities. It has taken over the role of the Welsh Office, created in 1964, being allowed to determine how Westminster legislation is implemented in Wales and to scrutinise Welsh administration. Its work covers agriculture, economic development, education, environment, health and social services, housing, industry and training, local government services, planning and transport, and sport and heritage.

Since the introduction of devolution, members of the National Assembly have urged a rethinking of the powers it has been granted. Review bodies have been established to examine the issue and, as a further indication of its ambitions, the Executive has adopted the nomenclature of the Welsh Assembly Government. It develops and implements policy and is accountable to the National Assembly which debates and approves legislation.

NB See also the reference to lobbying the new Welsh machinery in chapter 8 in connection with the hunting ban.

Westminster, lobbyists often obtain a better outcome by observing the protocol of approaching Welsh government ministers and AMs rather than ministers and MPs in London. The Welsh representatives then seek to convince their Westminster counterparts of what is appropriate for Welsh needs, themselves acting as a kind of pressure group to gain concessions or divergent policies for Wales. A further advantage of using the Welsh machinery is its greater accessibility. (Partly this is a matter of scale, the relative smallness of the country allowing Welsh ministers to develop a close knowledge of Welsh conditions; it is also a matter of style, the new machinery being designed to function in a more open manner than has traditionally been the case in Whitehall.) Should there be a need to lobby the British government directly, UNISON WALES would be more likely to lobby directly rather than operate through UNISON UK at the London headquarters, for this sharpens the focus on specifically Welsh concerns.

## Pressure groups in Northern Ireland

The situation in Northern Ireland is a confusing one. From 1969 until the signing of the **Good Friday (Belfast) Agreement** (April 1998), the province was under **direct rule** from Westminster. Once the new machinery created by the agreement was in place, a number of groups increasingly redirected their operations away from

---

**Box 6.6  The devolved machinery in Northern Ireland as it operated prior to the reimposition of direct rule**

The Good Friday Agreement provided for the following institutions:

- An assembly of 108 members (six from each multi-member constituency) elected by the single transferable vote. The membership was made large enough to accommodate a wide range of political opinions, both in individual constituencies and within the assembly as a whole. There was a requirement to receive cross-community assent in votes on contentious issues to guard nationalists against the any danger of unionist domination. The assembly had ten committees to support the work of the ten government departments. They provided advice and assistance to the departmental minister in the formulation of policy and undertook a scrutiny, policy-development and consultation role.

- An Executive, formed out of the assembly and responsible to it, was also to function on the basis of proportionality, so that decision-taking could not be dominated by one political grouping. It comprised a first minister and deputy first minister (one drawn from each of the unionist and nationalist communities) and up to ten departmental ministers. Offices were filled according to party strengths in the assembly, ensuring that all major groupings contributed to decisions at the executive level.

Devolution involved a substantial transfer of powers to Northern Ireland although Westminster alone remained responsible for the areas of security, civil defence and the raising of taxes. The assembly acquired primary law-making powers, enabling it to pass laws in the areas for which it was responsible.

One interesting feature in the Good Friday Agreement was the inclusion of a Civic Forum, a feature of the post-devolution Scottish settlement. The Belfast Agreement was vague about who would participate in the forum and what it would do, stating only that it would comprise representatives from the business, trade union and voluntary sectors to provide an arena for consultation on social, economic and cultural matters. In its final form, it had sixty members who were chaired by a nominee of the first and deputy first ministers.

Westminster and towards the Executive and assembly (see Box 6.6). The suspension on three occasions of the newly-created machinery – the third suspension has lasted until the time of writing– meant that direct rule was reintroduced. Accordingly, Westminster again became the target of group lobbying.

The approaches adopted by lobbyists during the period in which the devolved machinery was in operation were much the same as those employed by any pressure group – the preparation of written reports, submissions to the relevant departments, meetings with ministers and officials, meetings with members and committees of the assembly. (see Box 6.7 on the approach adopted by the Evangelical Alliance). As the legislature was granted law-making powers, it was a worthwhile target for lobbyists and campaigners. The precise access point they targeted varied according to what was appropriate for the issue. Bodies such, as the Ulster Farmers' Union, the BMA and the RSPCA were engaged in regular contact with the Executive, for this was the body with the power of decision. The Ulster Farmers' Union was heavily involved in lobbying ministers over the foot-and-mouth crisis in 2001.

## Box 6.7  The Evangelical Alliance and its campaigning

The Evangelical Alliance is the umbrella body which brings together Britain's 1 million plus evangelicals who are to be found in some 700 organisations and more than 3,000 churches. The Alliance has a public affairs team at Westminster but following devolution, it has employed public affairs officers for each of the devolved institutions in Scotland, Wales and Northern Ireland. Lobbyists use the full range of methods outlined in chapter 2, the choice depending on the issue, time-scale and personnel involved.

On some issues within its sphere of interest, the centre of decision-making is still very focused on Westminster/Whitehall. On issues such as human rights, it makes contributions to parliamentary committees, to MPs and to the relevant government departments. But, during the period of devolved rule, it had ongoing and regular contact with assembly committees and members, civil servants and statutory organizations, such as the Human Rights Commission. In particular, it:

- was actively involved in consultations during the early stages of the legislative process, wishing to help shape the development of policy rather than influence it later; this often involved providing evidence to assembly committees. Each government department was required to have an equality scheme and a list of organisations that it would consult over the development of policy. The Alliance was on the lists and would automatically receive consultation documents coming out of the departments. (Its spokespersons point to the danger that consultation can become merely a 'ticking of boxes' exercise, with ministers having already made up their minds and ploughing on with policies that fly in the face of the consensus of the inhabitants of Northern Ireland – education policy being one case in point, the introduction of civil partnerships another.);
- worked closely with a number of assembly members who were sympathetic to its viewpoint, networking with them being a useful means of getting its views more widely known.

Today, much of the Alliance's lobbying is conducted via the Northern Ireland MPs and with the government departments in Whitehall although, if there is something specifically related to events in the province, it takes up the issue with the Northern Ireland Office. As under devolved rule, it continues to make tactical alliances with other campaigning bodies in order to present a more formidable case, as is appropriate. For instance, on matters of human rights, it works closely with Care for Northern Ireland and the Evangelical Contribution on Northern Ireland (ECONI), now renamed the Centre for Contemporary Christianity in Ireland.

The work of lobbyists is in many cases, ongoing in that the causes for which lobbyists campaign are still relevant whatever the access point they target in their propaganda. The campaign to preserve Northern Irish grammar schools was mobilised following the announcement by the first Minister of Education of the new executive, Martin McGuinness, of his decision to phase out academic selection and introduce a comprehensive system for secondary education. Since the reintroduction of direct rule, the plans were still on the table and campaigners for grammar school education now concentrate their fire on ministers and their officials in the Northern Ireland Office (NIO) in Belfast. Many of the officials handling the issues are the same people who served in the years of devolved government.

The processes of consultation over policy formulation and implementation continue on the future of secondary education and other issues (such as the review of primary education and water charging) as before. As much of the legislation under direct rule is made by order in council (thereby not allowing for much debate or scrutiny in the House of Commons) the actual drafting stage of bills is crucial and this is where officials perform a significant role. Of course, there is now no point in approaching the 108 elected members of the assembly, their work having, at least temporarily, come to a halt. There are however, the eighteen MPs sent from the province to Westminster who may be worth talking to in the absence of devolution. They can approach the NIO and make representations on any group's behalf.

..............................................................................

## ✓ What you should have learnt from reading this chapter

- The creation of devolved machinery has provided new outlets for pressure groups to target.

- The extent to which individual groups lobby the devolved institutions depends in large measure on the powers granted to the new machinery. In other words, can the devolved institutions determine or influence policy?

- In Scotland, there was a clear intention that the new system of government would involve wide consultation with a range of interested bodies.

- Since 1998, consultation has been widespread in practice.

- In Northern Ireland and Wales, the impact of devolution on pressure groups has been less dramatic because of the suspension of institutions in the former and the relatively weak powers provided for under the Wales Act in the latter. Welsh groups contacted by the author, however generally had an ongoing relationship with the Welsh Assembly Government and the National Assembly and were consulted on issues of relevance to them.

## 🔍 Glossary of key terms

**Act of Union** The Act which united England and Scotland in 1707, thus forming Great Britain.
**Death with Dignity** The name given to the initiative adopted by voters in Oregon in 1994 to allow for doctor-assisted suicide (legalised euthanasia). Contested in the state supreme court, euthanasia has been legal in the American state since 1998.
**Devolution** The term used to describe the transfer of powers from London to Scotland, Wales and Northern Ireland. Although government is thereby decentralised, no transfer of sovereignty is involved for this remains in Westminster hands. In theory, what has been devolved can be retrieved.
**Direct rule** The method by which Northern Ireland was governed following the removal of the Stormont Parliament in 1969. The province was governed from Westminster, day-to-day decisions on the formulation and implementation of policy being made via the Northern Ireland Office, in Belfast. At the time of writing, direct rule remains in operation.
**Good Friday (Belfast) Agreement** The formal agreement reached by the Blair government with the unionists, nationalists and government of the Irish Republic to pave the way for the future government of Northern Ireland. The agreement created an executive and an assembly, both of which are currently suspended.

**Reserved powers** Those powers which are reserved to Westminster under the 1998 Scotland Act, such as the constitution, defence and national security, and foreign affairs.

**Souter referendum** Brian Souter privately funded a ballot of all Scottish people on the controversial Section 28 of the Local Government Act in 2000. On a 34 per cent turnout, 87 per cent wished to retain the section, 13 per cent wished to repeal it.

## Likely examination questions

How has the creation of devolved machinery in Scotland, Wales and Northern Ireland affected the operation of British pressure groups?

To what extent has the creation of new devolved institutions in Scotland introduced new opportunities for campaigners and lobbyists?

## Helpful websites

www.scotland.gov.uk  The Scottish executive

www.scottish.parliament.uk  The Scottish Parliament

www.civicforum.org.uk  The Scottish Civic Forum

www.ossw.wales.gov.uk  The Welsh Office

www.assembly.wales.org.uk  The Welsh National Assembly

www.nio.gov.uk  The Northern Ireland Office

www.nics.gov.uk  The Northern Ireland executive

www.ni-assembly.gov.uk  The Northern Ireland Assembly

www.careinscotland.co.uk/  Care for Scotland

www.scottishspca.org/  Scottish SPCA

## Suggestions for further reading

*Article:*

D. Watts, 'Pressure Group Activity in Post-Devolution Scotland', *Talking Politics* 18.2, Politics Association, 2006.

*Books:*

There are as yet no published works specifically concerned with the impact of devolution on pressure-group activity. See the relevant sections in:

W. Grant, *Pressure Groups and British Politics*, Macmillan, 2000.

P. Lynch, *Scottish Government and Politics: An Introduction*, Edinburgh University Press, 2001.

## CHAPTER 7

# Lobbying the European Union

## Contents

## Overview

The **European Union** has developed in size and importance since Britain first joined the **Community** in 1973. Following the **Fifth Enlargement** (2004), there are now twenty-five members with a combined population in excess of 450 millions. The full implications of membership have become more apparent to British politicians and people in the last twenty years. The Union has made a significant impact on various aspects of government and politics.

The relevance of the European dimension to the pressure-group activity has been increasingly recognised by writers on the British political scene over the last ten years. Many groups have found it necessary to adjust their lobbying techniques and the access points they target. In this chapter, we explore the scale of pressure group involvement with European institutions and the ways in which lobbyists seek to influence them.

## Key issues to be covered in this chapter

- Why the majority of British pressure groups have found it worthwhile to lobby extensively in Brussels and in Strasbourg
- The types of groups that engage in lobbying
- The early involvement of groups in the political development of the European Community
- Why groups are now more involved in the operations of the European Union than ever before
- In what ways key groups seek to influence European initiatives: the institutions they target
- The influence that lobbyists can wield
- The response of the institutions to a process never envisaged when the European Community was first conceived.
- Why some groups are more successful in lobbying European institutions than others

# Why pressure groups lobby in the European Union

Over the last three decades, Europe has played an increasing role in British politics. Particularly since the signing of the **Single European Act** in 1986, the momentum towards closer **integration**, especially in the economic and monetary union, has significantly increased. The completion of the **single market**, the ratification of the Maastricht and subsequent treaties, the signing of the **Social Chapter**, the launch of the single currency for Euroland, discussions in the Convention of a constitution for the Union and developments in a number of policy areas, such as asylum seeking, internal security, the environment, and defence and foreign policy, have all drawn attention to the growing importance of the Union. As a member since 1973, Britain has inevitably been involved in these developments.

In the light of such events, it is not surprising that British groups have felt the need to protect and promote their interests in Europe. Many decisions affecting key areas of our national life are now taken in Brussels (for details of the roles of the key institutions in decision-making, see Box 7.1 on pages 168–9). Many of our laws derive from regulations and directives (see page 170) of the Commission, so that 'in some sectors the bulk of new regulatory activity now takes place not in Whitehall but in Brussels'.[1] On topics ranging from food hygiene to the movement of live animals, from fishing to the outbreak a few years ago of bovine spongiform encephalopathy (BSE), the actions of British governments are much affected by what is laid down in the Commission. For instance, of the three hundred or so measures adopted in preparation for a single internal market (completed by the beginning of January 1993), sixty had animal-health and veterinary-control implications. Others affected the veterinary profession, having implications for such things as the freedom of movement and rights of establishment of veterinary surgeons. The British Veterinary Association and the Royal College of Veterinary Surgeons were inevitably going to be interested in such initiatives, while some of them were of relevance to the RSPCA, the NFU and the Euro-group for Animal Welfare.

Not surprisingly, the number of groups involved in EU affairs has increased dramatically over the last three decades. Recent research by

## Box 7.1 European Union institutions and decision-making: a brief summary

The five main institutions of the European Union are:

**The European Council**: gatherings of the heads of state or governments of the member states, usually held twice yearly. Not mentioned in the original treaties, the Council has come to play an increasingly important role in setting priorities, giving political direction and providing impetus for the development and resolution of contentious issues.

**The Council of Ministers** (the principal decision-making body in the Union machinery): made up of ministers from the member states with responsibility for the policy area under discussion, it adopts legislation and co-ordinates national policies. Most decisions are adopted by qualified majority voting (QMV) although, on some matters, there is still a need for unanimity.

**The European Commission**: initiates proposals for legislation, acts as guardian of treaties, manages and executes some Union policies, such as the Common Agricultural Policy.

**The European Parliament** (the only directly elected piece of Union machinery): traditionally dismissed as a talking shop, its members have acquired growing influence over legislation, the amount varying according to the issue being discussed. Its executive responsibilities are carried out by 25 Commissioners (in effect, the political arm of the Commission) and the administrative ones by the bureaucracy. Under the terms of the Amsterdam Treaty (1997), it has acquired the power of **co-decision** over a wide range of issues, including the free movement of labour, consumer protection, education, culture and trans-European networks. In addition, Parliament, whose plenary sessions are held in Strasbourg, has to approve the appointment of the Commission and shares budgetary powers with the Council.

**The Court of Justice**: deals with issues of interpretation and application of Community legislation. The judges lay down judgments on matters such as whether member states' legislation is in line with Community law and can impose fines on countries for non-implementation of legislation.

Other institutions referred to in connection with lobbying are:

**The Committee of the Regions (CoR)**: created under the Maastricht Treaty, its representatives – drawn from local and regional authorities – are consulted on regional policy issues by the Council and Commission.

**The Economic and Social Committee (ESC)**: a consultative body representing the various relevant categories of economic and social activity (including trade unions, employers and farmers' unions). As with the CoR, its opinions are not legally binding.

There are complicated rules to agree different types of EU legislation. In a growing number of policy areas, the European Parliament has acquired a more significant role. Under the increasingly important co-decision procedure, decision-making power is shared equally between Parliament and the Council.

One other body worthy of mention and explanation (not least because it is little known in Britain) is the **Committee of Permanent Representatives (COREPER)**: it comprises the Brussels-based ambassadors of the member states. Each country has an embassy in Brussels to manage its dealings with the various institutions of the Union, most especially its direct involvement in the legislative process through the Council of Ministers. **UKREP** is the acronym for the United Kingdom Permanent Representation, a large body noted for its professionalism. UKREP spends much of its time in meetings of COREPER and working groups within the Council structure. COREPER's most important task involves the preparations for meetings of the Council of Ministers.

**The decision-making process**
Legislation is usually initiated by the Commission. This is a simplified version of the decision-making process:

- Draft laws are drawn up by the Commission
- They are discussed and may be amended by the Parliament (under co-decision, they have to be agreed with the Council before they can become law)
- The Council of Ministers makes the final decision
- Checks on the proper implementation of laws are made by the Commission.

Wessels (1997) and Gray (1998)[2] has suggested that, across the Union, the overall number of trade associations, interest and cause groups, regions, think tanks, consultants and lawyers increased fivefold between the 1970s and the late 1990s. The number of lobbyists employed by groups operating in Brussels has similarly increased, to around 15,000. The European Union's *Directory of Special Interest Groups* lists over nine hundred lobby groups covering – in ascending order of numbers – agriculture, industry, services and general interest.

The many groups that engage in lobbying can be categorised into six main types:

1. Manufacturing groups, ranging from large, powerful, pan-European **euro-groups**, such as the Union of Industrial and Employers' Confederations of Europe (UNICE), latterly Business Europe, to less well-known bodies such as the Hearing Aid Association; from associations with influential members, such as those operating in the chemical industry, to ones of growing importance in the food and drink sectors. In addition, leading multinational companies are now lobbying strongly on their own behalf (see page 177).
2. Labour groups, ranging from the European Trades Union Confederation (ETUC), an influential euro-group, to major national umbrella groups, such as the British Trades Union Congress, as well as individual trade unions such as the Transport and General Workers Union.
3. Agricultural groups, ranging from the powerful euro-group, the Committee of Professional Agricultural Organisations (COPA),

## **Table 7.1  European Union legislation: regulations and directives

EU law may take the following forms:
- **Regulations**: The strongest type of EU law, these are directly applied in all member states without the need for national measures to implement them. An example in the area of animal welfare is the law prohibiting the use of certain traps for catching wild animals.
- **Directives**: This type of law lays down the rules, binding member states to the objective to be achieved, while leaving them the power to choose the form and means to be used in implementing them (by a certain date). An example is the law covering the conditions for rearing veal calves.
- **Decisions**: these are binding in all their aspects upon those to whom they are addressed. This can be any or all the member states, undertakings or individuals.

to groups representing specialised sectors such as organic farmers (e.g. the Soil Association in Britain).
4. Professional groups, including euro-groups representing national law, medical and veterinary associations, as well as individual law firms.
5. Public-interest groups, ranging from think tanks, such as the European Policy Centre, to organisations such as the European Blind Union; from environmental bodies, such as Greenpeace and the World Wide Fund for Nature (WWF), to organisations such as Human Rights Watch and the European Youth Forum. The EU decision-making processes provide greater access for a number of promotional, 'outsider' groups that normally lack influence in the inner-circle Whitehall group contacts.
6. Governmental organisations, including more than 160 accredited non-EU embassies and delegations (such as the United States Embassy) as well as regional governments (such as, the German *Länder*) and local authorities, some of which are very active on the European scene (for example, Birmingham).

## Why the amount of lobbying has increased in recent years

To a considerable extent, the reasons for the growth of group activity in recent decades lie in the explanation offered in the section above. The initiatives taken by the European Union have been of increasing relevance to British governments for they have introduced policies that ministers have to implement and from which Britain cannot easily opt out. European Union institutions are perceived by lobbyists as having more influence over domestic policy decisions than was previously the case. There are other factors that operate to make lobbying by British groups in Europe more extensive than ever before, however.

In the early years after Britain joined the European Economic Community in 1973, the full implications of membership were not always appreciated, particularly by some cause groups. Moreover, activists were faced with unfamiliar decision-making machinery and it took some time for them to find their way around the European institutions and to understand their relative powers. As they have gained more knowledge and experience of the decision-making process within the Union, they have been able to take more advantage of lobbying opportunities.

Moreover, institutions such as the European Commission have become more accessible and receptive to lobbyists. In part, this is because the expansion of Union responsibilities under the Single European Act (SEA) and Maastricht Treaty meant that bodies such as the Commission found that they required the knowledge, understanding and expertise that well-informed groups could provide. As a result, the Commission has made itself more open to influence. It maintains a large register of interested bodies whom it will regularly consult on matters of policy development.

The introduction of **qualified majority voting** in a growing number of areas has meant that groups wishing to exercise an influence on policy matters need to do so at an early stage in policy development. They need to gain concessions to their viewpoint as the policy is being developed, for they cannot have as much impact when it has been formulated into a directive that Britain must adopt. They have to ensure that policies they regard as hostile are defeated or modified for, once agreed by an appropriate majority, then there is no national veto to stop the policy from being introduced.

Finally, some groups found that in the 1980s they had lost much of their former influence over British ministers. Members of the Thatcher and Major governments were much less willing to meet, or respond to the pleas of, trade unionists and social groups representing the dispossessed, such as the homeless, the poor, children, and ethnic minority groups. Trade unionists who found the climate in British governing circles unwelcoming were inspired when the President of the European Commission, Jacques Delors, visited the TUC conference in 1988 and outlined his proposals for a social dimension to the single market. They were hopeful that some of the remnants of socialism killed off by Thatcherite ministers might be reintroduced via the back door, under pressure from Brussels. Their optimism was increased by the greater willingness of some EU institutions to challenge British governmental policies over a whole range of matters, from equal pay and retirement provisions to social security claims and water purity. It seemed well worth while to seek to influence their decisions.

# How pressure groups lobby in the European Union and the institutions they target

Powerful British interest groups representing agriculture, business and the professions have long been aware of the benefits of lobbying European Union institutions but so, too, have many cause associations. There are several different strategies open to the activists who conduct their lobbying activities. They can choose to adopt either a national or a European strategy, or a mixture of the two.

1. **A national strategy** This involves an attempt to influence the position taken by British ministers in European Union discussions and also to influence the implementation of EU directives. For some groups this is the most effective form of lobbying, for it is less expensive than lobbying directly in Europe on their own and, if they belong to a euro-group, then they may find that their counterparts from other countries do not share their viewpoint. British insider groups with a European interest will seek to build upon this channel of influence. The hope is that by meeting senior officials and junior ministers in Whitehall, then the secretary of state will advance their arguments and defend their cause in the Council of Ministers.

The National Farmers Union lobbies in Whitehall when the issue of reform of the Common Agricultural Policy rears its head in the anticipation that, when the minister goes to Brussels' meetings, he or she will resolutely defend the position of the agrarian community at home. Of course, as Butt Phillips[3] reminds us, 'the national pressure groups will be very much in the hands of government officials once the Council of Ministers' negotiations begin'. Many British groups pursue a national strategy, and writers such as Greenwood[4] have drawn attention to the fact that relationships between groups and national governments are 'stable, well-developed and reliable' Moreover, most groups carry more weight with their own government than with European institutions so that the impact of their lobbying is therefore maximised by focusing on Whitehall and Westminster. For the larger bodies, such as the Institute of Directors, however, this avenue is used in conjunction with others, the emphasis being on the strategy that is most likely to be effective in a particular case.

2. **A European strategy (a) Working via euro-groups**. Many British groups belong to euro-groups, European-level federations of national groups. More than a decade ago, Baggott's[5] survey showed that three-quarters of them were members of such an organisation. Many of these have operated from the early days of the original European Community, often being based in Brussels although some are to be found in Amsterdam, Cologne, London and Paris. The best-organised euro-groups are those concerned with representing the interests of big business, in particular the Union of Industries in the European Community (UNICE). In the Butt Phillips survey already referred to, the largest number represented employers, closely followed by those groups representing agricultural and food interests (such as the Committee of Professional Agricultural Organisations of the European Community, COPA). Other significant sectors dealt with issues such as consumers (for example, Bureau of European Consumer Organizations, BEUC), labour (for example, the European Trade Union Confederation, ETUC), the environment (for example, European Environmental Bureau) and animal welfare (for example the Euro-group for Animal Welfare and the Federation of Veterinarians of the European Community [see Box 7.2 below]).

Euro-groups can be useful to national groups in several ways: strengthening the case they wish to promote, putting pressure on the government of other EU countries to modify their position and

---

### Box 7.2  The Federation of Veterinarians of the EC (FVE): a case study of a euro-group

The FVE is an umbrella organisation for forty-four national veterinary bodies located across thirty-four European countries. Two British groups belong to it, the British Veterinary Association and the Royal College of Veterinary Surgeons. There is a central office in Brussels, comprising five people of whom three are veterinarians involved in work on lobbying files and two are administrative staff.

The FVE aims to inform its members of what is happening within Union organisations and also does lobbying work on behalf of the profession. For instance, when new legislation on veterinary inspectors is drafted, the staff at headquarters circulate the proposal to member organisations, form an ad hoc working group of experts, prepare and adopt a position paper and then begin lobbying the Commission, Parliament and the Council. In particular, with the Commission, work begins as soon as possible. Often, it invites the FVE's opinion in advance of releasing its draft proposals for legislation.

Currently, the main preoccupations of the FVE are:

- veterinary education and professional recognition
- animal health and welfare
- food safety
- good veterinary practice
- enlargement of the Union and its implications.

The FVE has a series of subgroups representing practising state veterinary officers, hygienists and industry and research. Britain is represented on all these groups which can provide the FVE with expert advice. One of its early committees dealt with animal welfare. Its representations on animal welfare and mutilation were accepted by the Federation and used to stimulate action.

influencing counterpart organisations elsewhere in the hope that they might lobby their own government. They are a strong means of lobbying the Union, a two-way channel representing national groups to the European institutions and a means of keeping national groups informed of Union proposals and initiatives. Their weakness is often their lack of resources, of which staffing is but one problem. Many are small-scale operations with only a handful of permanent staff and limited means for sustaining a long campaign. Some are influential and well resourced, however, among them the one featured below.

3. **A European strategy (b) Direct contact with Union institutions**. Most groups will have some form of communication with the machinery of the European Union, particularly the Commission. A much smaller number will also have an office in the Union to further their interests and to enable them to keep a close eye on key developments within the European Union. Such lobbying is usually a complement to that done in London, rather than a substitute for domestic action. An understanding of the institutions of the Union and how they operate is relevant to an appreciation of why groups

target particular access points. Box 7.1 on pages 168–9 provides a brief résumé. Lobbying of Community institutions can be carried out by several routes, among them:

- the Council of Ministers
- the Commission, including its officials and the twenty-five commissioners
- the Parliament and its committees, party groupings and intergroups (groups of MEPs who espouse a range of causes, such as the Friends of Israel or those concerned about animal welfare and the media)
- the Economic and Social Committee (ESC)
- the Committee of the Regions
- the Court of Justice

The Commission is the main target, for this is where proposals are drafted. It also supervises the day-to-day execution of EU policy (the executive tasks being spread among civil servants in its twenty-three directorates-general) and manages the Common Agricultural Policy.

Brussels is inevitably the most fertile location for the lobbyist. Not only is the Commission based there, but so also are the committees and party groupings of the European Parliament. It is where the Council of Ministers meets, as does the Economic Social Committee. For those groups that can afford the luxury of a European office, this is the place to be. Originally mainly viewed as listening posts/service centres for national association members and staff attending meetings in the city, these offices have over the last two decades played a more significant part in lobbying approaches. The CBI actually set up its Brussels base before British membership took effect in 1973.

Many groups who wish to influence Parliament rely on contact with their MEPs. For many associations, this is more easy to arrange and less costly than a visit to Strasbourg. Bomberg and Stubb[6] quote the long-serving British MEP who remarked, only half in jest: 'In 1979, we were begging people to come and see us. Now, we are trying to keep them away.' MEPs can make their views known in debates and questions within the chamber, but also via their political groupings and Parliament's committee structure. They also liaise with the Commission on behalf of associations with a point to put across. Many MEPs hold surgeries, otherwise they are willing and eager to receive representations from various organisations. The vastness of constituencies may make personal contact difficult to achieve. In this case, the lobbyist has to rely on e-mails, letters and phone calls.

Finally, we should mention the Court of Justice, based in The Hague. Lobbying of the Court does not apply in the sense that it does to other institutions, but individuals and groups can take legal action to challenge domestic law in the Court. Cases are also brought by the Commission. On a range of issues such as rights for part-time workers, retirement and equal pay, decisions taken by the justices have led to changes in domestic laws.

## Recent trends in European Union lobbying

The most obvious trend has been the growth in the number and influence of organised interests operating within the Union, as already outlined. Bomberg and Stubb have noted that 'different types of interests have congregated in Brussels in a series of waves', reflecting 'the deepening and widening of the European Union itself'. In the 1960s, the dominant actors represented commercial interests and agriculture. Employer – and later labour and consumer – interests followed and, by the 1980s, more public-interest organisations had European representation. Trade associations and remaining professional associations became more active in Europe after the passage of the Single European Act with the prospect of a single market. Some large companies also began to open their own offices in Brussels and take an interest in its decisions, examples being GlaxoSmithKline, Philip Morris and Six Continents (formerly Bass).

Particularly significant in recent years has been the increase in the lobbying carried out by regional and local governments, ranging from the German *Länder* to the Scottish and Northern Irish Executives and the Welsh Assembly. The development of cohesion (a policy concerned to reduce regional economic disparities) under the Single European Act and the formation of the Committee of the Regions under the Maastricht Treaty both pointed to increased EU concern for Europe's regional diversity and discrepancies. Representatives of such authorities have their eyes firmly set on the prospect of special funding for their pet regional and social projects but they are also interested in environmental policies and EU programmes for social inclusion, and support for business and cultural and tourism activities. The Brussels delegations of regional and local authorities maintain close links with all institutions, working closely with appropriate commissioners or staff of the directorates-general, and with sympathetic MEPs. The Committee of the Regions has estimated their number at around 190.

Think tanks have also increased in number although their numbers are more modest and their resources more limited than many of those operating in Washington DC, London or several other capital cities. Other areas of growth include environmental, animal rights, public health and human rights groups, the increase reflecting growing EU interest and responsibilities in these areas.

In recent years, the various groups have extended their lobbying to institutions other than the European Commission which was always the primary target of their activities. The European Parliament has gained powers latterly, giving it a more significant role in policy-making (for example, via co-decision). The Court of Justice has been used to resolve a number of issues: the National Union of Mineworkers and the Law Society have taken up causes such as pit closures and legal aid; and individual firms in the airline and car industries have taken cases to Luxembourg in protest against regulations that adversely affected their interests. In addition, the Committee of the Regions, the Economic and Social Committee and some other bodies have provided additional access points to the Union.

As lobbyists have acquired more knowledge and experience of the decision-making processes and the role of key institutions, so they see the point in making contact with the personnel who work in them. Those who work as parts of policy networks can also be identified. Policy networks have come to play an important part in sectors such as agriculture, chemicals, pharmaceuticals and technology. More often than not, they are wide and loose issue networks, rather than smaller policy communities in which relationships are particularly close and continuous. The impact of any group may vary from time to time, issue to issue, partly depending on the expertise it possesses. Peterson[7] points out that as the European Union has become a more important tier of governance in Europe, so 'EU policy networks have become a more important link between states and societies. A considerable amount of EU decision-making now occurs within policy networks.' This development is associated with the vagueness of some intergovernmental agreements that left the Commission and the groups with whom it had dealings a role in 'filling in the gaps'.

The other main development over the last decade has been the increasing professionalism of lobbying. As Bomberg and Stubb[8] point out, 'the art of lobbying has come a long way in the EU. In the view of one heavily lobbied MEP: "Now, we have far higher skills and standards in the lobbying industry. You very rarely get the utter fool you would have encountered some years ago." ' The Commission values well-presented, highly specialised information, and lobbyists need to demonstrate their expertise and carefully tailor their data and advice. Increasingly, they make links with other like-minded lobbyists, and establish alliances and networks across institutions and nationalities. E-mail has been used to develop and sustain dialogue with Commission officials and parliamentarians. It is used extensively by euro-groups, as they seek to maintain contact with their wide and highly dispersed membership.

## The findings of a 1993 questionnaire

A survey conducted by the author in 1993 highlighted the importance of the European dimension to many different British pressure groups. It indicated the way in which, from an early stage, business and agricultural interests had recognised the importance of the European dimension whereas unions and consumer organisations were slower to respond. It noted the growing importance attached by many professional interest groups to the activities of the European Union, in particular subsequent to the passage of the Single European Act with its emphasis on the harmonisation of qualifications, which enabled doctors, lawyers, vets and others to practise within the Union. The growing importance of lobbying in the field of animal welfare and the role of euro-groups were also indicated.

Sixteen out of twenty groups responded to the questionnaire and almost all of them saw value in maintaining regular contact with the EU institutions and their personnel. The general view of several representatives was that such contacts would develop in the future because of the growing relevance of the European Union to their operations and also because of their increased understanding of how the Union operated.

## The findings of a 2004 update

Of the sixteen groups that responded in 1993, two no longer exist as separate entities. Of the remaining fourteen, twelve replied to the questionnaire sent to them. They covered important areas, ranging from manufacturing to labour, farming to the environment, and animal welfare to the law.

All of the respondents agreed that the impact of the European Union had grown significantly over the last ten years although, in most cases, they pointed to the development of the single market as the major impetus to their involvement in matters European. The representative of the Transport and General Workers Union drew attention to the increasing amount of relevant legislation in recent years in the area of working conditions, notably that relating to hours of work and the conditions of part-timers and young people.

The officer for the Law Society also noted an increase in EU legislation of interest to its members, the establishment directive directly affecting the practice of law in the Union. Beyond that, he pointed to the European Union's increasing legislative competence in certain areas of civil and criminal law which affects the advice British solicitors give to their clients.

Not surprisingly, the two environmental groups, Friends of the Earth and Greenpeace, also felt that the European Union was more important in their work than ever before. FoE has recently been much involved with submissions on waste, while Greenpeace has taken up issues of emission levels and illegal logging.

The Policy Officer for the Society of Motor Manufacturers and Traders (SMMT) confirmed the growing impact of EU measures on national pressure groups. He drew attention to the way in which the number of interest-group offices established in Brussels has grown steadily and how the timing of these creations has broadly coincided with the acquisition by the European Union of new responsibilities covering a range of policy areas. In particular, he stressed the importance for the motor industry of environmental measures such as the REACH Chemicals Policy review, emission standards for new cars and safety issues such as pedestrian protection. He provided other explanations for the growing attraction of the European Union for interest groups, already implicit in what we have said with regard to EU institutions. He referred to its 'multi-level architecture', meaning that there are lots of opportunities to influence legislative outcome compared with some national arenas – for example, in the early drafting stage in the Commission, in the Council via national governments, and in the Parliament. He also referred to the EU's consciousness of its perceived '**democratic deficit**' and its recognition of the need to become 'closer' to its citizens. He noted that the Commission is taking an increasingly pragmatic approach to consultation. Its officials realise that there is little point in passing 'unworkable' legislation with which member states will have little interest in complying.

In the last few years, the SMMT has made increasing use of e-mail as a means of communication. It has also developed its programme of holding seminars and staging events in Brussels. Otherwise, it continues to employ a dual strategy in its lobbying programme. On the one hand, it holds regular meetings with British ministers and officials in key departments such as DEFRA, the DTI and DfT, in the hope that its concerns are taken into account, both when formulating the British negotiating position for the Council of Ministers and working-group meetings, and in transposing EU directives into national law. It also works through two euro-groups based on national automotive associations as well as having a more general input into manufacturing policy via its membership of the Confederation of British Industry, itself a member of UNICE.

Overall, of the twelve respondents, all of them lobby the national government in seeking to influence EU policy. All of them belong to euro-groups and engage in direct lobbying of EU institutions from Britain (such as via approaches to MEPs, or by contacting officials in Union institutions). Only two of them (the CBI and Law Society) have their own offices in Brussels although the RSPCA has a base at the Euro-group for Animal Welfare's headquarters. The survey of the RSPCA and its operations provides a fuller example of how one British group goes about its task of 'lobbying Europe' (see Box 7.3 overleaf).

## Box 7.3  The RSPCA: a case study of one cause group and its European activities

Animal welfare in an area of increasing concern, and groups such as Compassion in World Farming, are active lobbyists of the Community. The RSPCA seeks to influence European legislation in various ways: through the Euro-group for Animal Welfare, by seeking the support of sympathetic British MEPs, through contact with British commissioners and through contact with British ministers and the permanent representatives (UKREP) in the Council of Ministers. It has been involved in lobbying at Strasbourg and in Brussels since 1979, and this field of activity has increased considerably since then.

Much of the lobbying is co-ordinated through the euro-group, in which the RSPCA has a very strong personal input. The group has important contacts with the commission secretariat and with directorates-general VI (agriculture) and XI (environment) but it also works with the DGs responsible for enlargement, enterprise, fisheries, health and consumer protection, regional policy, research and trade. Not only does the euro-group have an office in Brussels, it has one in the RSPCA's own headquarters in Horsham.

The RSPCA is particularly interested in the latest enlargement of the European Union. The ten new countries have to adopt and implement European animal welfare legislation, as will Bulgaria and Romania, both due to join in 2007. This means that millions of animals will have the benefit of improved welfare standards. In preparation for this enlargement, the euro-group drew up its accession action programme that led to the establishment of links with national animal-protection organisations and governments in the candidate countries and monitoring the accession negotiations between the candidates and European institutions.

The Society is concerned about the variable enforcement of animal-welfare legislation across the European Union. Through its experienced team of undercover inspectors, it monitors standards of application across the Union. It also carefully monitors the implementation of European directives in Britain, ensuring that Union legislation is carried out in the way that, and as fully as, was intended.

## Conclusion

The European Union has encouraged the involvement of pressure groups – particularly those with a Europe-wide perspective – to become involved in its work. The Commission lists some nine hundred groups in its directory, most of them protective groups. The main peak associations, such as UNICE and ETUC, are examples of interest groups heavily committed to European lobbying. But not all euro-groups have their funds and resources, few being able to match their high profile. Several groups also find it difficult to adopt positions acceptable to members drawn from a wide range of countries.

In addition to euro-groups, national groups from member states have become increasingly involved in lobbying EU institutions, sometimes working in partnership with their home governments. Other lobbying comes from individual companies, regional and local governments, and external bodies, such as American multinational corporations and trade associations from countries as far away as China and Japan.

The European Union provides an additional and important channel for British lobbyists. Those well-known national insider groups, well-funded organisations equipped with excellent briefs, are likely to find that their views are much respected in Brussels. They can provide specialist information to those who develop policy. Aspinwall[9] and others have argued that the advantages of readily available resources work to the benefit of wealthy private companies in manufacturing and the professions, and to the detriment of smaller public bodies that cannot afford to employ professional agencies or commit extensive funding to their activities. But many groups that do not have access to policy-makers on the national scene now at least have an additional channel through which their lobbying can be conducted. Peterson[10] makes the point that campaigners concerned with consumerism, environmentalism and women's rights have all had the opportunity to pursue their cause at European level, perhaps by forging informal alliances with members of the Commission, Parliament or Court of Justice.

By the early 1990s, it was becoming increasingly apparent that much of what was happening within the Union was of direct interest to British pressure-groups. The trend to a Europeanisation of pressure group activity was gathering pace and the traditional view of Whitehall/Westminster as the centre of group attention needed to be revised. Over the last decade, various groups have become more confident and familiar with lobbying European institutions. To neglect them – at a time when EU competences have grown – would for groups operating over a range of sectors be a very risky approach. To rely on contacts with British ministers would be dangerous for, often, they have to concede on particular points in order to arrive at a compromise solution broadly satisfactory to the representatives of other member states. Hence Mazey and Richardson's[11] observation that 'a wise group will not rely on its ministry but will develop its own Brussels contacts'.

Few groups would now rely on a purely national strategy, even though many important decisions continue to be made by national governments. Most lobbyists recognise the need for a broader strategy, maintaining strong connections at the national and European level.

··········································································

### What you should have learnt from reading this chapter

* Many British pressure groups have lobbied the European Community/Union in recent years.

* The scale of lobbying has increased, an indication of the growth in importance which pressure groups have attached to the European machinery.

* As EU competences and the pace of integration were extended by the Single European Act and the Maastricht Treaty, so lobbying of European Union has intensified.

* Since the passage of the SEA, many decisions have been taken on the basis of qualified majority voting, making it necessary for groups to become more sophisticated in the access points they target.

* Broadly, as in all areas of pressure group activity, 'pressure-groups usually go where power goes'.[12]

### Glossary of key terms

**Co-decision**  A decision-making procedure written into the Maastricht Treaty (1991) and extended in the Amsterdam Treaty (1997) which has enabled Parliament to acquire greater powers. It has largely replaced the traditional co-operation procedure in most matters relating to the single market, allowing MEPs to share decision-making with the Council of Ministers.
**Democratic deficit**  The lack of democracy and accountability in the decision-making processes of the European Union and the obscurity and inaccessibility of its difficult legal texts. The Union is seeking to overcome these deficiencies via simpler legislation and better public information, and

by allowing organisations representing citizens a greater say in policy-making. But these do not address the demands of those who wish to see a more powerful Parliament and perhaps an elected Commission.

**Euro-groups** Federations of national pressure groups that represent sectoral interests within several, if not all, the member states of the European Union.

**European Community/Union** The European Economic Community was established by the Treaty of Rome in 1957. It was merged with two other organisations to become the European Community (EC) in 1967. Technically, it remained as the European Community until the implementation of the Maastricht Treaty in November 1993. This turned the EC into the European Union (EU).

**Fifth Enlargement** The most recent enlargement allowing for the entry of ten new states into the European Union, taking its membership from fifteen to twenty-five. In 2007, the Sixth Enlargement is due to provide for the admission of Bulgaria and Romania.

**Integration** The process of making a community into a whole by strengthening the bonds between its component parts. In this case, building unity between nations on the basis that they pool their resources and take many decisions jointly, thereby leading to a deepening of the ties that bind the European Union.

**Maastricht Treaty** The treaty on European Union negotiated and signed at Maastricht in December 1991, designed to achieve 'an ever closer union among the peoples of Europe where decisions are taken as closely as possible to the citizens'. It was particularly noted for its timetable for movement towards the adoption of a single currency, a common foreign and security policy, and co-operation in the areas of justice and home affairs within the European Union.

**Qualified majority voting (QMV)** The most widely adopted method of voting in the Council of Ministers, involving the according to each member state a 'weighting' very broadly reflecting its population.

**Single European Act (SEA)** An act which committed member states of the European Union to work towards the creation of a single market in 1992. This would be a fulfilment of the original concept of the European Community, that there should be a Common Market, a free-trade area without any restraints to trade. An aspect relevant to pressure groups was the agreement to allow qualifications attained in one country to be applicable elsewhere in the Community, a provision that made it possible for lawyers and other professionals to work in Europe.

**Single market** An 'area without frontiers' in which the 'free movement of goods, persons, services and capital' was ensured, as planned in the Single European Act 1986, for completion in 1992.

**Social Chapter** Originally known as the Social Charter, a programme to provide the European Community with a 'social dimension' via which workers' rights were secured. It became the Social Chapter at Maastricht, although Britain opted out from the relevant protocol. On coming to office, the Blair government quickly signed up to the document which became part of the Amsterdam Treaty of 1997. Among its provisions, directives have been concerned with the introduction of European works councils, parental leave and the rights of part-time workers.

## Likely examination questions

To what extent and why do British pressure groups now focus attention on the political institutions of the European Union?

In what ways has lobbying of the European Union by British pressure groups changed in recent years?

## Helpful websites

www.europa.eu.int The massive site of the European Union, providing basic information about the organisation, its institutions, policy areas, enlargement, etc.

www.europa.eu.int/comm/civilsociety/coneccs/index  The European Union's Directory of Special Interest Groups

www.cec.org.uk  The British office of the European Commission

www.europarl.en.int/uk  The British office of the European Parliament

www.rspca.org  The RSPCA

## Suggestions for further reading

*Articles*

W. Grant, Pressure groups and the EC, *Politics Review* 31, 1993.

D. Watts, 'Lobbying Europe: an Update', *Talking Politics*, September 2004.

*Books*

E. Bomberg and A. Stubb, *The European Union: How Does it Work?*, Oxford University Press, 2003.

A. Geddes, *The European Union and British Politics*, Palgrave, 2004.

J. Greenwood, *Interest Representation in the European Union*, Palgrave, 2003.

N. Nugent, *The Government and Politics of the European Union*, Palgrave, 2003.

## CHAPTER 8

# The Abolition of Hunting with Dogs: an English, Welsh and Scottish Case Study

## Contents

## Overview

The contentious issues of fox hunting and hunting with dogs in general have been much in the news over the last decade. North and south of the border group activists on either side of the dispute – those wanting a ban and those seeking to resist one – have been heavily involved in campaigning to achieve their goals. In Scotland (2002) and in England and Wales (2005), bans were finally achieved.

In this case study, we examine the ways in which lobbyists have been involved prior to the introduction of legislation, during its passage and after it became law.

## Key issues to be covered in this chapter

- The controversial nature of the issue
- The development of the campaign to abolish hunting with dogs in England and Wales
- The groups involved on either side
- The Countryside Alliance, its nature and approach
- The reasons for the success of the anti-hunting campaign
- The development of the campaign in Scotland
- How the issue of hunting was handled by the Scottish Parliament, its members and its committees
- Reflections on the campaigns north and south of the border

## Introduction

Hunting with dogs has been practised across rural Britain for many centuries. It involves the pursuit and usually killing of animals (deer, foxes, hares and mink) with one or more dogs frequently followed by riders on horseback. It is variously viewed as a recreational pastime, a method of pest control, or a cruel and inhuman sport. All forms of hunting are contentious, but fox hunting is the most divisive issue, one that attracts public and political attention.

Supporters of hunting see it as providing an essential service in rural communities. They see hunting as a component of rural culture and the rural economy. In the eyes of many farmers, huntspersons are welcome on their land because they help control pests. But not all farmers and not all people living in the countryside take this view. Neither do many people in the towns, particularly those concerned with animal welfare. They fail to see what sport is involved and point to the alleged cruelty of hunting with dogs. They also note the environmental damage that it can cause.

## The campaign to end hunting with dogs in England and Wales

Opponents of hunting are to be found mainly in Centre-Left political parties (although not all members of the Labour and Liberal Democrats are opposed to it, nor are all Conservatives in favour); in a range of pressure groups, some of which engage in direct action over the issue and – according to the opinion polls – among a substantial majority of the voters.

The setting of animal against animal for entertainment has for more than two centuries been a cause of parliamentary concern. Around that time, a bill to ban bull-baiting was passed by Parliament. Bans on cockfighting, dogfighting and badger-baiting were later enacted. Since World War II, MPs have focused their attention on ending the practice of hunting wild animals with dogs. For many years a variety of groups have existed to articulate their points of view. A bill to ban **hare coursing** was passed by the House of Commons in 1970 but it ran out of parliamentary time and so did not become law.

Much of the campaigning has been conducted peacefully, via traditional means of lobbying or non-violent protest. But in the 1960s and 1970s some activists began to employ forms of direct action. These 'hunt saboteurs' sought to disrupt hunts, their activities sometimes leading to violent clashes with hunters.

The issue of hunting became particularly high profile after 1997 because, with an overwhelming Labour majority in the House of Commons, there was at last the opportunity to achieve a ban on hunting with hounds. A number of private member's bills were unsuccessful. When ministers gave MPs a choice of options – a ban, stricter regulation or maintenance of the status quo – the initiative failed because of the irreconcilable differences between people on either side of the dispute and the differing views taken by members of the Lower House and Peers. (see below). Meanwhile, hunting with dogs was banned in Scotland by the Scottish Parliament.

In an attempt to resolve the issue, the government reintroduced a bill on hunting in 2004. It was rushed through the House of Commons in a day and then despatched to the Lords, with ministers warning that outright rejection would be met by the use of the **Parliament Act**. In November, the Parliament Act was invoked. After abortive challenges in High and Appeal Courts launched by the Countryside Alliance, the umbrella organisation that led the opposition to the ban, the ban came into force in mid-February 2005.

## Table 8.1  Time-line of the main initiatives in the attempts to ban hunting with dogs

| Date | Initiative |
|------|------------|
| 1949 | Two private member's bills to ban or restrict hunting fail. Labour government appoints committee to investigate all forms of hunting – it recommends the continuation of fox hunting as a means of controlling foxes without cruelty. |

## Table 8.1 (Continued)

| Date | Initiative |
|------|-----------|
| 1970 | Commons votes for legislation to ban hare coursing: bill runs out of time. |
| 1992 | Commons rejects private member's bill to ban hunting with dogs. |
| 1993 | Commons rejects Fox Hunting (Abolition) bill, introduced by Tony Banks (Labour), animal rights campaigner |
| 1995 | Lords rejects private member's bill to ban hunting with hounds. |
| 1997 May | New Labour government elected on promise to promote animal welfare and have a free vote on 'whether hunting with hounds should be banned'. |
| 1997 November | Labour MP Michael Foster publishes private member's bill to ban hunting with dogs, but government refuses to grant legislation any parliamentary time. Bill 'talked out' by opponents of ban in March. |
| 1998 March | Pro-hunting Countryside Alliance organises massive protest against Foster bill and threats to other aspects of the traditional rural way of life. At least 250,000 take part. |
| 1999 July | Tony Blair announces that he plans to make fox hunting illegal, preferably before the next election. |
| 1999 November | The government announces it will support a backbencher's bill on fox hunting. Home Secretary Jack Straw announces the **Burns Inquiry** into the effect of a fox-hunting ban on the countryside. |
| 2000 May | Labour MSP Mike Watson introduces bill to ban hunting with dogs in Scottish Parliament. |
| 2000 June | Burns Inquiry says some 6,000–8,000 jobs would go in the event of a ban, half the number usually suggested by the pro-hunt lobby. |

## Table 8.1  (Continued)

| Date | Initiative |
|---|---|
| 2001 February | MPs vote by a majority of 179 for an outright ban. Bill fails in the following month, in the Lords: runs out of time, as the election looms. |
| 2001 October | MPs in new Parliament urge ministers to make parliamentary time available for a vote on banning hunting. |
| 2002 February | Scottish Parliament bans hunting north of the border. |
| 2002 March | Ministers ask both Houses of Parliament to choose between three options: a complete ban, the preservation of the status quo and the compromise of licensed fox hunting. MPs vote for ban, peers opt for the so-called 'middle way'. |
| 2002 September | Countryside Alliance organises Liberty and Livelihood march through central London; 400,000 attend, the focus being on the likely ban on fox hunting although other rural issues are also publicised. |
| 2002 December | Hunting bill unveiled, allowing some fox hunting under strict licensing, and banning hare coursing and stag hunting: ministers hope that this compromise would avoid a prolonged Commons–Lords dispute. |
| 2003 June | Tony Banks MP proposes an amendment in favour of a complete ban: passed overwhelmingly. MPs vote in July to turn hunting bill into an outright ban on hunting with dogs. |
| 2003 October | Bill goes to Lords where peers reject the complete ban and opt for a licensing regime for all three forms of hunting. Anti-hunt MPs vote to reinstate the outright ban. Lords rejects the bill. |
| 2004 September | Ministers announce plans to give MPs a free vote on the hunting bill by the end of November. Vote for an outright |

| Table 8.1 (Continued) | |
| --- | --- |
| **Date** | **Initiative** |
| | ban, as protesters involved in violent demonstrations outside Parliament: pro-hunt demonstrators manage to break into Commons chamber. |
| 2004 November | After period of parliamentary ping-pong between the two houses, and a further Lords rejection, Speaker invokes Parliament Act. Bill due to become law in February 2005. |
| 2005 January | Pro-hunt campaigners lose a High Court challenge and a further appeal is rejected in mid-February when the judges reject the argument by the Countryside Alliance that the Hunting Act is unlawful. Meanwhile, act comes into effect on 18 February. |

## The pressure groups involved on either side of the dispute and the methods employed

Over the last ten years, as the prospect of a ban on hunting became an imminent possibility, pressure groups were involved on either side of the argument at every stage.

### The pro-abolition lobby

On the pro-abolition side, the key group was the umbrella organisation Campaigning to Protect Hunted Animals (Box 8.1 opposite) which acted on behalf of the International Fund for Animal Welfare (IFAW), the League Against Cruel Sports and the RSPCA. The coalition was formed to campaign for 'the end of the cruel, unnecessary sports of fox, deer, hare and mink hunting with dogs'.[1]

### The pro-hunting lobby

Ranged against the abolitionists was the Countryside Alliance, another umbrella group which was born out of pro-hunting bodies such as the now-defunct British Field Sports Society. Several other

## Box 8.1 Groups supporting the coalition to protect hunted animals

The International Fund for Animal Welfare is a leading international animal welfare organisation, with over two million supporters world-wide. It seeks to motivate the public to prevent cruelty to animals and to promote animal welfare and conservation policies. It works for the welfare of wild and domestic animals.

The RSPCA is the world's oldest and largest animal-welfare charity, its aim being to prevent cruelty and promote kindness to all animals. It campaigns in Britain and elsewhere to educate the public and to secure legislative changes that improve the welfare of all animals.

The League Against Cruel Sports combines campaigning with conservation. It was at the forefront of the campaign to ban hunting with dogs and liaised closely with politicians in pressing for govern-mental action. Enjoying cross-party support, the League backs up its campaigning work with a conservation programme.

organisations listed in the table below (see page 194) were prominent in the campaign.

The Countryside Alliance was formed in 1997 by a combination of interest groups committed to defence of the rural way of life. It comprised those who earned their living from the land and those who enjoyed country pursuits. The primary issue was fox hunting, although many inhabitants of rural areas were troubled by: the general decline in farming; grievances ranging from falling farm incomes and the handling of the BSE episode; the particular prob-lems of small holdings which found it increasingly difficult to compete in global markets despite the range of support and subsidies available from the European Union; the decline in public-transport provision in the countryside; high petrol prices; the closing of local branches of banks and building societies, hospitals, schools and post offices; plans to build houses on greenfield sites previously considered safe from development; the recently enacted right to roam legislation; and a range of other local issues. Here was ample cause of complaint, sufficient to inspire leaders of the Countryside Alliance who could rail against London-based politicians and members of New Labour who failed to understand the rural way of life.

The Alliance organised its first rally in 1998, a well-organised protest which gained massive support from rural Britain, well over 250,000 meeting to draw attention to their concerns and show how widespread and strong was the feeling in the countryside. The Countryside March, as it became known, shocked many politicians and Londoners with its scale and careful organisation. Four years later, some 400,000 attended a similar Liberty and Livelihood demonstration. Protesters stressed how the proposed ban showed a lack of understanding of rural issues; it was a threat to personal freedom, supporters of abolition showing intolerance of the rights of a minority to pursue their interests without interruption from the majority on whom it had little impact. Moreover, if enacted, it would imperil jobs for workers in allied occupations such as gamekeeping. This was an influential demonstration, illustrating as it did the strength of feeling in rural constituencies. A former Conservative media spokesperson[2] was quoted in a national newspaper as remarking: 'I don't think any political leader would ignore something like this. It's absolutely unprecedented . . . You'd ignore that kind of public outpouring at your peril.'

There was also a militant, extremist wing of the Alliance – completely disowned by the mainstream organisation – whose members called themselves the Real Countryside Alliance. A shadowy body, its members were balaclavas in a manner akin to past Northern Irish

## Table 8.2  Some organisations actively supporting the Countryside Alliance

The Association of Masters of Harriers and Beagles
The British Association for Shooting and Conservation
The British Field Sports Society
The British Society
The Clay Pigeon Association
The Country Land and Business Association
The Federation of Welsh Packs
The Masters of Basset Hounds
The National Coursing Club
The National Farmers Union
The Timber Growers' Association

terrorists, and anonymously threatened that they would 'hound to their graves' MPs and ministers who were campaigning for abolition. Supporters began a campaign of defacing buildings and signposts. They were especially keen to target pro-abolition MPs and undermine their chances of re-election.

## Campaign approaches

Lobbying was stepped up after the election of the Labour government in 1997, as campaigners sought to define the arguments in the politicians' and members of the public's minds. It intensified whenever a bill was produced. When abolition finally reached the statute book in early 2005, the Alliance was already involved in taking their case to the courts, a process that continued on various grounds, over several months and via appeals at every opportunity (see Box 8.2, on pages 196–7).

In both cases, lobbyists were active in targeting MPs, providing sympathetic members with material that they could use in parliamentary discussions. They were also keen to influence the public. The pro-abolitionists regularly commissioned opinion polls indicating the level of support they had. Pro-hunting campaigners in the Alliance were keen to demonstrate mass support by organising large demonstrations in the capital and smaller ones elsewhere.

Parliamentary lobbying was particularly relevant in the case of a piece of private member's legislation. The executive was less relevant although some individual ministers and the Prime Minister were seen as being open to persuasion. A feature of the parliamentary lobbying was the use made of the House of Lords. As we have seen in chapter 2, the second chamber has been an access point used by campaigners more frequently in recent years, as its effectiveness and reputation have increased. In this case, there was the real prospect of the various abolition bills being blocked by peers. Or again, they might be – and were – persuaded in large numbers that a 'third-way' solution based on licensing hunts was at the very least preferable to an outright ban.

Ministers involved in finding a solution that would finally resolve the thorny issue of abolition found themselves between two strong forces. Alun Michael was appointed as the junior minister in DEFRA after the 2001 election and given a special brief to develop policies for the regeneration of rural life. He and some others in the Labour Party were keen to find a middle way, a policy that had a natural compromise appeal as a means of taking the sting out of the campaigning on either side. In the ministerial bill introduced in December 2002 there was provision for local tribunals to adjudicate on whether in particular circumstances hunting provided a useful service to farmers and the countryside, outweighing considerations of animal suffering. From the ministerial point of view, the unfortunate fact was that it did not have strong support in the House of Commons and neither did it have much popular support. In the summer of 2003 Labour MPs rejected this preferred option on a free vote. The Lords rejected a ban and reinstated the government proposal for regulation.

Ministers – who had previously criticised the wrecking tactics of many Labour MPs – now accepted the overwhelming wish of the House of Commons and decided to invoke the Parliament Act. Their decision was an indication of the determination to settle the issue and end the town–country divisions with which it was associated. They argued that the attempt at abolition had had such a tortuous history and consumed so much parliamentary time that a decisive step was needed. As a result of this action, hare coursing, beagling, and fox, mink and stag hunting were banned in England and Wales.

## Box 8.2  The Countryside Alliance and the courts

**The challenge to the Parliament Act**
The Alliance went to court in December 2004 to challenge the legitimacy – indeed, the legality – of the 1949 Parliament Act which was being used by New Labour ministers to get the hunting ban on to the statute book. They claimed that the original 1911 Parliament Act conferred no power to amend that act by legislation passed under its terms. In other words, any amending measure should have been passed by Parliament in the usual way that a bill is passed (passage through the ten parliamentary stages in one session, prior to the Royal Assent) something that would probably not have happened as peers would have probably obstruct any further attempt to curtail their powers.

It was never likely that the case presented by the Alliance was going to be victorious, not least because it would have been no light matter for judges to set aside the provisions of an act that had already been used on three occasions to pass legislation through

Parliament. The case was lost in the High Court and the Court of Appeal and then went to the House of Lords where it was heard by nine instead of the usual five law lords, an indication of its significance. It was lost in the Lords, a verdict against which there was no further possible appeal.

### The challenge under human rights legislation and European Union law

A further challenge was mounted by the Alliance to challenge the Hunting Act's compatibility with the European Convention on Human Rights in the High Court. It was argued that a ban was incompatible with various Convention rights protected under the Human Rights Act of 1998, specifically: Article 8 (the right to private life); Article 11 (the right to freedom of assembly); Article 1, Protocol 1 (the right to peaceful enjoyment of possessions); and Article 14 (the right not to be discriminated against). At the same time as the Alliance challenge, a number of individuals used European law in the courts in a challenge to the Hunting Act. Two claimed that it was incompatible with the Human Rights Act and failed to comply with several British international treaty organisations. Others claimed that it interfered with the free movement of goods, the free movement of workers and the freedom to provide and to receive services, as guaranteed in the laws and treaties of the European Union.

The challenge under human rights legislation was lost in the High Court. Judges found that the ban was 'rational, necessary and proportionate', their conclusions being highly damaging to the case mounted by the Countryside Alliance.

As the three cases were lost in the High Court, they were then taken to the Court of Appeal with the ultimate option of an appeal to the House of Lords or even the European Court of Human Rights in Strasbourg. In June 2006 the Appeal Court rejected the challenge brought under Human Rights and European law, ruling that the ban was lawful and did not breach human rights, trade and employment laws.

The League Against Cruel Sports mounted a private prosecution against a huntsman of the Exmoor Foxhounds in August 2006, to test the exemption concerning **flushing** a fox to hounds. In the so-called Wright case, the District Judge – having viewed film of the relevant incident – decided that it was not exempt hunting.

The Hunting Act 2004 was a piece of primary legislation of the British Parliament. It operates on an England and Wales basis, the issues involved not having been devolved to Cardiff. The measure cannot be modified by the Welsh Assembly government or the National Assembly for Wales. Neither has any role in the implementation of the act, responsibility lying with DEFRA in London. If those working in the Welsh machinery wished to amend the legislation to suit Welsh conditions, they would need firstly to have the approval of the Westminster government and that is unlikely to be forthcoming in the near future. Accordingly, Welsh pressure groups have not been involved in discussions leading to the passage of the bill, lobbying being conducted by British groups.

### Why was the anti-hunting lobby victorious?

For a long time, the bulk of Labour MPs had wanted to see outright abolition and the landslide electoral victories of 1997 and 2001 made its introduction very likely. Whatever the anxieties and doubts of the Prime Minister over such a contentious move, he and other ministers wanted to resolve the issue once and for all. The government's willingness to apply the Parliament Act made any further opposition from the second chamber irrelevant. From a ministerial point of view, for an administration that had run into major difficulties over Iraq and tuition fees, the abolitionist position had some attraction. It might rally some of its disillusioned backbenchers who wondered what the point of a large majority was if ministers were unable to achieve a much-wanted reform. In the words of one opponent,[3] the government 'needed to throw them a bone to keep them happy'.

## The campaign to end hunting with dogs in Scotland

### Background

Hunting with dogs was well established in Scotland which had nine mounted packs, four hill packs and twenty-eight fox destruction clubs. Much of Scottish fox hunting was concentrated in the Borders, where the prospect of legislation ignited a fierce debate. Many of the leading hunt supporters were key figures in the Scottish Countryside Alliance.

Responsibility for legislation in the areas of land use and the environment transferred from Westminster to the Scottish Parliament on 1 August 1999. Labour MSP Mike Watson had already announced his intention to introduce a members bill in the new Parliament to ban hunting with dogs. The introduction of the bill was sponsored by the

Scottish Campaign Against Hunting with Dogs (SCAHD), a coalition of Advocates for Animals, the International Fund for Animal Welfare (IFAW) and the League Against Cruel Sports. SCAHD issued a press release in August 1999 stating the bills intentions:

The legislation would outlaw:

* Hunts, mounted or otherwise, which employ dogs to pursue, attack and kill wild mammals
* Hare coursing
* The use of terriers to attack wild animals underground.

The co-sponsor of the bill was Tricia Marwick (SNP), a choice made to indicate broad cross-party support for the proposal.

The Scottish Conservative and Unionist Party appointed Alex Ferguson MSP to establish a co-ordinated campaign of opposition to the planned Watson bill. Although Tory MSPs were given a free vote on the legislation, the appointment indicated a general lack of Conservative support for the measure.

By 2 September 1999, the proposal had secured the support of more than the eleven MSPs necessary before a members bill may be introduced under Rule 9:14 of the Standing Orders.

The legislation became law in February 2002 in the form of The Protection of Wild Mammals (Scotland) Act.

### Early support and consultation

The rigorous consultation required for the introduction of an executive bill – as described in chapter 6 – was not required for legislation planned by a private member. Watson did, however, secure the financial support of a charitable organisation, Advocates for Animals, to fund the bill's introduction. The organisation works with politicians to secure long-term changes to improve existing legislation and to introduce new laws to protect animals. In order to place animal protection issues high on the political agenda, Advocates lobbies the Scottish, British and European Parliaments.

Watson met a variety of groups, including the Scottish Countryside Alliance, the Scottish Hill Packs Association, the National Working Terrier Federation and the Scottish executive, to discuss the likely consequences of the legislation.

The views of the majority of Scots had already clearly emerged in a number of polls. Among several others it conducted, MORI had conducted a telephone poll of 1,000 Scots aged eighteen and over (June 1999) to ask their views on a ban on hunting with dogs. The percentage findings were:

Strong support 55
General support 19
Neither 9
General opposition 6
Strong opposition 4
Don't know/no opinion 6

Rounded up, 75 per cent of the public offered their support for a ban. MSPs were similarly polled by MORI in the same month. In response to the question 'If appropriately framed legislation to ban hunting wild animals with dogs were to come before the Scottish Parliament, would you be prepared to vote for it, or not?', the percentage responses were:

Would be prepared 71
Not prepared 15
Unsure 14

**Consultation during the legislative process**
The Watson bill was examined by two parliamentary committees. The Rural Affairs Committee had the lead role in taking evidence and scrutinising the legislation. But Parliament also invited the Justice and Home Affairs Committee to consider the bill because it would create a new criminal offence and therefore have implications for law enforcement.

The Rural Affairs Committee allowed four days for oral evidence on the bill. It had already opened consultation with twenty-three, organisations, resulting in the submission of more than 300 pages of evidence from twenty-two of them. It had also received more than 4,000 letters from members of the general public. Oral evidence was then heard from the Scottish Campaign Against Hunting with Dogs and a wide range of other organisations listed in the adjacent box.

The Justice and Home Affairs Committee took oral evidence from representatives of the Scottish Countryside Alliance, SCAHD, the

## Table 8.3  The twenty-two organisations that provided oral evidence to the Rural Affairs Committee on the Watson bill in Scotland

Advocates for Animals
Borders Foundation for Rural Sustainability
British Association for Shooting and Conservation
Countryside Alliance
Deer Commission for Scotland
Deerhound Club
Game Conservancy Trust
International Fund for Animal Welfare
League Against Cruel Sports
Macaulay Land Use Research Institute
National Farmers Union of Scotland
National Working Terrier Federation
Royal Society for the Protection of Birds
Scottish Agricultural Science Agency
Scottish Association for Country Sports
Scottish Campaign Against Hunting with Dogs (SCAHD)
Scottish Crofters Union
Scottish Executive Rural Affairs Department
Scottish Gamekeepers' Association
Scottish Hill Packs Association
Scottish Landowners Federation
Scottish Society for the Prevention of Cruelty to Animals (SSPCA)

Scottish Society for the Prevention of Cruelty to Animals (SSPCA), the Royal Society for the Prevention of Cruelty to Animals (RSPCA) and the Association of Chief Police Officers in Scotland (ACPOS). It received written submissions from the Law Society of Scotland and the Scottish Gamekeepers' Association, and took sight of the relevant written evidence submitted to the Rural Affairs Committee.

### The aftermath

Pressure groups have been monitoring the 2002 legislation since its introduction to see how it works in practice. Pro-hunt groups are keen to argue that it is 'business as usual' for hunts in Scotland, whereas monitors of the anti-hunt organisations claim to have detected little or no activity for much of the time. In their view, huntspersons saddle up as soon as cameras or journalists are in the vicinity.

SCAHD has uncovered breaches of the act and has made complaints to the police about the behaviour of members of some hunts. Whereas some hunters are willing and eager to use the courts to test any loopholes in the law, SCAHD is keen to see that the judicial system ensures that its provisions are fully obeyed. On its own, Advocates for Animals continues to monitor the effectiveness of abolition, though intermittently rather than continuously. It has some fears about inadequate enforcement.

Some anti-abolition organisations have similarly maintained a watchful eye on what is happening. The Scottish Rural Property and Business Association[4] 'monitors at a low level and will give support to Scottish Countryside Alliance which is a single issue organisation with substantial resources behind it, on particular challenges or issues as they arise'.

## Conclusion

The issue of whether hunting should or should not be legal has been a bitterly contentious one for many years. It is an interesting one in its own right for the arguments involve sharply contrasting attitudes about what is acceptable in a civilised society; a clash between town and countryside; and a division between the attitudes of modernising New Labour ministers and the forces representing the traditional activities of rural Britain.

Fox hunting is also an interesting issue in discussion of pressure groups. The number and nature of the groups involved on either side of the campaign in north and south of the border and their organisation into broad umbrella movements illustrate how an effective campaign can be waged; the range of targets they accessed shows how groups can concurrently operate at different levels as they seek to create backing for their cause; and the outcome indicates some of the reasons why groups can achieve success.

The phenomenon of the Countryside Alliance and its mass demonstrations is particularly interesting as an example of the politics of populist pressure that have become more widespread in recent years. It provides a striking example of the new style of mass political participation that has come to bypass political parties and instead mobilise young and old to take part in a major protest. Like other eruptions of popular feeling, such as those of the fuel protesters and the anti-handgun campaign, the Alliance:

- emerged suddenly, creating what McNaughton[5] has called 'a forest fire of passion' about the issues involved;
- was able both to create and to articulate a widespread emotional response, helped in this by the coverage in newspapers and the images they carried of huge demonstrations;
- used conventional lobbying, such as participation in public inquiries and contact with members of the lower house and peers, to make its point but,
- supplemented the above forms with direct action to make a striking impact, the television scenes of vast numbers of voters expressing their discontent being used to place pressure on ministers to listen to their demands;
- succeeded in turning their own interest and preferences into a popular cause.

Yet the Alliance campaign was not victorious. If it was successful in generating publicity and mobilising support in some sections of the community, it failed to shift public opinion on the issue. Urban Britain remained unconvinced. The Centre-Left parliamentarians who represented its inhabitants and were dominant in the House of Commons were determined to see fox hunting abolished. If the groups campaigning on their side made less impact in popular debate, it was because they were articulating views that already had widespread popular support. To some extent, their job had already been done.

The issue of hunting continues to make the news from time to time, particularly on Boxing Day, the traditional day on which hunters pursue their interest. Supporters have been pleased that hunts have not been disbanded and hunting with dogs continues, even if they are not allowed to pursue foxes to their death. Members of anti-hunting organisations claim that much of the cruelty of hunting has been removed, while maintaining vigilance over any alleged breaches of the law. For pressure groups, lobbying for their respective viewpoints is but one part of their activities. When legislative changes are made, monitoring of the implementation of the law becomes the new priority.

## ✓ What you should have learnt from reading this chapter

- Hunting with dogs and in particular, fox hunting have been contentious issues for many years.

- Numerous attempts have been made in Parliament to abolish such field 'sports'.

- In England, Scotland and Wales, the legislation that brought about the ending of fox hunting was introduced by private members.

- MSPs and MPs were the focuses of detailed lobbying by a variety of groups.

- In Scotland, the parliamentary process involved extensive consultation with the many groups on either side of the debate.

- In England and Wales, the campaigns for and against abolition were fought via broad umbrella organisations of interested groups.

- In both cases, the weight of parliamentary and public opinion in favour of abolition proved to be overwhelming.

## 🔎 Glossary of key terms

**Burns Inquiry** Established by Labour ministers in 1999 to investigate the differing aspects of hunting with dogs, the implications of a ban and how any ban might be implemented, the inquiry, headed by Lord Burns, reported in 2000. The report was seized upon by campaigners from both sides who claimed it validated their arguments. It had something for everyone, in that: it concluded that hunting 'seriously compromised the welfare of the fox'; accepted that other methods of control could be considered equally cruel; agreed that hunting contributed to the cohesion of rural communities; estimated that around seven hundred jobs were directly tied to hunting, with some 6,000 to 8,000 more dependent on it; felt the effects of a ban were 'unlikely to be substantial and would be dissipated within a decade'; but accepted that the short-term effects would be more serious.

**Flushing** Traditionally, in some uplands areas, foxes were flushed by packs of dogs to be shot, a practice still permitted under Scottish law. Schedule 1 of the 2004 Hunting Act produced a tight curb on such flushing, not least because it is difficult to control a large number of hounds in dense woodland of the type where it had previously taken place. A restriction to two dogs was written into the Act to ensure that foxes were flushed to be shot rather than being chased. In the Wright case, the judge questioned 'whether it could ever be possible, save in some limited areas of woodland or similar cover, to utilise the exemption with foxhounds'.

**Hare coursing**  A 'sport' in which hounds are matched against one another in pairs for the hunting by sight of hares.

**Parliament Act**  A measure passed in 1911 which removed the permanent veto power of the House of Lords. Peers would in future be able to delay any other bill for only two years, after which it automatically became law. In 1949, the post-1945 Labour administration further reduced this delaying power to one year.

## Likely examination questions

What does the campaign to abolish hunting with dogs in England, Scotland and Wales tell us about the organisation and operation of pressure groups in Britain today?

## Helpful websites

www.scotland.gov.uk/Consultations/Archive  The devolved institutions in Scotland contain useful material

www.scottishparliament.uk/business/research/date/2000

www.huntinginquiry.gov.uk/  The Burns Inquiry

*Pro-abolition*

www.banhunting.com  Campaigning to Protect Hunted Animals

www.ifaw.org  IFAW

www.league.uk.com  League Against Cruel Sports

www.respca.org  RSPCA

www.advocatesforanimals.org.uk  Advocates for Animals

*Pro-hunting*

www.basc.org.uk/ The British Association for Shooting and Conservation

www.countryside-alliance.org The Countryside Alliance

www.cla.org.uk The Country Landowners Association (Country Land and Business Association)

www.nfu.org.uk The National Farmers Union

www.scottishgamekeepers.co.uk The Scottish Gamekeepers' Association

## Suggestions for further reading

As yet, no studies have appeared on the campaigning for and passage of this legislation.

## CHAPTER 9

# Pressure Groups and Democracy

## Contents

## Overview

As we have seen in the Introduction, there are different schools of thought on the role of pressure groups in a democracy. For some, they are both inevitable and desirable in a pluralist society. For others, they distort the democratic process.

In this chapter, we examine the merits and demerits of group activity, in order to reach some conclusions about the ways in which groups contribute to or undermine democracy in Britain and elsewhere.

## Key issues to be covered in this chapter

- The problem of reaching any assessment of the merits or otherwise of group activity
- The case against group activity
- The case for group activity
- Recognition of the inevitability of pressure-group lobbying
- The conflicting outlook of writers upon the value of pressure groups in a democracy

## Assessing group activity

The difficulty in assessing the role of pressure groups in the democratic process derives from their multiplicity and diversity. We are dealing with thousands of organisations whose aims, composition and methods vary significantly. Some may be guilty of the charges often laid against group activity, others not. Some may serve the public good for much of the time, others have only a marginal benefit. Moreover, it is important to remember that pressure groups are social organisations and, unlike political parties, they do not engage in continuous political activity. For some of them, their creation has little or nothing to do with political attitudes and only intermittently do they interact with the political process. In the light of these substantial differences, we can only make generalised comments that do not apply to all groups in all circumstances.

### A matter of balance

In any democracy, groups have rights to freedoms of speech, assembly and association, as long as these are pursued peacefully and in a way that does not harm other people. They have a right to express their opinions, to be heard and to try to influence those policy-makers who make decisions affecting their interests. They are, therefore, an inevitable and indispensable feature of pluralist democracies where political decisions are the outcome of the competition and conflict between groups. But, if they are undemocratic in their internal arrangements, become too powerful and 'capture' and control government policy to their own advantage, they may be seen as threatening to democratic values. Governments ought to be willing to listen to those who represent group demands and ideas and express them in a reasonable manner, but should only make decisions which are in the overall public interest.

What is needed is a balance of power. Too little group power poses the threat of government behaving high handedly and ignoring people's legitimate needs and preferences. Excessive group power creates the possibility of organised interests foisting their particular views upon those ministers who are elected to carry out public policy in a way which is as fair as possible to all sections of the community. Opinions differ on exactly where one draws the line between excessive and reasonable influence.

## The case against pressure groups: how they undermine democracy

There are several allegations made against pressure groups in Britain and other democracies. They are sectional in outlook; the better resourced and organised are at an advantage over those lacking such assets: some groups have unrepresentative leadership; some use methods that threaten the rest of society; much lobbying is done behind closed doors; and finally groups slow down the process of policy-formation and thwart necessary social progress.

### A sectional interest

By definition, a pressure group represents the viewpoint of a number of broadly like-minded citizens in society. That is why it is established. In other words, it is a sectional interest; the NFU represents farmers, the NUT teachers. But governments have to govern in the 'national interest', and consider the views/needs of all sections of the community, not the voice of the powerful only. Thus, the TUC still represents a substantial proportion of working people but by no means all workers; the union voice on pay may be strong but it is consumers who may have to finance inflationary pay awards by spending more for the goods and services they purchase.

The criticism goes further than stating that groups have a sectional interest. They are alleged also to be self-interested, as indeed protective groups are; they exist to defend the interests of their members. They would also argue, however, that in protecting the interests of those who work in their sector, they also serve the general good. Contented teachers and doctors are necessary to provide effective services in education and health. Moreover, they engage in campaigning activities designed to promote a better quality of provision, arguing for more governmental commitment and funding, and contributing their views on the preferred ways of operating the services in which they are involved. The sectional interests they represent may, in this way, be of value to the whole community.

There is a danger that, in consulting on a regular basis with representatives of certain groups, ministers and officials may find themselves sympathetic to the group's attitudes. But governments, and those who aspire to form them, are aware of the dangers of being captured by special interests and of the need to articulate the general interest, hence, the Blair observation of 'no special favours' to trade unions. It limits the appeal of any party if it is seen to be the prisoner of a particular interest. Especially in the 'corporatist' 1960s and 1970s, and arguably through until the 1990s, Labour was damaged by the perception that it was 'too close to the unions'. The age of corporatism has passed away in Britain, and with it some of the opportunities for behind-the-scenes secret understandings, pacts and deals. Some groups have been forced into more open methods of campaigning.

Faced by such an answer, the critic of groups may move on to a second argument, that some are richer or better organised than others, putting certain sections of the community at a disadvantage.

**The better resourced and organised are at an advantage**
This is a frequent criticism, that not all sections of the community are equally capable of exerting influence. In other words, 'God is on the side of the big battalions' and might is right. As a generalisation, protective groups are stronger than promotional ones, insider groups at an advantage over outsider ones. Business and professional groups have better resources and access than do welfare ones. Those that can present a strong case are at an advantage over those with less funds.

There is a danger that ministers may be prepared to accept too uncritically the advice of a powerful interest group. They may accede to the requests of those groups that can afford to present their case most effectively, even if there are substantial objections to what they propose. Among protective groups, the voices that are less frequently heard in Whitehall are those of taxpayers and consumers. Both are difficult to organise, other than via the ballot box, for they are diffused throughout society. They are not a homogeneous group anyway, some having leanings to the Right, others to the Left and many more having no obvious political affiliation at all. Their voice is heard less frequently in Whitehall whereas the producer groups, the unions and the industrialists in particular, have easier access.

But there is no necessary correlation between wealth and resources and the amount of publicity a group receives or the reception its representatives get in Whitehall. Moreover, any government which was not susceptible to consumer pressure would be jeopardising its chances of re-election and, in recent years, their voice has been listened to more, and with greater attention, and treated with greater consideration.

## Unrepresentative leadership

Groups are often oligarchic in tendency. Most are dominated by a handful of leaders who, to a large extent, determine the attitudes and behaviour of the organisation. They may achieve domination because of their experience and long-standing involvement, many members not having the time or the inclination to be so actively involved. Many groups do not have sophisticated systems of election that link the leadership of a group with its membership. In cases where they do have such internal democracy, it may be the case that the proportion that exercises the right to vote is very small, as is often true of trade-union elections.

The leaders of some groups are unrepresentative and may, on occasion, misrepresent the views of the supporters so that the opinions expressed and the demands made may not fully reflect the inclinations of the membership. This was the case with a number of unions before the Thatcherite changes in the law on industrial relations forced them to hold elections for the post of general secretary. It is important that any government knows that the people it talks to do genuinely reflect their members' wishes, and that deals made with leaders will stick because they have the backing of group supporters.

It is true that the leadership of some organisations may tend to act in a dominant, even an autocratic, way. It is true of parties as well as pressure groups. In the case of groups, it is difficult to see how the oligarchical tendency can be reversed other than by encouraging all who have the opportunity to be as actively committed as possible. In the case of organisations, such as unions, it is possible to legislate for periodic elections, as has been done. Governments would prefer to speak with those who are representative of the membership and, indeed, of any in the same line who do not belong to the organisation. They want to please as many people as possible. If government departments are uneasy about the views being expressed, they are free to seek out a range of other viewpoints as well.

In the case of some groups – such as NIMBY groups seeking to stave off some unwanted development – the tendency for certain domineering personalities to take over and impose a sense of direction is largely inevitable. There is no answer to the danger of leaderships being unrepresentative other than for members to be active in seizing opportunities to express their own views, and those who take account of a group's position at least to be aware of the danger and to recognise that it may be worth consulting others before making their decision.

Of course, it would be possible to legislate to ensure that all pressure groups operate in a democratic manner, perhaps requiring that all officers must be elected each year either by postal vote or at an annual general meeting. But to do so would involve governmental interference in the internal affairs of voluntary organisations.

Finally, it should be remembered that, with regard to some of our most well-known and influential pressure groups, their leadership is representative. Governments do know that, in speaking with the leaders of the BMA or the NFU, they are receiving the views of the memberships of those organisations. Moreover, they are dealing with groups that dominate the fields in which they operate, so that the BMA speaks not only for those doctors who belong to it but for almost all doctors.

**Threatening methods**
The very word pressure conjures up an image of intimidation and coercion which is why some NGOs, in particular, are unhappy with the nomenclature. The anxiety about undue pressure has usually been related to the activities of trade unions, however, particularly in the days when strikes were more prevalent than they have been over the last two decades. Certain categories of workers have the capacity to 'hold the country to ransom' for, by exercising their right to withdraw their labour, they impose difficulties on everyone else. In crucial areas of the economy, withdrawal of labour may be very disruptive to productivity and the provision of services. In the public sector, a threat by doctors to withdraw from the National Health Service or by nurses to go on strike may lead to serious consequences, at worst death, for those who are sick at home or in hospital. Similarly, any failure to attend calls by members of the fire service could have appalling repercussions.

Trade-union use of strikes as a form of pressure is a long standing form of direct action. We have seen in chapter 5 that the use of other forms of direct action has mushroomed in recent years. Some are legal but the actions may cause inconvenience to others. Some may be not only illegal but also violent and get out of hand. The right to make a protest, particularly when other forms of contact are yielding no adequate results, is a fundamental one in any democracy. In most cases, sensitive policing and co-operation by the key players involved can ensure that the exercise of free speech and the right to demonstrate is not incompatible with the right of those with an alternative view or approach to go about their own lives without undue disruption.

The alleged disruption and harm to the economy and society may seem less of a danger today than at times in the past. But whenever there is a flexing of muscles by aggrieved workers (as in the dispute concerning the firefighters, 2002), the charge of endangering the lives or livelihoods of others, is repeated.

Of course, the groups involved, mainly unions, disclaim any intention of threatening the rest of society, and their spokespersons repeat the line that they are merely protecting the interests of their members who have suffered grave disadvantages in recent years. But it remains the fact that strikes by workers in key services either do put others at risk or else exercise such leverage that ministers are under great pressure to yield to their demands.

In recent years, governments have not tended to back down in the face of strike action by workers. If necessary, they can usually operate an emergency service (as in the fire dispute when the old-fashioned 'green goddess' fire appliances were brought back into action). On occasion, the union involved allows some of its members to operate a very basic service.

### Secrecy, lobbying behind closed doors

Some people worry about the secrecy under which bargains between powerful interest groups and Whitehall departments are made. This was the theme of Samuel Finer's[1] study, *The Anonymous Empire*. He pointed to the way in which much lobbying was conducted in Whitehall, emphasising that there was a closed relationship between group representatives and senior civil servants and ministers in Whitehall. The details of what was discussed were not examinable. Parliament, the media, parties, other pressure groups and other representatives of the public were excluded. He concluded his analysis with a plea for 'Light, More Light'.

Many of the most successful examples of lobbying do involve private negotiations and these may arouse suspicion of the motives of those involved. Secrecy may provide a cover for unpopular actions and policies, decided without being subject to wider public scrutiny. It may conceal manipulation of those who make decisions by interested parties or be used to mask inefficiency. It denies the public the chance to be fully informed of the motivations for certain policies and of the groups who are exercising influence. Such ignorance is said to be detrimental in an open society.

Other critics have expressed the fear that too many MPs are beholden to outside groups and business commitments; such anxieties fuelled the desire for a register of MPs' interests [*Register of Members' Interests*], as established in 1975. They resurfaced in the 1990s, when the growing use of professional lobbying provided opportunities for MPs to act as paid consultants. As a result of the '**cash for questions**' allegations, that register was monitored more closely and new means were introduced to ensure that people could be reassured that MPs were not operating in a way that endangered the public interest. The taint of corruption has at least been mitigated by the new emphasis on standards which ensures that members do not have a conflict of interests because of their over-familiarity with outside interests. Media and public vigilance and scrutiny, assisted by new freedom-of-information legislation, are the antidote to secret deals and excessive scrutiny.

Some of the abuses outlined have been tackled, but the concern remains that those groups with access to the corridors of power in Whitehall – Grant's[2] insider groups – are still able to exercise a stronger influence than others in society. The groups involved, however, can hardly be blamed for employing the methods that best suit their requirements and enable them to reach accommodation with government. They are inevitably attracted to the locations where power resides and, in a centralised country such as Britain, this is in Whitehall. As we have already seen in chapter 2, government departments encourage such contacts for it brings them several benefits. The officials who work in them probably prefer to operate under conditions of secrecy for they are supposed to be anonymous in the performance of their tasks. In any case, if the discussions were more transparent and open to the public gaze, many people would be uninterested in – indeed, probably apathetic towards – the highly technical and detailed information under consideration.

## Slowing down the work of decision-making and acting as a barrier to social progress

As we saw in chapter 4, governments can be highly critical of group activity, particularly when relevant groups are finding out and publicising information and expressing attitudes that are critical of ministerial claims. As former Home Secretary, David Blunkett, and his successor, Charles Clarke, sometimes found, the civil-liberties lobby could be a thorn in their flesh as they tried to introduce legislation on asylum seekers and the prevention of terrorism. As we have seen, one of their predecessors[3] found them to be 'strangling serpents' that slowed down and distorted the work of government. Each of these home secretaries was convinced that the policies upon which they had embarked were necessary for the protection of society. They regarded many of their group opponents as being out of touch with the real concerns of members of the public about the abuses associated with asylum seeking and the dangers to security in an age of terrorism.

As Baggott[4] points out, according to this view 'groups tend to oppose developments such as new roads, industrial installations and power plants, even though these are in the broader public interest'. In the same way, professional groups and trade unions are portrayed as impeding the introduction of necessary changes in working practices. Sometimes, groups needlessly fuel public alarm. The criticism was expressed in strong terms by Michael Dobbs in *The Times*[5] a few years ago: 'Militant pressure groups . . . rush to judgement exaggerating their case and in expressing themselves in simplistic terms designed for easy headlines, they undermine both balanced decision-making and Parliamentary democracy.' In July 2006, Prime Minister Blair noted that NGOs and groups with single causes can be benevolent, but can also exercise a kind of malign tyranny over the public debate on much-needed policy changes.[6]

Governments stand above pressure groups. They are uniquely authorised by the voters and are accountable to Parliament and to the people for their actions. The fact is that prime ministers and their colleagues are aware of their responsibilities to listen to all views. In recent decades, it has made them wary of entrenched interests. For Margaret Thatcher, it may have been organised labour that was the target of much of her criticism of group activity but industrialists in the CBI also found that their voice was not always heeded as once it had been and that their influence had diminished. Her successors have been unwilling to reverse her stand, and ministers have been critical of groups. They acknowledge their rights to be heard and to try to influence public policy. But they are vocal in pointing out that their voices are not those of the majority and that they are often narrowly self-interested players who have no right to receive particular access or privileges.

## The case for pressure groups: how they sustain and enhance democracy

Those who take a positive view of pressure-group activity feel that: they enhance our democracy and have an important role in the political process; suggest that they represent the right of like-minded individuals to band together to make their voice heard; widen participation in public life and the decision-making process, allowing for continuity of representation between elections; act as a link between the people and the government, a useful intermediary between the electors and those whom they elect, allowing a variety of views to be expressed; provide specialised, often technical, information useful to those charged with making decisions on matters of public policy and assist them in the implementation of policy; and help to hold the government to account, providing an important check against over-mighty executives and legislatures.

### The right of individuals to band together to express their views

The existence of groups allows individuals to associate with one another and proclaim their views, essential rights in any democracy. They provide a safety valve enabling any person with a grievance to feel that he or she is able to vent their disenchantment. They act as a defence for minority interests, especially those connected with parties not in government. This function is particularly important in the case of ethnic and gender minorities and other disadvantaged groups. It allows them to express their distinctive points of view, providing an opportunity to express any resentment about their treatments, and to outline any ideas that would help overcome obstacles that prevent them from fulfilling their potential.

Of course, not all communities are as well organised as others. Certain minorities may feel that their cause is neglected in some larger organisations. Even if views can be expressed, it is no guarantee that they will be taken seriously and acted upon by those with the power of decision.

### Encouragement to wider participation in public life and the decision-making process

Pressure groups allow participation in decision-making by ordinary individuals. Many people participate directly in political life only at election time but elections are held only every four or five years and do not allow voters to express a preference on individual issues. People can play a part in, and make a contribution to, the workings of democracy however, by joining groups which can influence the decisions of public bodies. To those who favour a more participatory form of democracy, this is a significant virtue. Certainly far more people belong to a pressure group – sometimes to two or three – than belong to a political party. Members receive the benefits of honing their political skills and making new contacts (networking) as well as enjoying the fellowship of people who share their visions and goals for society.

Furthermore, groups provide an outlet for political recruitment. In chapter 2, we have noted the overlap between politicians of the Centre-Left and active involvement in campaigning activity, particularly in the civil rights and social arenas. Many a political career was launched via prominence in group activity.

It is easy to overstate popular involvement in groups, however. Politics is a voluntary activity, of course, and many people are uninterested in becoming involved in political action. They have no wish to participate, in some cases not even at election time let alone via other forms. Many voters are content to let others, whose broad approach they support, make the decisions.

Many who do join have no desire to play an active role and often see their membership of organisations, such as FoE and Greenpeace, as short term – hence their high turnover in membership. They join without anticipating playing a regular part and limit their involvement to signing the occasional petition or joining a march. For many, writing out their cheque or giving their credit card number is the limit of their participation.

## A link between the people and those who govern them

Groups provide an outlet for people with little interest in party politics who may find themselves galvanised into action over an issue that is of direct concern to them. Sometimes, traditional party attitudes seem irrelevant to their concerns whereas, via group activity, they feel that they have a chance to realise their goals.

Groups therefore counter the monopoly of the political process by political parties. Sometimes, they raise items for discussion which fall outside the realm of party ideas and policy and which do not tend to get in to the manifestos. They made the running in the 'green' arena before the parties took up ecological issues. As part of the two-way link, they inform government of how members feel and they help to inform their members about governmental attitudes and the difficulties involved in making and carrying out policy.

Baggott[7] has summarised their value effectively: 'The views which pressure groups convey are legitimate interests . . . Modern democracy would not exist without pressure groups. As a channel of representation, they are as legitimate as the ballot box . . . They can mediate between the government and the governed.'

## The provision of specialist information to government and help in the implementation of policy

In formulating, legislating on and implementing policies, governments need information. Groups provide valuable and continuous information to government departments, based upon their specialist knowledge and understanding of their field. In some cases, this is backed by co-operation in administering a particular policy and monitoring its effectiveness. They are indispensable to governmental decision-making because they are available for regular consultation. Indeed, this may be on a very frequent basis, there being continuing dialogue between a government department and a key interest group such as the CBI or the BMA. As we have seen, the government knows that a group of this type represents the bulk of people in that particular sector. Most farmers are in the NFU and therefore its voice is representative.

It is not just via dialogue with ministers and officials that information can be conveyed. Governments create an array of consultative committees, working parties, advisory groups and commissions and, through their involvement in these bodies, group representatives can offer advice and technical information and assistance.

### A valuable check upon those who exercise political power

Groups can help keep a government in check. In Des Wilson's[8] words, they 'improve the surveillance of government', helping to expose information that would otherwise remain secret. Even governments with a large majority, as in 1997 and 2001, can be vulnerable to the probing activities of lobbyists who publicise/leak information and highlight governmental lapses or attempted cover-ups. Groups function as a check upon their intentions and actions. Also, when government seems to be resistant to popular demands, activists can resort to direct action to ensure that their views are taken into account. In the words of one campaigner:[9] 'I was one of those imprisoned for protesting at Twyford Down. Sometimes, when the shady avenues of bureaucracy have been exhausted, there is no choice but to throw yourself in front of the digger.'

The counter-argument, of course, is that group involvement cannot only slow down the process of government but make it more difficult to make decisions. They encourage a questioning approach, use information selectively and play down the difficulties inherent in decision-making. In emphasising the civil-libertarian concerns involved in legislating on asylum seeking or terrorism, the effect could be to make any worthwhile, effective legislation more difficult to devise and implement.

## Conclusion

From the above review, it is easy to assume that the dangers of group activity are mainly associated with the activities of powerful protective groups that have special access to government. By contrast, promotional groups are seen as advancing worthy causes, acting in a

## Table 9.1 Pressure groups for and against: a summary

| Pressure groups are a threat to democracy | Pressure groups benefit our democracy |
| --- | --- |
| Groups represent the sectional interest of their own members, but governments have to consider the needs of the whole electorate. | The existence of a wide range of groups is a fundamental precondition for democracy, allowing as they do individuals to associate in order to express their opinions. |
| Organisations that are better resourced and organised possess an advantage over those less resourced and organised, including consumers, ethnic minorities and women. | Groups encourage wider participation in public life and in the decision-making process in the period between elections. |
| Too many vested sectional interests negotiate policies in secret and impose their views which may be contrary to the public interest. Indeed, governments can be 'captured' by special interests. | Groups are a useful channel of communication between the government and the governed, allowing views to be passed in either direction. |
| Groups slow down the work of decision-making and make the work of government more difficult, especially if many groups wish to be consulted and/or where the protection of individual rights is concerned (e.g. anti-terrorism legislation). | Groups assist the process of government by participating in consultative exercises, providing specialist information, helping in the implementation of policy and keeping issues on the political agenda. |
| In some cases, groups employ threatening methods in order to coerce government and the public into acceptance of their viewpoint. | The existence of groups serves to disperse political power and act as a counterweight to any excessive concentration of it in too few hands. In other words, they are a check upon those who hold ministerial office. |

noble and public-spirited way. In his study of campaigning methods, Wilson[10] who has represented many causes in a high-profile way, (Shelter, lead-free petrol, freedom of information, among them) was critical of 'vested interests, whose cause is usually maintenance of the status quo irrespective of the implications for the community'.

There is a danger in viewing groups in this way. There is no harm in groups looking after the interests of their members. In some cases, sectional interests will coincide with the public good however that term is defined. Moreover, we have seen that protective groups can also do valuable campaigning work. Such groups have a right to be heard. Similarly, because promotional groups are not self-interested, this does not make them morally superior. Indeed, some of the causes they espouse are highly contentious, not least on issues such as abortion, euthanasia and other right-to-life issues. Moreover, it is the activists of campaigning groups who sometimes use methods that can frustrate progress or spill over into violence. Yet again, whatever their outlook, they, too, have a right to get their message across and to seek to influence public policy.

Group activity is a feature of every democracy and, indeed, of many authoritarian states as well. Groups are an inevitable feature of a free society so that the issue of their desirability or otherwise is in a sense irrelevant. They have a very long history; they exist today and will continue to do so into the foreseeable future. They are an established and visible part of our democracy. They have many opportunities to influence policy and, although some have greater access to those with the power of decision than others, nonetheless the situation is not a fixed and immutable one. Group influence waxes and wanes, new groups come along, established ones may lose some of their former influence. The world of pressure-group influence is a fluid one, and governments in recent years have shown a greater willingness to consult widely with those representing a wider range of viewpoints than ever before.

The work of pressure groups is pervasive in established democracies. Their existence is testimony to human kind's natural associative tendency. By joining them, many people acquire a sense of belonging and of community. For minorities, in particular, they are an effective way of organising and protecting their interests. But, as we have seen, their activities raise issues about the distribution of power and influence in society.

For critics, the world of group interests is at best an impediment to, at worst almost a corruption of, democratic government. The late Hugo Young[11] portrayed the admittedly seductive appeal of the single-issue campaigner as a 'failure not a triumph of democracy'. Journalist Melanie Phillips[12] recognises that 'the formidable specialist expertise of many lobbyists makes them an invaluable resource for a generalist civil service', but goes on to say that this has sometimes made them 'become their captive . . . Vested interests – farmers, teachers, police officers, whoever – are locked in fatal embrace with Whitehall, corrupting the process of disinterested government.'

For supporters, groups are an emblem and bastion of a healthy society. They represent the fundamental right of freedom of expression, allowing people to organise with other like-minded individuals so that their views can be heard by others and taken into account by those with the power of decision. As such, in Wilson's[13] words, they 'are not a threat to a genuine democracy, but a real contributor'. For Finer[14], lobbying 'embodies two basic democratic procedures: the right to participate in policymaking and the right to demand redress of grievances'.

Groups flourish in liberal democracies, performing essential functions of aggregating and articulating public opinion. But they do also exist elsewhere. In some parts of central and eastern Europe, environmental, gender and peace groups had already developed prior to the ending of Communist rule. In the case of Solidarity, the trade union organisation in Poland supported by the Roman Catholic Church, it actually played a role in bringing about the removal of the regime. Since the break-up of the Soviet system in that region, they have become a feature of life in the 'new democracies' created after the overthrow of authoritarian rule. By contrast, the role of groups in existing dictatorships is very different, for rulers continue to see opposition as a threat to their own power and seek to clamp down on any organised focuses of opposition.

. . . . . . . . . . . . . . . . . . . . . . . . . . . . . . . . . . . . . . . . . . . . . . . . . . . . . . . . . . . .

## What you should have learnt from reading this chapter

- It is difficult to reach a conclusion about the merits or demerits of groups that applies to their many diverse forms.

- The value of pressure-group activity is much debated.

- Views vary from the highly positive to the deeply negative about the contribution made by groups to our democracy.

- Groups are an inevitable feature of a democratic country, their existence distinguishing free countries from those that seek to clamp down on the right of association.

## Glossary of key terms

**Cash for questions**  A reference to the allegation in *The Guardian* that, in the 1990s, ex-Conservative minister, Neil Hamilton MP, had received cash for asking parliamentary questions on behalf of Harrods owner Mohamed Al Fayed. In a report published soon after the 1997 election, the first Parliamentary Commissioner for Standards, Sir Gordon Downey, concluded that there was 'compelling' evidence that up to £25,000 had been received by the MP.

## Likely examination questions

'Pressure groups are undemocratic and therefore bad for democracy.' Discuss

In what ways do pressure groups (a) undermine and (b) advance democracy?

Discuss the view that, far from being suppressed, the pressure-group system should be extended to cover all possible interests, even those which are currently not well organised.

Discuss the view that governments should not allow themselves to become too dependent on pressure groups.

Comment on the view that pressure groups are indispensable to the efficient running of the modern state.

## Helpful websites

There is nothing additional to the sites already referred to earlier in the book.

## Suggestions for further reading

B. Coxall, *Pressure Groups in British Politics*, Pearson, 2001.

W. Grant, *Pressure Groups and British Politics*, Palgrave, 2000.

D. Judge, *Representation: Theory and Practice in Britain*, Routledge, 1999.

# References

## Introduction

1. A. de Tocqueville, *Democracy in America* (trans.), Doubleday, 1969.
2. G. Wilson, *Interest Groups*, Blackwell, 1991.
3. P. Lowe and J. Goyder, *Environmental Groups in Politics*, Allen & Unwin, 1983.
4. D. Held, *Models of Democracy*, Stanford University Press, 1997.
5. R. Baggott, *Pressure Groups Today*, Manchester University Press, 1995.
6. G. Peele, *Governing the UK*, Blackwell, 2004.
7. W. Grant, *Pressure Groups in British Politics*, Pearson, 2001.
8. D. Truman, *The Governmental Process*, Knopf, 1951.
9. R. Hague and M. Harrop, *Comparative Government and Politics: An Introduction*, Palgrave, 2004.
10. A. Bentley, *The Process of Government*, University of Chicago Press, 1908 (re-issued, ed. by P. Odegard, Belknap, 1967).
11. D. Truman, *The Governmental Process*, Knopf, 1951.
12. R. Dahl, 'Pluralism' in J. Krieger (ed.), *The Oxford Companion to Politics of the World*, Oxford University Press, 1993.
13. J. Galbraith, *The New Industrial State*, Pelican, 1974.
14. D. Truman, *The Governmental Process*, Knopf, 1951.
15. C. Lindblom, *Politics and Markets*, Basic Books, 1977.
16. R. Dahl, 'Pluralism' in J. Krieger (ed.), *The Oxford Companion to Politics of the World*, Oxford University Press, 1993.
17. R. Hague and M. Harrop, *Comparative Government and Politics: An Introduction*, Palgrave, 2004.
18. M. Olson, *The Logic of Collective Action: Public Goods and the Theory of Groups*, Schocken Books, 1968.
19. R. Miliband, *Capitalist Democracy in Britain*, Oxford University Press, 1992.

## Chapter 1

1. S. Finer, *Anonymous Empire*, Pall Mall, 1966.
2. J. Walker, *Mobilising interest Groups in America*, University of Michigan Press, 1991.

3. C. Jillson, *American Government: Political Change and Institutional Development*, Harcourt Brace College Publishers, 1999.
4. J. Stewart, *British Pressure Groups*, Oxford University Press, 1958.
5. A. Heywood, *Politics*, Macmillan, 1997.
6. B. Coxall, *Pressure Groups in British Politics*, Pearson, 2001.
7. British Toilet Association website www.britloos.co.uk.
8. W. Grant, ideas originally advanced in Working Paper 19, 'Insider groups, outsider groups and interest group strategies in Britain', 1978, but first published more widely in *Pressure Groups, Politics and Democracy in Britain*, Philip Allan, 1989.
9. R. Benewick, 'Politics without ideology: the perimeters of pluralism' in R. Benewick, *Knowledge and Belief in Politics: The Problem of Ideology*, Allen & Unwin, 1973.
10. W. Grant, *Pressure Groups, Politics and Democracy in Britain*, Philip Allan, 1989.
11. R. Baggott, *Pressure Groups and the Policy Process*, Politics Association, *Politics 2000* series, 2000.
12. G. Jordan, W. Maloney and A. McLaughlin, 'Insiders, outsiders and political access', British Interest Group Project Working Paper No. 4, University of Aberdeen, 1992.
13. G. Almond and G. Powell (eds), *Comparative Politics Today: A World View*, HarperCollins, 2000.
14. K. Newton and J. Van Deth, *Foundations of Comparative Politics*, Cambridge University Press, 2005
15. M. Moran, *Politics and Governance in the UK*, Palgrave, 2005.
16. D. Marsh and R. Rhodes (eds), *Policy Networks and British Government*, Oxford University Press, 1992.

## Chapter 2

1. R. Hague and M. Harrop, *Comparative Government and Politics: An Introduction*, Palgrave, 2004.
2. T. Matthews, 'Interest Groups' in R. Smith and L. Watson (eds), *Politics in Australia*, Allen & Unwin, 1989.
3. R. Hague and M. Harrop, *Comparative Government and Politics: An Introduction*, Palgrave, 2004.
4. C. Secrett, Friends of the Earth press release, 31.5.01.
5. The findings of the Study of Parliament survey, as reported in M. Rush (ed.), *Parliament and Pressure Politics*, Clarendon Press, 1990.

6. The findings of the Study of Parliament survey, as reported in M. Rush (ed.), *Parliament and Pressure Politics*, Clarendon Press, 1990.
7. For example, R. Baggott, 'The measurement of change in pressure group politics', *Talking Politics* 5:1, 1992.
8. R. Baggott, *Pressure Groups Today*, Manchester University Press, 1995.
9. W. Grant, *Pressure Groups in British Politics*, Pearson, 2001.
10. P. Jenkins, *The Guardian*, 12.5.2001.
11. The findings of the Study of Parliament survey, as reported in M. Rush (ed.), *Parliament and Pressure Politics*, Clarendon Press, 1990.
12. G. Jordan, *Government and Pressure Groups in Britain*, Clarendon Press, 1987.
13. W. Grant, *Pressure Groups, Politics and Democracy in Britain*, Philip Allan, 1989.

## Chapter 3

1. R. Hague and M. Harrop, *Comparative Government and Politics: An Introduction*, Palgrave, 2004.
2. W. Grant, *Pressure Groups, Politics and Democracy in Britain*, Philip Allan, 1989.
3. R. Hague and M. Harrop, *Comparative Government and Politics: An Introduction*, Palgrave, 2004.
4. R. Hrebenar and R. Scott, *Interest Group Politics in America*, Prentice Hall, 1997.
5. The findings of the Study of Parliament survey, as reported in M. Rush (ed.), *Parliament and Pressure Politics*, Clarendon Press, 1990.
6. R. Baggott, *Pressure Groups Today*, Manchester University Press, 1995.
7. R. Baggott, *Pressure Groups and the Policy Process*, Politics Association, *Politics 2000* series, 2000.

## Chapter 4

1. A. Heywood, *Politics*, Macmillan, 1997.
2. *Directory of British Associations* 17, A CBD Research Publication, 2005.
3. D. Hurd, *The Daily Telegraph*, 20.9.1986.
4. *Modernising Government*, White Paper, Cm4310, 1999.
5. J. Straw, *The Times*, 8.4.1998.
6. *Electronic Telegraph*, 1366, 20.2.1999.
7. A. Woolf, 'Pressing Problem', *Guardian Society*, 12.5.1999

8.  A. Blair, Interview in *The Times*, 23.7.1994.
9.  C. Secrett, Friends of the Earth press release, 31.5.01.
10. R. Garner, *Environmental Politics*, Harvester Wheatsheaf, 1994.
11. P. Lowe and J. Gogden, *Environmental Groups in Brtain*, Allen & Unwin, 1983.
12. J. Porritt, *The Times*, 21.6.1994.
13. J. Porritt, 'Blair's green record condemned', BBC website, 26.8.2002.
14. 'Labour's blind spot', editorial in *The Guardian*, 11.10.1999.
15. J. McCormick, *British Politics and the Environment*, Earthscan, 1991.
16. R. Grove-White, press release, Centre for Environmental Change, Lancaster University.
17. C. Secrett, Friends of the Earth press release, 31.5.01.
18. G. Jordan, paper delivered to Political Studies Association, 1994.
19. P. Rawcliffe, *Environmental Pressure Groups in Transition*, Manchester University Press, 1997.

## Chapter 5

1.  R. Baggott, *Pressure Groups Today*, Manchester University Press, 1995.
2.  J. Vidal, *The Guardian*, 1998 as quoted in B. Coxall, *Pressure Groups in British Politics*, Pearson, 2001.
3.  J. Vidal and A. Bellos, *The Guardian*, 27.8.1996.
4.  J. Curtice and R. Jowell, *British Social Attitudes*, 12th ed.,1995.
5.  D. Hoad, *Talking Politics*, 10:3, The Politics Association, 1998.
6.  R. Baggott, *see* 1 above, quoting *The Campaigning Handbook*.
7.  K. Dunion, *Troublemakers: The Struggle for Environmental Justice in Scotland*, Edinburgh University Press, 2003.
8.  As quoted in S. Steingraber, *Living Downstream*, Addison-Wesley, 1997.
9.  As quoted in S. Lash 'Risk Culture', in B. Adam, U. Beck and J. van Loon (eds), *The Risk Society and Beyond*, Sage, 2000.
10. K. Dunion, *Troublemakers: The Struggle for Environmental Justice in Scotland*, Edinburgh University Press, 2003.
11. Furhers 4 Justice website.
12. N. McNaughton, 'Populist Movements', *Talking Politics* 4:1, 2001.
13. R. Garner, *Animals, Politics and Morality*, Manchester University Press, 1993.
14. N. McNaughton, 'Populist Movements', *Talking Politics* 4:1, 2001.
15. A. Dobson, *Green Political Thought: An Introduction*, Allen and Unwin, 1990.
16. P. Melchett, *BBC News*, 27.7.1999.

17. B. Martin (FoE activist), as quoted in D. Wilson, *Pressure: The A–Z of Campaigning*, Heinemann, 1984.

18. D. Wilson, *Pressure: The A–Z of Campaigning*, Heinemann, 1984.

19. K. Milne, *Manufacturing Dissent: Single-Issue Protest, the Public and the Press*, Demos, 2005.

## Chapter 6

1. G. Jordan, 'Redemocratising Scotland', paper for symposium at Graduate School of Law, Hokkaido University, Sapporo, 28/29.9.2004.

2. P. Lynch, *Scottish Government and Politics: An Introduction*, Edinburgh University Press, 2001.

3. Civic Forum website www.civicforum.org.uk.

4. Interim report of Cultural Commission (established by Executive), 4.11.2004 (www.culturalpolicy.arts.gla.ac.uk).

5. J. Allardyce and B. Brady, 'God on their side?', *Scotland on Sunday*, 12.5.2002.

6. T. Hopkins, as quoted in J. Allardyce, 'Christians plot political infiltration', *Scotland on Sunday*, 12.5.2002.

7. D. Miller, as quoted in J. Allardyce and B. Brady, 'God on their side?', *Scotland on Sunday*, 12.5.2002.

8. G. Jordan, Redemocratising Scotland, paper for symposium at Graduate School of Law, Hokkaido University, Sapporo, 28/29.9.2004.

9. P. Cairney, course notes made available to author, now published on www.abdn.ac.uk/pir/notes/Level3/P13546/TheQuestion ofAccess.doc.

10. H. Marshall, response to questionnaire and telephone conversation with the author 21.10.2005.

## Chapter 7

1. B. Coxall, *Pressure Groups in British Politics*, Pearson, 2001.

2. O. Gray, 'The Structure of Interest Group Representation in the EU: Some Observations of a Practitioner' in P.-H. Claeys et al., *Lobbying, Pluralism and European Integration*, European Interuniversity Press, 1998; and W. Wessels, 'The Growth and Differentiation of Multi-Level Networks: A Corporatist Mega-Bureaucracy or an Open City?' in H. Wallace and A. Young, *Participation and Policy-Making in the European Union*, Clarendon Press, 1973.

3. A. Butt Phillips, 'Pressure Groups in the European Community', Occasional Paper, University of Bath, 1985.
4. J. Greenwood, *Representing Interests in the European Union*, Macmillan, 1997.
5. R. Baggott, 'The measurement of change in pressure group politics' in *Talking Politics*, autumn 1992.
6. E. Bomberg and A. Stubb, *The European Union: How Does it Work?*, Oxford University Press, 2003.
7. J. Peterson, 'States, societies and the European Union', *West European Politics*, 20:4, 1997.
8. E. Bomberg and A. Stubb, *The European Union: How Does it Work?*, Oxford University Press, 2003.
9. M. Aspinwall, 'Collective attraction: the new political game in Brussels' in J. Greenwood and M. Aspinwall (eds), *Collective Action in the European Union*, Routledge, 1998.
10. J. Peterson, 'States, societies and the European Union', *West European Politics*, 20:4, 1997.
11. S. Mazey and J. Richardson, *Lobbying in the European Community*, Oxford University Press, 1993
12. N. Nugent, *The Government and Politics of the European Union*, Palgrave, 2003.

## Chapter 8

1. Campaigning to Protect Hunted Animals website at www.ifaw.org.
2. *The Guardian*, 24.9.2002.
3. Representative of the National Gamekeepers' Organisation, in response to author's questionnaire, September 2005.
4. Representative of the Scottish Rural Property and Business Association, in response to author's questionnaire, September 2005.
5. N. McNaughton, 'Populist Movements', *Talking Politics* 4:1, 2001.

## Chapter 9

1. S. Finer, *The Anonymous Empire*, Pall Mall, 1966.
2. W. Grant, ideas originally advanced in Working Paper 19, 'Insider groups, outsider groups and interest group strategies in Britain', 1978, but first published more widely in *Pressure Groups, Politics and Democracy in Britain*, Philip Allan, 1989.

3. D. Hurd, *The Daily Telegraph*, 20.9.1986.
4. R. Baggott, *Pressure Groups Today*, Manchester University Press, 1995
5. M. Dobbs, *The Times*, 13.9.1995.
6. A. Blair, speech to the News Corps, Pebble Beach, CA, 30.7.2006.
7. R. Baggott, *Pressure Groups Today*, Manchester University Press, 1995.
8. D. Wilson, *Pressure: The A–Z of Campaigning*, Heinemann, 1984.
9. E. Must (of Alarm UK), *The Guardian*, 27.12.1994.
10. D. Wilson, *Pressure: The A–Z of Campaigning*, Heinemann, 1984.
11. H. Young, *The Guardian*, 15.6 1995.
12. M. Phillips, *The Observer*, 24.3.1996.
13. D. Wilson, *Pressure: The A–Z of Campaigning*, Heinemann, 1984.
14. S. Finer, *The Anonymous Empire*, Pall Mall, 1966.

# Index

Bold indicates that the term is defined